Transforming Health Sciences Library Spaces

MEDICAL LIBRARY ASSOCIATION BOOKS

The Medical Library Association (MLA) features books that showcase the expertise of health sciences librarians for other librarians and professionals.

MLA Books are excellent resources for librarians in hospitals, medical research practice, and other settings. These volumes will provide health care professionals and patients with accurate information that can improve outcomes and save lives.

Each book in the series has been overseen editorially since conception by the Medical Library Association Books Panel, composed of MLA members with expertise spanning the breadth of health sciences librarianship.

Medical Library Association Books Panel
Kristen L. Young, AHIP, chair
Dorothy Ogdon, AHIP, chair designate
Michel C. Atlas
Carolann Lee Curry
Kelsey Leonard, AHIP
Karen McElfresh, AHIP
JoLinda L. Thompson, AHIP
Heidi Heilemann, AHIP, board liaison

About the Medical Library Association
Founded in 1898, MLA is a 501(c)(3) nonprofit, educational organization of 3,500 individual and institutional members in the health sciences information field that provides lifelong educational opportunities, supports a knowledge-base of health information research, and works with a global network of partners to promote the importance of quality information for improved health to the health care community and the public.

Books in the Series:

The Medical Library Association Guide to Providing Consumer and Patient Health Information edited by Michele Spatz

Transforming Health Sciences Library Spaces

ALANNA CAMPBELL

ROWMAN & LITTLEFIELD
Lanham • Boulder • New York • London

Published by Rowman & Littlefield
An imprint of The Rowman & Littlefield Publishing Group, Inc.
4501 Forbes Boulevard, Suite 200, Lanham, Maryland 20706
www.rowman.com

6 Tinworth Street, London SE11 5AL

British Library Cataloguing in Publication Information Available

Library of Congress Cataloging-in-Publication Data

Names: Campbell, Alanna, author.
Title: Transforming health sciences library spaces / Alanna Campbell.
Description: Lanham : Rowman & Littlefield, [2019] | Series: Medical Library
  Association books series | Includes bibliographical references and index.
  Identifiers: LCCN 2018041611 (print) | LCCN 2018053195 (ebook) | ISBN
  9781538114681 (Electronic) | ISBN 9781538114674 (cloth : alk. paper)
Subjects: LCSH: Medical libraries. | Libraries—Space utilization. | Library
  buildings—Design and construction.
Classification: LCC Z675.M4 (ebook) | LCC Z675.M4 C36 2019 (print) | DDC
  026/.61—dc23
LC record available at https://lccn.loc.gov/2018041611

Printed in the United States of America

Contents

List of Illustrations

LIST OF FIGURES

LIST OF TABLES

Acknowledgments

I would like to thank all of the authors for their contributions to this book. It was a pleasure and privilege to learn and work with everyone. Kelsey Grabeel, who contacted me about editing *Transforming Health Sciences Library Spaces* and the Medical Library Association's Books Panel, of which she represents; Andrew, Charles, and Michael at Rowman & Littlefield for their advice and guidance through this process; my colleagues and director at the Health Sciences Library, who let me bounce ideas off them and encouraged me as I edited this publication. The fine doctors at Health Sciences North. Thank you from the bottom of my heart. Team OAX, thank you for pushing me to learn and never give up in pretty much every way possible professionally and personally. Finally, thank you to my husband, family, and friends for their support and for always cheering me on.

Preface

Library spaces have been a hot topic since the early 2000s. The evolution of digital resources has led library administrators, users, and other stakeholders to question the form and function of the physical library space. Some organizations have responded to technology, tight budgets, and a need for space by reallocating portions of their library spaces to other organizational functions. As Thibodeau describes, the Duke University Medical Center Library was approached in 2007 regarding their "prime real estate" for reallocation.[1] Their entire top floor, 29 percent of their total space, was ultimately converted into offices.[2] Other libraries, such as Saul's Memorial Virtual Library at Piedmount Atlanta Hospital, went completely virtual in 2012 as a response to a change in usage patterns, budget cuts, and staff reductions.[3]

At the same time, some libraries have been able to harness the uptick of digital collections to respond to the evolving needs of patrons. Many are now acting upon latent demand for an increase in diverse study spaces and integrated services within the library such as copy services, IT support, writing centers, and cafés. Cunningham and Tabur argue that students are "still choosing the physical library as much as ever and even in increasing number in renovated libraries."[4] This even though the majority of the core collection can be accessed online.

There isn't one right way to respond to the changes technology has spurred, or evolving user demands. As librarians who support the library space, it is our responsibility to learn about and act upon how we can transform and enhance our spaces to better meet the needs of our users. That's who we're here for, right?

This book aims to provide firsthand case studies and practical advice on transforming health sciences library spaces in the twenty-first century. Health sciences library spaces differ across a wide spectrum of variables. We include academic, health care, consumer, and special libraries. We are distributed, local, and in between. Our user populations vary from students, residents, interns, patients, physicians, nurses, and other health care professionals. We have different budgets and funding sources and the list goes on.

Many of us however have the same issues and interests related to our space. This includes but is not limited to the following:

- Identifying and overhauling dated spaces that lack flexibility.
- Gathering information on usage behavior and user feedback in relation to our spaces.
- Working with feedback to increase satisfaction, and use of the library space with little funds.
- Removing a large percentage of the physical collection and deciding what to replace it with.
- Maximizing relationships with stakeholders such as leadership and external departments to transform the library space.
- Understanding what going 100 percent virtual means in practice.
- Managing usage of materials not traditionally well suited to online access.

Collected here are the experiences and thoughts of librarians on the transformation of health sciences library spaces. As both seasoned leaders and fresh new voices they provide insights into planning, budgeting, collecting and integrating user feedback, collaborating with leadership and architects, and thriving in the good times and the tight times.

This book has been divided into three main sections. Part I, Library Spaces That Work for Users, includes the perspective of Stevo Roksandic and Allison Erlinger, who address the transformation of the consumer health library spaces at Mount Carmel Health Services' multiple sites. They discuss the design, planning, and execution of these projects as well as the relationship between library users and the design and function of the library space.

Roksandic and Erlinger also provide their experience renovating the Mount Carmel Health Sciences Library, which serves employees and learners affiliated with Mount Carmel. They speak to the demand for the library space to meet users' contemporary information behaviors and diverse user populations. Mellanye Lackey and colleagues review the experience of the Spencer S. Eccles Health Sciences Library (EHSL) at the University of Utah with Ithaka S+R. The library employed Ithaka S+R to collect and analyze how people were using the library space including their engagement, sense of ambience, and other tangible and intangible assets of the library. This chapter reviews the project's methodology, shares results of the study, and assesses the study's value to an academic health sciences library in setting its future strategic directions. Valrie Minson and colleagues look at the University of Florida's Marston Science Library from a traditional collection-centric library to a reinvigorated collaboration and learning hub. While not a health sciences library, Marston serves agricultural, biological, chemical, and physical sciences, as well as engineering, mathematics, and statistics. They are a great example of a large budget renovation that transformed their space through new technologies, services, and user conveniences.

In part II, Working in Unique Spaces, Lisa Blackwell addresses the transition of staffing, resources, and services from a physical campus-based library to a cohesive, primarily virtual, enterprise-wide operational infrastructure at Chamberlain University. Helen-Ann Brown Epstein examines showing leadership in virtual library spaces. She looks at the library website "as place," the virtual librarian's role in library services, marketing, leadership styles and assessment, and librarians as leaders and information stewards. Esther Carrigan and Nancy Burford from Texas A&M University provide the perspective of the special collections space, having completely renovated theirs. They discuss the standard space issues related to housing special materials as well as global and local issues influencing the decision to renovate a special collections space.

In part III, Library Spaces Working with What They've Got, Jessica Decaro and Shannon Butcheck of Cleveland Health Sciences Library discuss losing 50 percent of their space at Case Western Reserve University in 2014. The authors outline how this initial loss has generated subsequent space transformations and ultimately has contributed to a highly efficient space. Margaret Hoogland looks at surviving tight budgets and proving value added in library spaces based on current literature. She discusses the trends and technology in library spaces and the retooling and rethinking of librarian roles, including the necessary professional development, to prove value added. Hoogland also takes a look at how MLS education is responding to these trends and the rethinking of roles to produce new librarians equipped for the modern landscape. Last, Patty Fink and I explore making space improvements by nickel and diming the annual library budget in the Health Sciences Library at the Northern Ontario School of Medicine. Specifically, we deal with how to maximize a budget that has no budget line for space improvements.

I have thoroughly enjoyed working on this book and reading the diverse perspectives and experiences of the contributing authors. I hope the content of these chapters inspire, inform, and motivate readers in planning and transforming their library spaces.

NOTES

1. Patricia L. Thibodeau, "When the Library Is Located in Prime Real Estate: A Case Study on the Loss of Space from the Duke University Medical Center Library and Archives," *Journal of the Medical Library Association* 98, no. 1 (2010): 25. doi: 10.3163/1536-5050.98.1.010.

2. Thibodeau, "When the Library," 26.

3. Stacie Waddell, "The Road to Virtual: The Sauls Memorial Virtual Library's Journey," *Medical Reference Services Quarterly* 33, no. 1 (2014): 92–101. doi: 10.1080/02763869.2014.866493.

4. Heather V. Cunningham and Susanne Tabur, "Learning Space Attributes: Reflections on Academic Library Design and Its Use," *Journal of Learning Spaces* 1, no. 2 (2012): par.1. http://libjournal.uncg.edu/jls/article/view/392.

I

LIBRARY SPACES THAT WORK FOR USERS

1

Consumer Health Library Spaces

"If You Build It, Will They Come?"

STEVO ROKSANDIC AND ALLISON ERLINGER

INTRODUCTION

In this chapter, we share our experience with consumer health library (CHL) services at the Mount Carmel Health Sciences Library (MCHSL), primarily focusing on the design of CHL spaces at multiple operating sites within the Mount Carmel Health System (MCHS). We explain why the elements of space planning and design are vitally important in establishing a consumer health information (CHI) business and providing CHL services. We also share how our CHL operation was impacted by the emergence of both budgetary and staffing issues. In our experience, the existence of a designated CHL space strongly influenced the sustainability of our CHL services under the expansion of general austerity measures at the corporate level. We believe that our experiences and lessons learned can provide guidance not only to CHLs located on hospital campuses, but to other libraries and librarians who are considering providing CHI to health care organizations or to the general communities that they serve.

CONCEPT AND OVERVIEW

The concept of establishing the CHL as a branch of the existing MCHSL was based on the results of a survey of librarians in the public libraries in Franklin County, Ohio, conducted in 2008.[1] The completion of this survey project initiated further analysis of the community and organizational need for the establishment of CHL services within MCHS. During the period from 2007 through 2011, the concept of offering CHI services to both MCHS patients and the local community was further developed and garnered support from MCHS organizational leaders.

With a clearly defined concept for CHI services in mind, the first phase in the life cycle of the Mount Carmel Consumer Health Library (MCCHL)—define, design, deploy—officially began in 2010. Following the completion of a needs assessment, research of best practices in CHI, and the definition of the scope and focal targets, the idea was aligned to the mission and vision of both MCHS and MCHSL. The details of the needs assessment process and action plan for the establishment of CHL services at MCHS are highlighted as a case study in the second chapter of *The Medical Library Association Guide to Providing Consumer and Patient Health Information* edited by Michele Spatz.[2] After completing a design of the physical space and defining the business operational design of the future MCCHL as a branch of MCHSL, the scope of services to be provided was assessed and established. The plans included the provision of reference services, circulation of diverse bibliographical materials, a roving patient library, participation at local health fairs and festivals, and one of the most important services in the eyes of the library, the organization and provision of CHI education to the local community, K–12 schools, and other librarians.

All of these plans were successfully executed thanks to the establishment of partnerships, both internally, within the MCHS organization, and externally, with local community organizations. Finally, in March 2011, MCCHL opened its doors to users and organizational and community partners. With

FIGURE 1.1

MCCHL sequential workflow.
Photo reprinted with the permission of Mount Carmel Health system Supervisor of Audiovisual services, Frank Shepherd

the provision of CHI services at MCHS underway after phase one, the newly established MCCHL continued to evolve through two subsequent phases of development: rethink, reinvent, redefine (2013) and reorganize, refine, reposition (2014–2016). The following sections describe each phase in greater detail in order to serve as a guide for the reader who is interested in establishing CHL services at their own institution.

DEFINE, DESIGN, DEPLOY

Following the development of a clear vision, grounded in assessment and research, and the establishment of internal and external partnerships, the first phase of CHL services at MCHS truly began with the opening of the MCCHL in March 2011, with the goal of providing CHI services to both MCHS patients and the surrounding local community. Here, we focus on the original design of the physical space and the specific services offered during phase one of MCCHL.

Space

The original MCCHL that opened in 2011 was located on the Mount Carmel West (MCW) campus of MCHS in the Franklinton neighborhood of Columbus, which is among the poorest and most underserved populations in Franklin County. At the time of its opening, MCCHL was located in an existing room within the Lower Lights Christian Health Center Nursing Clinic, on the second floor of a medical and administrative building adjacent to the main hospital. This location was not on the typical walking path of hospital patients or visitors and consequently MCCHL was primarily providing personalized CHI services to patients at the Lower Lights Clinic, and MCW hospital patients through the roving patient library.

This original space was comprised one three-hundred-square-foot room that had formerly served as an office. We designed the layout of this space based on information gathered through Medical Library Association (MLA) CE courses and research on best practices in providing CHI services. The design was intended to provide comfortable and user-friendly areas to accommodate users' needs and meet the standards set forth by the Planetree Health Resource Center, on the San Francisco campus of California Pacific Medical Center (Pacific Presbyterian Medical Center) and existing MLA recommendations. Planetree is a nonprofit consumer health organization founded on the philosophy that people should have access to the information they need to make informed health-care decisions.[3]

The space was furnished with a library front desk, two computer stations, shelves for books, periodicals, and other reading materials, a pamphlet display, a designated children's area, and adult visitor seating. Considering the popularity of mobile technology and available access to accurate and authoritative CHI online, a dedicated MCCHL website was developed to provide direct links to recommended health websites, and a catalog of books, magazines, and CHI-themed DVDs and videos. As an added visitor attraction and educational material, basic three-dimensional anatomy models (pregnancy, heart conditions, orthopedic procedures, etc.) were displayed in the library space. A large wall-mounted television screen allowed for the screening of hospital patient education channels and/or animated film screening for child visitors. Photographs of the original MCCHL space are shown in figures 1.2–1.4.

FIGURE 1.2

Reading display and 3D anatomy model in the original CHL space.
Photo reprinted with the permission of Mount Carmel Health system Supervisor of Audiovisual services, Frank Shepherd

FIGURE 1.3

Pamphlet displays in the original CHL space.
Photo reprinted with the permission of Mount Carmel Health system Supervisor of Audiovisual services, Frank Shepherd

FIGURE 1.4

Children's area in the original CHL space.
Photo reprinted with the permission of Mount Carmel Health system Supervisor of Audiovisual services, Frank Shepherd

Services

From its earliest beginnings, MCCHL was designed to offer a variety of services to meet the needs of consumers and health information professionals alike. With the goal of reaching not only the MCHS patient and visitor population, but also the larger community, we extended CHL services well beyond the bounds of the physical library space.

The results of the survey Enhancing Health Information Services in Franklin County, Ohio Public Libraries: Consumer Health Information Project (CHIP), conducted in 2008, revealed a need among public librarians in Ohio for organized education on the provision of CHI. In order to meet this identified need, MCCHL began organizing and offering National Network of Libraries of Medicine (NNLM)–sponsored CHI classes for librarians. This initiative was marketed not only to hospital and medical librarians, but also to any interested CHI providers, including school, public, state, and other special librarians. These educational offerings provided an opportunity for librarians to accumulate the CE hours needed to receive MLA Consumer

FIGURE 1.5
A well-attended interactive class sponsored by MCCHL.
Photo reprinted with the permission of Mount Carmel Health system Supervisor of Audiovisual services, Frank Shepherd

FIGURE 1.6
Speaker providing education to library professionals.
Photo reprinted with the permission of Mount Carmel Health system Supervisor of Audiovisual services, Frank Shepherd

FIGURE 1.7
Hands-on small group education session.
Photo reprinted with the permission of Mount Carmel Health system Supervisor of Audiovisual services, Frank Shepherd

Health Information Specialist (CHIS) certification at two different levels. MCCHL also organized and offered classes to educate MCHS employees about CHI pertinent to their specialty areas of practice. A selection of photographs from these classes, shown in figure 1.5, demonstrates the consistently high level of attendance that they garnered.

In order to extend services to the MCW hospital inpatient population, MCCHL instituted a patient library service. This service involved MCCHL librarians and volunteers taking a rolling cart with selected materials into the hospital and visiting patients in their rooms to offer leisure reading materials (books, magazines, DVD movies, etc.) and personalized CHI on request. Upon arrival on each clinical unit, the MCCHL staff or volunteer checked in with the nursing staff on duty to determine which patients may benefit the most from the service and those who should not be disturbed for any reason. To promote infection control, the patient library was not offered to patients on any kind of clinical isolation precaution and the cart used for the transportation of MCCHL materials was regularly disinfected.

When visiting hospital patients, staff and volunteers provided a specially created MCCHL pamphlet, shown in figures 1.8 and 1.9, and offered to obtain and provide appropriate CHI related to current illness, general health, or wellness, based on patient request. In order to keep this process organized, interested patients were asked to fill out or dictate to MCCHL staff, a locally designed CHI literature research form. After completing patient library rounds for the day, librarians returned to the library space, conducted the

FIGURE 1.8
MCCHL pamphlet exterior.
Photo reprinted with the permission of Mount Carmel Health system Supervisor of Audiovisual services, Frank Shepherd

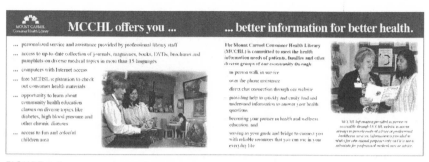

FIGURE 1.9
MCCHL pamphlet interior.
Photo reprinted with the permission of Mount Carmel Health system Supervisor of Audiovisual services,
Frank Shepherd

requested CHI searches, and then returned to the inpatient unit to share the results with the patient on the same or following day. All patient information requests and results received through the MCCHL patient library, including any attached consumer information materials, were shared with the appropriate nursing unit coordinators prior to being completed and returned to the

FIGURE 1.10
Patient Library staff with materials cart.
Photo reprinted with the permission of Mount Carmel Health system Supervisor of Audiovisual services,
Frank Shepherd

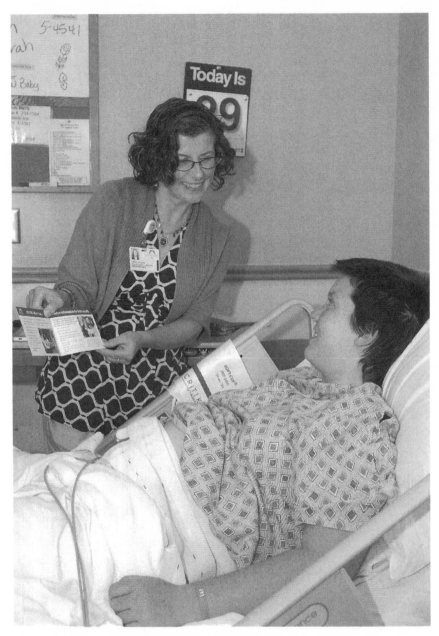

FIGURE 1.11

Patient library interaction in a hospital room.

Photo reprinted with the permission of Mount Carmel Health system Supervisor of Audiovisual services, Frank Shepherd

patient. This process was regulated through the creation of specific MCCHL policies and procedures, developed by the library and chief nursing officer of the MCW Hospital. These policies and procedures also included provisions for information requests received in the MCCHL library and online through the website. Figures 1.10 and 1.11 show the patient library materials cart and a sample patient interaction.

Finally, in an effort to reach the local community outside of the MCHS system, MCCHL librarians and volunteers also participated in fairs, festivals, and community events put on by local schools, churches, and community organizations. We actively sought out information about upcoming events that offered the opportunity for outside institutions to set up information tables. CHI materials that were selected and brought to these events were tailored to meet the particular health needs, cultural and/or religious preferences, literacy level, age group, and language of the expected attendees. MCCHL

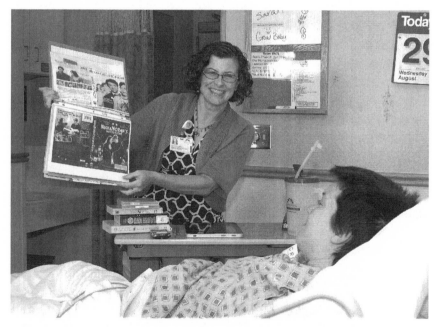

FIGURE 1.12

Patient library interaction using an easily portable binder with images for material selecting.
Photo reprinted with the permission of Mount Carmel Health system Supervisor of Audiovisual services, Frank Shepherd

marketing materials, such as an informational pamphlet with the location and contact information, were also distributed in order to raise awareness and usage of MCCHL services following such events. A sample of the MCCHL tables and client interactions at such community events appear in figure 1.13.

During the first year in which MCCHL was in operation, these diverse services reached a wide variety of patrons, including MCHS patients and staff, local community organizations and the public, as well as other health information professionals across the state. The success of this first year set the stage for the growth and development of MCCHL.

RETHINK, REINVENT, REDEFINE

In the following year (2012), under the sponsorship of the Mount Carmel Foundation, MCHS planned the construction of a new Community Health Resource Center (CHRC) on the MCW Hospital Campus. The concept for the CHRC was developed on the model of similar facilities existing in other neighborhoods in Franklin County, where MCHS is a primary health-care provider. These existing facilities, however, were located primarily in neighborhoods with high socioeconomic profiles, very unlike the Franklinton neighborhood that surrounds the MCW campus. MCHS created the CHRC with the goal of engaging the local Franklinton community and meeting the particular needs of its residents by providing education, health, and wellness services to its members. By taking health-care information and education beyond the inpatient hospital setting, the CHRC was positioned to prevent and manage chronic medical conditions, encourage healthy lifestyle habits, and promote holistic wellness, resulting in a healthier community. In order to meet this goal, the CHRC would bring together a variety of health, educational, and support resources and make them readily available to the local community, patients, their families, and MCHS colleagues and physicians.

The vision of the new CHRC included a new state-of-the-art consumer health library, the healthy living center, a demonstration kitchen for cooking and nutrition classes, and spaces to be used for exercise classes, childbirth education and outpatient lactation support, diabetes education, oncology nurse navigators, survivorship programs, and financial education classes. The concept of such a facility was very compelling and the idea gained support from leaders of MCHS and of the Franklinton neighborhood and City of Columbus. It reflected the mission and vision of MCHS, and clearly aligned

FIGURE 1.13

Library staff providing CHI to members of the public at a community event.
Photo reprinted with the permission of Mount Carmel Health system Supervisor of Audiovisual services,
Frank Shepherd

FIGURE 1.14

MCCHL table display used at public events.
Photo reprinted with the permission of Mount Carmel Health system Supervisor of Audiovisual services,
Frank Shepherd

FIGURE 1.15

Library staff working directly with children at a local event.
Photo reprinted with the permission of Mount Carmel Health system Supervisor of Audiovisual services, Frank Shepherd

to the Healthy People 2020 initiative by bringing services to a neighborhood in need.[4]

The construction of such a facility was also very timely in the larger health-care environment: new health reform on the horizon emphasized a focus on prevention and wellness; fast-paced development of technology was changing relationships and communication between health providers and patients; and the Internet was drastically changing the ways in which individuals sought health information. All of this change, however, relied on the accessibility of services and technology, both of which were comparatively lacking in the neighborhood immediately surrounding the MCW hospital campus. Thus, establishing a people-centered CHRC at MCW was an ideal opportunity to proactively engage a community in need with emerging trends in health care and to support the health and wellness of its residents.

FIGURE 1.16
Library staff helping to select culturally appropriate materials for community members.
Photo reprinted with the permission of Mount Carmel Health system Supervisor of Audiovisual services, Frank Shepherd

At this time, MCCHL was already active in the community, providing educational support, participating in local health and community events, and fostering partnerships with both vital community organizations such as the State Library of Ohio, Columbus Metropolitan Library, Ohio Department of Development, and Columbus Community Relations Commission, and MCHS departments and programs including the Mount Carmel College of Nursing (MCCN), Live Your Whole Life employee wellness program, Women's Health Center, and the office of Diversity and Inclusion. In its first year of existence, MCCHL had already become recognized by the Midwest Chapter of NNLM and other peers as a leader in organizing CHI education for librarians and providing diverse support and services extending beyond those previously established elsewhere. Of particular note was the highly personalized CHI that was selected from a wide variety of sources in order to accommodate specific cultural and language needs.

The construction of the new CHRC, which was to be located on the first floor of the same building in which the original MCCHL was already located, provided an incredible opportunity for the expansion and development of the library as an integral component of the MCW hospital campus. A new space for MCCHL was included in the plans for the CHRC, which comprised 2,200 square feet positioned directly inside one of two primary entrances to the facility. We worked closely with the CHRC architectural team to design the space and the existing "mini-version" of MCCHL finally had the opportunity realize the long-time vision of its creator. A modern state-of-the-art shelfless library was planned with features designed to meet the identified needs of its target user populations, and to be able to serve as the "main branch" in the future, when CHI services and resources would hopefully be offered at other MCHS locations.

Thanks to generous support from the Mount Carmel Foundation in combination with a grant, MCCHL was also able to hire its first dedicated consumer health librarian. Up until this time, consumer health services had been provided by the MCHSL staff in addition to their existing job roles and duties. Due to the constraints of available financing, the original position was limited to a term of one year, but library staff strongly believed that demonstration of MCCHL librarian engagement, results, industry trends, and the ongoing need for CHI services would provide the support needed to secure permanent staff financing.

FIGURE 1.17

Community members browsing selected materials at a local event.
Photo reprinted with the permission of Mount Carmel Health system Supervisor of Audiovisual services,
  Frank Shepherd

FIGURE 1.18
Display of hand-washing education available in several languages.
Photo reprinted with the permission of Mount Carmel Health system Supervisor of Audiovisual services, Frank Shepherd

This positive thinking had its foundations in strong advocacy of information services and health-care organizations to meet the demands of recent health-care reform, the demonstrated need of our local community, the national Healthy People 2020 initiative, and the MCHS mission and vision. Support for and understanding of the need for people-centered CHI services expanded at the organizational level and two other MCHS Hospital campuses expressed interest in establishing similar services at their operating sites. We had already been considering the expansion of MCCHL services to the MCHS patients, visitors, and local communities at all operating sites across Central Ohio. Supported by the increasing interest of organizational leaders at some of these other MCHS sites, the idea of having satellite Consumer Health Information Centers (CHIC) on the other MCHS hospital campuses began to take shape.

The first priority, however, was the completion of the new MCCHL space in the MCW CHRC, which would serve as the primary location of MCCHL and the hub of CHL services within MCHS. This would be a space where the local community could find needed CHI and receive health-related education designed to meet their needs and interests. The organizational and operational business model essentially mimicked that of the already well-established MCHSL, which has a fully staffed main library branch at MCW and smaller, unstaffed library virtual commons at the other MCHS operating sites to support the medical staff and academic departments across all MCHS.

The plan for the new MCCHL took into consideration its position within the CHRC and accommodated the eventual sharing of space to support growing CHRC programs and services. During the final mapping of the CHRC floor plan, it was determined that additional space would be needed to accommodate the activities of the diabetes educator group, and the library offered a portion of its dedicated space to meet that need. With the final plans settled, construction of the new CHRC began.

While the construction of the new CHRC and MCCHL was underway, a grant from the NNLM provided MCCHL an opportunity to purchase several laptops and a hotspot connection device for mobile Internet access. This allowed MCCHL staff to begin offering CHI services out in the community, utilizing mobile technology to provide education and services outside the walls of the library. Through collaboration with MCCN students and faculty, MCCHL was also able to include a licensed registered nurse in its community visits to provide basic health screenings, such as point of care blood pressure, blood glucose, and cholesterol measurements.

The most successful example of this service model was the establishment of regular visits to the Hawthorn Village Senior Apartment Homes, located only a few blocks from the MCW hospital campus. Despite being very close to the MCW campus, many residents of Hawthorn Village have limited mobility and transportation, making it difficult for them to come to MCCHL for services. Through interaction and conversation with these users during our visits, it became apparent that they also felt more comfortable asking questions about their health and receiving needed services and access to CHI in their home environment. Further discussions with librarians at the Franklinton branch of the local Public Library revealed this to be a very common and well-established method of proactively engaging community members with education, information, and services. Our ongoing commitment to provide basic health screenings, CHI information, and education at Hawthorn Village was very warmly welcomed and produced a successful long-term service relationship with its residents.

Once the basic structure of the new CHRC was complete and the new MCCHL space began to take form, we were able to view the space and begin brainstorming and discussing ideas for positioning all the previously identified elements and service points that would make up the new MCCHL. In addition to a large front desk for the librarians, pamphlet displays, storage for mobile technology, eleven hardwired PC stations, a children's area, and reading and study/teaching spaces, an enclosed consultation room was added, which provided a private space to meet with visitors and clients to discuss sensitive health topics. To complement the ample natural light in the space,

FIGURE 1.19
Library staff providing computer literacy training to Hawthorn Village residents.
Photo reprinted with the permission of Mount Carmel Health system Supervisor of Audiovisual services, Frank Shepherd

FIGURE 1.20

Display of materials provided at regular visits to Hawthorn Village.
Photo reprinted with the permission of Mount Carmel Health system Supervisor of Audiovisual services, Frank Shepherd

FIGURE 1.21

Registered nurse performing blood pressure screening on a Hawthorn Village resident.
Photo reprinted with the permission of Mount Carmel Health system Supervisor of Audiovisual services, Frank Shepherd

the warm and bright wall colors, and comfortable modern furniture, the designers suggested adding a fireplace, which would give MCCHL a home-like
feel. A beautiful wall display was also created, telling the story of Mount Carmel's 125 years of history in the Franklinton neighborhood and Central Ohio.
This display also listed the major donors who contributed to the building of
the CHRC. The library was very proud to find on that list some of our own
business partners, whose financial contributions helped to make the CHRC
a reality and establish MCCHL as an anchor for CHI services within MCHS.

During discussions about the design of the new MCCHL, the professional
designers quite reluctantly accepted our vision of building a shelfless consumer health library. Based on the previous years' experience in providing
CHI information and services, including the emphasis on delivery of information and education to our users in their own community settings, and a
noted disinterest in borrowing available books, the new MCCHL became
the first Library in the area whose space did not contain bookshelves. A very
small collection of books, consisting largely of illustrated items, resided on the
counter behind the library front desk.

FIGURE 1.22
Reading and study space in the new MCCHL.
Photo reprinted with the permission of Mount Carmel Health system Supervisor of Audiovisual services,
Frank Shepherd

FIGURE 1.23
Librarian front desk in the new MCCHL.
Photo reprinted with the permission of Mount Carmel Health system Supervisor of Audiovisual services, Frank Shepherd

The major source of CHI information in print was a large collection of pamphlets that were displayed in clear plastic pamphlet holders positioned on the walls throughout the library without taking up large sections of floor space as traditional shelving does. Their visibility and ease of access created the opportunity for MCCHL clients to self-serve, and with the advice of professional library staff, to choose items that would meet their specific information needs and expectations.

This collection of pamphlets was developed by the librarians during the construction of the new library space. The librarians contacted various government and health care organizations, associations, and institutions with ready made CHI pamphlets and handouts available to ship. The National Institutes of Health (NIH), NNLM, MLA, and many national, state, and local cancer, diabetes, and other specialty associations and organizations were happy to provide these materials in bulk quantities, only charging for the cost of shipping. We also worked with the MCHS Patient Education Department to print electronically accessible materials written at varying literacy

FIGURE 1.24
Public computer stations and consultation room in the new MCCHL.
Photo reprinted with the permission of Mount Carmel Health system Supervisor of Audiovisual services,
  Frank Shepherd

levels and in several languages, other than English, that are common among the Central Ohio population. These strategies significantly reduced costs for initial collection development and resulted in a very minimal operating budget for acquiring informational materials. This allowed the library to direct available funds toward hiring additional staff in order to further develop the MCCHL collection and services, educational offerings, and engagement in community activities. A request for an additional librarian was approved, bringing the total MCCHL staffing level to 1.5 full-time employees by the time the new space was ready to open.

The elimination of traditional shelving units from the design of the new MCCHL meant more space was available for specialized service points to accommodate user activity. As mentioned above, the librarians had workstations at a large and open front desk, positioned directly inside the entry and in the center of the library. Since the MCCHL entrance was also a main entrance to the CHRC and medical and administrative offices on the upper floors of the building, library staff were able to greet and offer CHI services to all visitors coming through the building. They also recorded the number of visitors, both visually and using an electronic door traffic counter, and the type of interaction (CHI services, directional assistance, etc.).

A dedicated children's area was designed using smaller-sized furniture and kid-friendly materials. This space included two PCs with integrated software and games designed to enhance their learning about health and wellness, as well as a wall-mounted television to play children's health education videos or age-appropriate entertainment, while parents or other accompanying adults received CHI services. The area also had a collection of toys, coloring and picture books, and group and individual games, all of which were primarily donated by MCHS employees to meet the needs of our younger visitors. A policy was established that all minors needed to be accompanied by an adult, and for their safety this area was always under the observation of library staff or volunteers. This visually appealing space was also frequently used in photographs and marketing materials.

FIGURE 1.25
Children's area in the new MCCHL.
Photo reprinted with the permission of Mount Carmel Health system Supervisor of Audiovisual services, Frank Shepherd

The enclosed consultation room, which was not built into the architectural footprint of the library, was constructed using modular panels featuring frosted glass walls and door. The room was equipped with a desk, two chairs, a computer, and life-sized anatomy models for education.

Eight additional computer stations with Microsoft Office software and hardwired Internet access were located in the main space of the library for visitor use. Printing was made available upon request and librarian approval, using a printer located behind the staff front desk. Use of the computers for entertainment and leisure activities was limited to one hour in order to keep computers available for users wanting to access health information. Librarians and volunteers were also available to assist library users with online information searches. Additionally, a total of twenty laptops and Chromebooks, which were used during community visits as described above, were also available to be checked out and used in the library. These items were stored in a locked cabinet behind the front desk with built-in charging stations.

The main space of the library also featured tables and chairs for reading, studying, or consultation. The fireplace that the professional designers had recommended adding became the focal feature for a comfortable seating area in one corner of the library. This area was furnished with a sofa and upholstered chairs with movable desk-surfaces for writing. A television with DVD player was mounted above the fireplace. When it was not being used for educational programming, local television stations were played on mute with closed captions.

One wall adjacent to the comfortable seating area was dedicated to the MCHS employee health and wellness program, Live Your Whole Life. The official program logo was displayed on the wall using decals, and pamphlet displays held information for MCHS employees about activities and initiatives related to the program. MCCHL was very pleased to add this to the space and to be able to offer pertinent health and wellness information for MCHS employees as well as patients and visitors.

The patient library service that had been established during the first year of MCCHL continued and remained the primary venue for the provision of CHI services. The majority of visitors who came to the library for CHI services were attendees of the CHRC programs and patients of the Lower Lights Clinic that was still located on the second floor of the building. CHRC program attendees were regularly brought to MCCHL and were introduced to the available space and services. A number of MCHS departments and staff, including educators, nurses, and physicians working in the MCHS Mobile Coach, which provides basic health care and education to the homeless population in Columbus, and resident physicians practicing at MCW, also came to MCCHL to gather information materials for their patients and visitors. During this phase of development, the majority of educational events hosted by MCCHL were directed at library and information professionals looking to learn more about the provision of CHI services. Frequent attendance of MCCHL staff and volunteers at local festivals and health fairs such as the Columbus International Festival, Columbus Pride Festival, FamJam, and various local church, school, and community group events continuously created new opportunities to offer CHI services and support, actively engaging in health promotion and advocacy for prevention and wellness activities.

This second phase in the lifecycle of MCCHL brought a brand new and significantly expanded, state-of-the-art consumer library space and the opportunity to further expand upon the services that had been offered from the beginning both at MCW and in the surrounding local community. The final phase would bring even bigger changes, some of them quite unanticipated.

REORGANIZE, REFINE, REPOSITION

By 2014, the evolution of MCCHL services and the corporate landscape of MCHS brought about the opportunity to further expand on the original vision of the library, by offering CHI services at multiple operating sites in the MCHS system and reaching all of its patient and visitor populations. In addition to new dedicated spaces at two other MCHS operating sites, a major redesign of the website was also undertaken as a priority project in order to better connect with potential users and communities in need for CHI services and resources.

The first new MCCHL space was to be created at Mount Carmel St. Ann's hospital (MCSA), which was already undergoing a large-scale campus renovation. The plans for the new design of this hospital included the addition of a designated space for CHI materials and services. Working collaboratively with the professional designers, we developed an economic and visually appealing model for the first MCCHL satellite Consumer Health Information Center (CHIC). The space measured 200 square feet, very similar to that of the original MCCHL library at MCW and was ideally located in a brand-new lobby area, just inside the main entrance of the hospital. This new open space consisted of a small librarian desk, pamphlet wall display, glass case to display illustrated books and anatomy models, two standing and two sitting PC stations, and designated reading areas for adults and children. The design of this first CHIC offered a visually appealing and welcoming space to all hospital visitors. The selection of pamphlets and other CHI materials to be made available here was based on information from the hospital's Patient Education Department and known demographics of the surrounding community.

Mount Carmel East Hospital (MCE), located in another area of the city, was also preparing for a major renovation, and similar positioning and design were used to add a second CHIC on that hospital campus. Prior to the renovation, the MCE Patient Education Department already operated a visitor information desk offering patient education materials. Despite being well-positioned for visitor traffic in the hospital, this space was outdated and offered a limited collection of information materials. MCCHL collaborated

FIGURE 1.26
Librarian desk and pamphlet display at the MCSA CHIC.
Photo reprinted with the permission of Mount Carmel Health system Supervisor of Audiovisual services, Frank Shepherd

FIGURE 1.27
Entrance to MCSA CHIC with clear signage.
Photo reprinted with the permission of Mount Carmel Health system Supervisor of Audiovisual services, Frank Shepherd

FIGURE 1.28
Public computer workstation at the MCSA CHIC.
Photo reprinted with the permission of Mount Carmel Health system Supervisor of Audiovisual services, Frank Shepherd

Figure 1.29
Newly renovated CHIC at MCE.
Photo reprinted with the permission of Mount Carmel Health system Supervisor of Audiovisual services,
    Frank Shepherd

with the MCE Patient Education Department to develop a model for a new shared space that would be remodeled with space designated for a CHIC similar to the one that had recently opened across town at MCSA. Without engaging professional designers, we created this space under the leadership of the Hospital Facilities Department, and the second CHIC was soon open, giving MCCHL a third branch within MCHS.

During this time, MCCHL librarians also developed an education curriculum to meet the needs of community members. This resulted in the creation of seven discrete classes:

- Basic Computer Skills
- How to Search for Health Information on the Internet
- Talking to Your Doctor
- Figuring Out Food Labels: What Is a Nutrition Facts Label and Why You Should Care
- Complementary and Alternative Medicine
- Safe Use of Medication
- Advance Care Planning

These classes were designed for delivery in a variety of settings and had started to be offered at local public libraries and schools. Further interest from local civic and community organizations, such as the Parks and Recreation Department, was actively developing.

This expansion of MCCHL and the new opportunities that it created for engagement at two additional hospital locations and the surrounding communities was very promising and exciting. However, it also created the need for an expanded budget and additional staffing. An additional MCCHL librarian position was approved and filled. Unfortunately, at this same time, the effects of general austerity measures were creating financial difficulties across the health-care system. Although MCHSL and MCCHL operated under the corporate umbrella of MCHS and were providing services at multiple MCHS hospitals, financing for MCCHL was only being provided by MCW.

Having established MCCHL as an integral part of MCW and beginning to expand it to other MCHS operating sites, the staffing and financial needs of this business operation began to exceed the scope of support for CHI services that had been defined when the MCW leadership first agreed to undertake the project. With three employees, the potential for further expansion, and no further grants for outside support since the original one (which had supported only the first year), it was time to reevaluate the MCCHL operations. Furthermore, the CHRC was in need of additional space for its operations and programming. The visitation data that had been carefully recorded by MCCHL staff was reviewed by MCW leadership and it was determined that the number of visits for the utilization of MCCHL services did not justify the continued use of the library space for this purpose. The apparent gap in securing ongoing systemwide support for MCCHL can be attributed to early budgetary limitations, which negatively affected staffing levels and made it necessary to concentrate efforts on service provision rather than administrative work, as well as sweeping organizational austerity measures affecting departments across the health system.

In 2016, the decision to close the MCCHL business and repurpose the newly designated spaces was made by organizational leadership and given as a clear directive to the library. This resulted in the elimination of all three MCCHL librarian positions and the loss of all designated MCCHL space. Without dedicated spaces or staffing, the majority of MCCHL activities came to an abrupt halt. Despite this very disappointing outcome, MCHSL staff still receive and answer consumer health requests and enquiries from MCHS patients and visitors and residents of the Franklinton neighborhood almost two years after the official closing of MCCHL. The former consumer health library space at MCW is now used by the Von Zychlin Healthy Living Center, previously known as the CHRC, for their programs, activities, and classes.

SUMMARY

In the five years of providing people-centered CHI resources and services to meet the needs of patients and consumers alike, MCCHL librarians and volunteers custom tailored CHI to clients' needs using evidence-based research and expanded from operating out of a small repurposed office to designing and occupying three state-of-the-art consumer library spaces across the city of Columbus. Community engagements reached residents who would have otherwise been unable to access CHI services and the development of an original community education curriculum resulted in the creation of seven unique classes.

Looking back on our experiences, we believe that one of the best strategies employed by MCCHL was the proactive promotion of our services through the patient library service and participation in organizational and community events and outreach initiatives. By having an active presence at CHRC classes and activities, MCHS employee health screenings, and community-, school-, and church-sponsored events targeting diverse populations, MCCHL implemented a holistic and wide-reaching approach to providing CHI resources and services aligned to the MCHS mission, vision, and strategic initiatives.

Designing spaces for two iterations of MCCHL and two satellite CHIC spaces from the ground up and seeing them come to life was an unparalleled opportunity and learning experience, but our anecdotal experiences and carefully collected usage data consistently demonstrated better results when services were offered in community environments rather than library spaces. Our MCHSL staff also continue to successfully provide requested CHI using primarily electronic resources. Accepting limitations and taking advantage of opportunities when they were presented, collaborating with professional designers, architects, and other members of MCHS development teams exceeded all of our expectations. Unfortunately, they also outpaced efforts to secure ongoing financial support for a very rapidly growing business operation, particularly in light of widespread health system austerity measures.

The rapidly evolving technological landscape, the ongoing transformation of health care delivery and payment systems, and the evolution of the role of libraries as information providers and community gathering spaces should all be carefully considered when developing new library spaces and services. MCCHL learned this lesson the hard way through the rapid growth and eventual discontinuation of consumer health services at MCHS. We hope that by sharing our experiences, we can help other libraries and information professionals avoid making some of the same mistakes and successfully develop their own CHI services.

NOTES

1. Stevo Roksandic, "Enhancing Health Information Services in Franklin County, Ohio Public Libraries: Consumer Health Information Project (CHIP)" (unpublished manuscript, 2008).

2. Nicole Dettmar, "Where to Start? Needs Assessment," in *The Medical Library Association Guide to Providing Consumer and Patient Health Information*, ed. Michelle Spatz (Lanham, MD: Rowman & Littlefield, 2014), 11–26.

3. Tracey L. Cosgrove, "Planetree Health Information Services: Public Access to the Health Information People Want," *Bulletin of the Medical Library Association* 82, no.1 (1994): 57–63, http://www.ncbi.nlm.nih.gov/pubmed/8136762.

4. Office of Disease Prevention and Health Promotion, "HealthyPeople.gov," Office of Disease Prevention and Health Promotion, accessed February 6, 2018, https://www.healthypeople.gov/.

2

Space Utilization Study by Ithaka S+R

MELLANYE LACKEY, JEAN P. SHIPMAN,
CAMILLE SALMOND, AND DARELL SCHMICK

INTRODUCTION

The Spencer S. Eccles Health Sciences Library (EHSL) at the University of Utah, stands at the intersection of two major forces of change. One is the change sweeping over libraries as print collections are removed and new technologies and other environmental factors transform the ways people work and how they seek and use information. The other change is the transformation of several health sciences buildings on the University of Utah campus, with demolition and new construction creating innovative environments for teaching, learning, research, and clinical care.

The EHSL, a 34,000-square foot building, opened in 1971, and is located on the health campus near the schools of medicine, nursing, and pharmacy and the campus hospital. The library has three floors, called the Upper Level, Main Level, and Garden Level. The EHSL is connected via an elevated foot bridge to a 158,000-square-foot education building, the Spencer F. and Cleone P. Eccles Health Sciences Education Building (HSEB) that opened in 2005. In 2014, the librarians at the EHSL removed most of the print collection of books and journals to create additional space for the Center for Medical Innovation, and to install a skills-building simulation center to join a fabrication laboratory, and the Therapeutic Games and Apps Laboratory (The GApp Lab). Locating these facilities in the EHSL building, most of them on the Lower or Garden Level of the EHSL, brought many operational and

FIGURE 2.1
Upper Level of the Spencer S. Eccles Health Sciences Library.

FIGURE 2.2
Main Level of the Spencer S. Eccles Health Sciences Library.

use changes to the EHSL. Personnel who were not EHSL faculty or staff were regularly present after operational hours, requiring changes in building access and security. More people, such as student competition teams, began using EHSL space for meetings rather than to study or use the EHSL's information resources.

Following the removal of most of the print collection, the EHSL has become a community center for the campus with activities such as yoga, weekly book readings, dog therapy during finals, themed art shows, and other collective activities, and designated safe space for all students. Most of these activities happen during regular business hours. The foot bridge from the HSEB connects to the EHSL's Upper Level, serving as an indoor path to the adjacent health sciences buildings. This pathway greatly contributes to the social feel and community environment. Usage of the physical space in the EHSL has changed dramatically since 2014, with more individuals visiting for these community and group activities. (See usage and building statistics in table 2.1.) More about the transformation of the EHSL's collection and physical space and the resulting innovative partnerships may be found in several publications.[1, 2]

In conjunction with these changes, the university has undertaken a major transformation of multiple physical spaces on the health campus. The main School of Medicine building and other buildings are being demolished to be replaced between 2018 and 2021, with a new medical education and discovery building, an ambulatory care clinic, a rehabilitation hospital, and a discovery and innovation center. These four buildings will be connected to each other, and the discover and innovation center will connect to the Garden Level of the EHSL.

As old buildings are demolished, relocated personnel will need work space, which is already at a premium. Consequently, usage and function of the EHSL

Table 2.1. Usage and building statistics

Number of seats	419
Public access computers	25
Average number of community read events per year	25
Average number of grand rounds for research reproducibility per year	25
Average number of other community events per year	10
Average number of art exhibits per year	5

and surrounding buildings are being carefully examined. Since the EHSL is in the heart of the Health Sciences Campus, it is prime for assessment of use and for temporary relocation of personnel.

In the face of these changes, library leaders and staff wanted to develop a more complete understanding of the use of the EHSL building to support our visioning and data-driven decision making. The need for assessment prompted the EHSL's then-executive director to consult with Dr. Nancy Fried Foster, a design anthropologist who was then senior anthropologist at Ithaka S+R, to investigate the physical use of the EHSL. Dr. Foster proposed an ethnographic study as a promising approach.

OBJECTIVES

The EHSL study had three objectives. The first was to develop a clear picture of who uses EHSL spaces, the activities people engaged in while in these spaces, and the tangible and intangible assets, including the ambience, which draw them there. The second objective was to explore the choices and motivations of individuals who do not use library spaces when they work. The third objective of the study was to investigate ways in which off-site patrons communicate with the library and whether those communication methods needed improvement, alteration, or expansion. The EHSL contracted Dr. Foster through Ithaka S+R to help set up the study, collect and analyze data, and derive insights from the analysis to support better use of EHSL spaces and enhanced communication. The seven-month project culminated in a final report to be shared with health campus administrators and building planners.

METHODOLOGY

Formation of the Project Team

In fall 2016, EHSL formed a team to plan and implement the EHSL study. The group consisted of Darell Schmick (project lead), Jean Shipman (project sponsor and coordinator), Mellanye Lackey, and Camille Salmond (project team members). Dr. Foster was the project's consultant.

Planning Phase

Dr. Foster provided the team with a project plan including steps and target deadlines for the study. Throughout the fall and winter, the team met monthly with Dr. Foster via Skype to tailor the suggested study design to meet the unique needs of the EHSL. The project team selected behaviors to observe, oriented Dr. Foster to the physical library space, reviewed specific details of the study methods, applied for IRB approval, and decided to conduct the study in late March and early April 2017.

Literature Review

There have been many ethnographic studies in colleges and universities as well as in academic libraries.[3, 4, 5, 6, 7, 8, 9, 10, 11, 12, 13] Many of these projects have followed the lead of the original University of Rochester studies, which used ethnographic methods in software and, later, space design projects.[14, 15, 16, 17] Recently, academic health sciences libraries have also used the methods pioneered at the University of Rochester to understand the work practices and needs of the people who use their libraries.[18, 19] Based on the success of these studies, an approach was drafted for use by the EHSL.

Study Design

The project team used several methods because we had many different questions. Some would best be answered by direct observation, others using a targeted survey, or face to face.

To get a sense of what was happening in the EHSL, the team conducted observations of library spaces. To do this, the team divided the EHSL physical space into several sections for observation. Over seven consecutive days, we walked through the library at three preselected times and marked codes on floorplan printouts to indicate where and how people were using the EHSL. We coded for the following activities: concentrated work by an individual, taking a break, participating in an event, viewing a display, doing group work, or attending a meeting. For this study, concentrated work meant someone studying from a book, using a computer, reading a newspaper, or similar. Taking a break included people who were casually talking with each other, putting together a jigsaw puzzle, or using their phone. We also coded people who were present but not evidently engaged in any previously coded activity (e.g., sleeping, walking through the space on their way elsewhere). We also decided to code unattended belongings (e.g., laptops, books, papers). On the floorplans, we drew a circle around individuals who were engaged with each other. We determined that individuals were engaged with each other by observing behaviors such as talking to each other or sharing a screen.

We decided that individuals who were sitting near each other or at the same table, but who were not talking to each other or sharing a screen, were doing concentrated work.

To gain more detailed information about what people were doing in the EHSL, we distributed brief survey cards. We set a goal to distribute and collect 150 cards (30 cards at 5 scheduled times over 5 days) to survey EHSL users. These cards requested a small amount of demographic information and asked eight questions about the respondents' activity (e.g., choice of location, solitary or group work, length of time in the chosen location, alternative locations if they had to leave the building). We chose to print the survey on half sheets of paper with the hope that respondents would be more likely to agree to take the survey if they perceived it as short and not a big interruption of their time.

While the previous two methods elicited information from people already in the EHSL, we also had questions to ask people who rarely, if ever, come into the building. Some of these questions had to do with receiving communications from the EHSL about changes, events, services, and resources. To acquire this information, we scheduled interviews for Dr. Foster to conduct with nine faculty members who are known to be remote users of the EHSL. They represented a range of health sciences departments and programs.

Finally, we wanted to know more about the information practices of a wide range of university students, staff, and faculty members regardless of whether they ever came into the building. To get this information, Dr. Foster conducted thirty interviews with individuals recruited at random from nonlibrary campus locations. In these interviews, she asked respondents where they had conducted their most recent information study or work session using warranted information, what specific activities they had engaged in, and what it was about their locations that made them desirable for those information-related activities. She also asked them more generally about information search and retrieval practices, such as the use of library resources and search tools. These interviews were conducted at several locations around the EHSL, such as the College of Nursing, the adjacent HSEB, the hospital cafeteria, Starbucks, lunchrooms, study spaces, and so forth. Data about the types of input methods used and number of participants for each can be found in table 2.2.

Table 2.2. Number of participants by method

Method	Number of participants
Observation	721
Reply cards	132
Space use interviews	30
Communication interviews	9

FINDINGS

The information collected in this study provided us with insights in the following areas: current use of the physical space at the EHSL, reasons to use the EHSL or choose alternative spaces, remote use of the EHSL, and preferred user communication modes.

Current Use of the EHSL Physical Space

The data from the observations and surveys showed that the people who used the EHSL in person were mainly students. They used the facility more in the afternoon than either the morning or the evening. They made more use of the Upper and Main Levels than the Garden Level (see photographs of the Upper and Main Levels in figures 2.1 and 2.2, respectively).

The EHSL is primarily used for concentrated work by individuals. In observations, 82 percent were engaged in academic work. In reply cards, 79 percent of respondents reported that they were conducting academic tasks. This was corroborated in the space use interviews: eleven of the eighteen individuals who remembered being in EHSL said they had been there to study.

Most respondents worked alone even if they were sitting with people they knew. With regard to working with others, about 10 percent of observed individuals were interacting but not necessarily working with each other. According to reply card responses, 40 percent were sitting with people they knew, and most of them were studying. Only 16 percent had worked with someone else in EHSL on their current visit.

Fewer than 10 percent of respondents had an interaction with a staff member, and of those who did, most interactions had to do with reserving or checking out equipment and supplies. Only one individual consulted a staff member about academic resources during their visit to the EHSL.

Reasons to Use the EHSL or Choose Alternative Spaces

With regard to why people used the EHSL building versus going elsewhere, individuals responding to reply cards reported choosing to work in the building because it was quiet, provided a good work environment with enough seats, and offered plenty of space to spread out one's belongings. Dr. Foster asked about where they would go instead of the EHSL if they had to leave their spot. Respondents reported they would go to the adjacent HSEB (42 percent) or to their home (22 percent) to seek a quiet place, where they could be comfortable and have room for their study materials.

The thirty space-use interviews that were conducted with randomly selected members of the university's health community provide clues to general attitudes toward the EHSL. Note that the small sample size means that findings are suggestive rather than conclusive. One third of the thirty space use interview respondents had been in the EHSL within the past week, and about another third had never been in the EHSL or could not remember when they might have been there. The remaining third were occasional users of the EHSL, but they did not have a preference for being there. Similarly, to the reply card respondents, space use interview respondents described wanting a space that was conveniently located, open when they needed it, and amenable to quiet, focused work.

Of the two thirds of respondents who were not regular users, eight avoided using the physical EHSL space because it was inconvenient (by schedule or location) or because they did not feel comfortable there. The other twenty-two respondents either came to EHSL regularly or did not expressly avoid using it, but instead used other spaces. As one respondent said, "Because that's where I already am." In many cases, respondents sought and used information or conducted other library-type activities in their workplaces because they wanted to be where they may be needed for clinical care or experimental work in a laboratory.

Remote Use of the EHSL

With regard to respondents who rarely or never come to EHSL, five of the thirty interviewees (17 percent) reported that they simply do not access library resources remotely. That is, they have experienced no need to make use of the EHSL in any form or through any channel. Of the remaining twenty-five respondents, a little more than a third (40 percent) start at the EHSL homepage and navigate to resources through links they find there. Another five respondents (17 percent) start on the website of the main campus library or a health campus intranet page, where they log in to begin their navigation. Other respondents clicked browser bookmarks to access specific databases, publisher sites, or to use Google or Google Scholar.

Preferred User Communication Modes

With regard to receiving information from the EHSL, remote users look to the EHSL website and to the weekly Research Update, published by the Office of the Vice President for Research (VPR), more than other channels (eight and five out of nine respondents, respectively). None of the nine respondents to the communication interview regularly used the EHSL YouTube channel, EHSL Instagram account, or calendars to get information about the EHSL. In addition to the EHSL website and VPR Research Update, announcements on the health sciences intranet and email messages from EHSL emerged as the preferred and stickiest means of communication. However, three respondents mentioned in passing that they are exposed to too much information in their environment on a daily basis, and that the EHSL may be able to help by consolidating information or making it easier to filter information to receive the most useful items.

DISCUSSION

Impact of the Collected Data

The study conducted at the EHSL constitutes an initial effort to better understand who uses the building's spaces, users' activities, and preferences for the EHSL's current communication channels. Based on what the study revealed, there are several programmatic and policy implications to be considered.

The most frequent finding we observed was people who use the EHSL physical space for studying or to meet with others do not use the electronic resources or staff assistance while in the building. The majority of respondents counted in this project, surveyed, or interviewed used the EHSL building to study. While group work accounts for only a small proportion of the work that was observed or surveyed, the ability to have a meeting in EHSL seems desirable. Most reported not utilizing other library services while in the building. However, they value the availability of the building for study and meeting space. Many who study in EHSL, especially medical students, look to EHSL spaces to meet needs that are not adequately met elsewhere. These users would benefit from extending EHSL hours both earlier and later in the day, as they retreat to the EHSL as a place to go when not attending class.

The Upper Level pathway, providing access to other health sciences buildings, is a great convenience, and it is also a way for us to attract people to view art exhibits and signage about database trials, new electronic purchases, or building changes among other topics. While the space is busy with passers-through, it offers an opportunity to draw attention to our space. People sometimes stop to talk to their colleagues as they pass through the space. The EHSL Upper Level pathway offers different environments for people like places to study alone or in small groups while still being in a social setting.

We hope this data shows EHSL is valued, partly because of its function as a study hall and community meeting place. The study data showed our users value the library as a place, which might have implications for the expenditure of resources to support the place. What kinds and numbers of rooms are needed, and how they should be equipped, are things we will consider if we further remodel the building. Future renovations should increase or preserve the academic affordances of the current space, such as the quiet atmosphere, spaces to be social or conduct meetings, and space for spreading out belongings, all of which supports user focus and concentration.

The data collected highlighted one particular function that the EHSL performs for the community; we offer access to electronic resources. A large majority of respondents reported they use academic information resources and associated technologies to help them find and access those resources. We invest considerably in education and outreach efforts, connecting people with resources wherever they may be, and will continue to do so. We know from web usage statistics that our online presence is by far our most highly used real estate.

Before the study, we wondered how administrators and space planners viewed the EHSL building, as they must negotiate competing pressures to rehouse faculty offices or develop classroom spaces when adjacent buildings are demolished for campus construction projects. Sometimes the seats are full of students immersed in concentrated work, while other times study carrels and tables sit unoccupied and the building seems empty. The data from this study shows that users value access to the physical building for quiet study.

A small but significant number of respondents reported being hesitant to enter the EHSL because they were afraid they would not know anyone or be confused about where to go and what to do. We strive to make the EHSL an inviting place for everyone. Adding welcoming language to existing orientation activities may improve this situation. Additional signage located outside of the physical building may help alleviate these concerns as well. Information kiosks are something we could add to offer guidance to the facilities and services to those too timid to ask in person.

Interviews with nine remote users asked their preferred communication channels for updates about the EHSL. They reported preferring weekly emails from the vice president for research (VPR) or visiting the EHSL website to get updates. We believe a multipronged approach that uses several communication channels is best. Due to the small sample interview size, we will continue to push content to the VPR's office, and future EHSL website content will include news, events, and updates about the EHSL. We will also continue to use social media, even though the respondents did not report using YouTube, Twitter, Instagram, or other EHSL social media communication channels. Several of the platforms cross-post, easing the workload when we need to broadcast a message. Usage statistics from these applications show moderate to high use, so messaging does reach some users.

Impact on the University of Utah Campus Transformation

The final report of the EHSL Study was shared with key health campus administrators. Unfortunately, the report was delivered immediately before several major leadership changes, including the expected retirement of the executive director, the sudden and unexpected resignation of the administrator to whom she reported, and the accelerated retirement of the president of the university. Therefore, we have seen no impact as a result of the report to date. However, as new administration is hired at the university and EHSL, and as the campus building transformation progresses, we anticipate the report will be useful to illustrate the need for quiet space for students. Whether this quiet space needs to be in the EHSL building or in another space remains to be seen.

Some of us feel that retaining a physical building holds us back from being seen as information management experts, particularly if people perceive the library profession as diminishing. People continue to need our assistance whether on campus or remotely. If we were embedded librarians throughout the campus, would our expertise be better used or could we see opportunities to insert our expertise if we were in closer proximity to our colleagues and their research, clinical care, education, or administrative activities? Would our location matter if our users are also located remotely? Others of us feel that we are stronger if we remain together as a collective library faculty and staff to be able to learn from one another, to assist those who do enter the building or use us remotely, and to retain a physical location designated as the library, a brand still treasured by many as a quiet retreat and demonstrated by the survey results.

EHSL AND OTHER LIBRARIES

The results of the EHSL study are generally consistent with those of other academic libraries conducting similar ethnographic studies, including the University of Nevada, Reno (UNR), Montgomery College, Auburn University, and Purdue University. Like the University of Utah, UNR, Auburn, and Purdue are large, public research universities. Montgomery College is the community college system of Montgomery County, Maryland. According to previously published reports, the four institutions received largely similar student responses to the questions used in the EHSL study.[20, 21, 22, 23]

The rate of academic work reported by EHSL respondents was in the same range as the others. The greatest similarity was seen with Montgomery College, where all students commute, are older than the average four-year college student, and have few alternatives to the library. At the University of Utah health sciences campus, students largely commute and are older than the average graduate student. The rate of group work was slightly lower, the biggest difference being with Purdue, where the study was done in conjunction with a project to increase active learning. More Auburn students appeared to sit together (about 40 percent), although fewer than one in five worked together on the same assignment or project. Across all sites and projects, respondents working in the library do so for three main reasons: (1) it is convenient, (2) there is enough space, and (3) the surroundings enable them to do good work. Note that the availability of physical library materials is no longer a primary reason for respondents in any of these studies to use library spaces.

We encourage other libraries, especially academic health sciences libraries, to replicate our study to add more collective data to determine how physical library buildings are used in today's digital information world. Are there collective results that can drive university administrators' perspectives of the future of libraries? Many libraries are being asked to demonstrate their value in an information-rich, digital society. Additional data may help to demonstrate how users value their library buildings.

SMALL STUDY SIZE LIMITS CONCLUSION VALIDITY

The main limitation of this study is the low study selection numbers. Because of the low numbers, findings and discussions are only suggestive rather than conclusive. Scheduled times for surveys and observations were varied over several days to offer a well-rounded representation of who uses the EHSL and for what purpose. Usage statistics would better represent the number of people who visit the building, though we do not currently ask people the purpose of their visit. Our survey numbers are small and in the case of how to best communicate with our users, very small.

The selected study design does an excellent job of collecting accurate data at specific points in time in a way that is unobtrusive, efficient, and easy to implement and replicate. It is a snapshot from a particular point in time, as if we took a picture of the space and the individuals and groups that were there at that second. However, the data from the study does not capture the full range of uses of the library as a building. If we had selected survey response times or observation times during special events, then the data and resulting analysis might look very different. For example, if we had made observations during a yoga session or during one of the weekly book discussion meetings, then more participants would be observed in group activities rather than concentrated work as defined in this study. Another example is the single interviewee who said they had used a library resource during their time in the building. Taken alone, this finding might suggest that library resources are not in high demand by our users. However, web-usage data shows that people use the library's electronic resources regularly and with great frequency. When reporting the study results, we had to repeatedly make the distinction that this study, and the data collected were about the physical building rather than all of the functions of the EHSL. To illustrate the true impact of the EHSL, a different approach and study design would need to be implemented.

LESSONS LEARNED

If we were to conduct the study again, we would likely make some changes. We might spread the surveys and observations collection times and days farther apart. Some survey respondents told us that they had already completed a survey on a previous day or time. We asked them to fill out a second survey, and they all agreed. During the observations, we coded every person we saw in the library, even if we had counted them in a previous observation. Collecting the data in this way was appropriate because they indicated single, though not unique instances of library usage. Sometimes visitors to the library would stay in the same spot for several hours in one day, or they would return to the same spot for several days in a row. Increasing the spread of days between the surveys or observation times may have lessened the number of repeat users. Unique data may in turn have returned a different analysis.

During observations, it was challenging to know if individuals who were talking to each other with computers in front of them were doing group work or if they were taking a break. To keep with the spirit of the observation, we did not listen to their conversations, interrupt them, nor watch them for any length of time. We had to make a quick decision as if we had taken a photograph of the area and had to record our observations based on the information in the photo. The project team met with Dr. Foster for a training session before beginning the study where we talked through this process and similar issues.

Via a casual observation, one would say the majority of people use the EHSL for quiet study, group meetings, or events. We have years of usage statistics taken daily at selected times. These two elements combined could reveal similar information as the data collected in the study. As a group, we discussed what the benefit would be to having study data that showed information that we, in the EHSL, anecdotally knew. The culture on the health campus is to apply data to drive decisions. We ultimately decided that having the ethnographic data added enough value to our experiential knowledge that the project was justified.

Colleagues asked why we did not follow study methodologies already used by peer libraries to generate the study instruments and to conduct the study on our own, without the use of a consultant. This certainly might have been an option if any members of the team were experienced in qualitative survey design or had conducted a similar study elsewhere. Additionally, Ithaka S+R and the consultant are well-known for their research, which helped to speed along the study as past experiences and methodologies could be applied.

Two last items that warrant mentioning include the sharing of the study instruments and a modified study design. While sharing the instruments used in the study would increase transparency, due to the consultancy nature of the project, actual tools are not being shared due to their intellectual property value. If we had the opportunity to redesign the study, we would address the question about accessing communication channels as a separate survey, in order to focus on the topics of space and remote use of resources and services.

CONCLUSION

We did not offer monetary compensation to the survey respondents or interviewees. Rather, we relied on their enthusiasm to help the EHSL and offered our thanks as rewards for their participation. People were very willing to take our survey when we approached them. No one refused to take the survey, though some interview candidates declined because of scheduling conflicts. Many survey respondents offered additional details about how having the library space available benefited them, and they noted their support for keeping it available.

We anecdotally knew some users greatly valued the EHSL as a space for quiet study. However, we learned the extent to which they value it over the course of this study and during the events that followed.

The study period in late March and early April 2017 coincided with three key events: (1) medical students studying for board exams, (2) preparation for the 2019 Liaison Committee on Medical Education (LCME) reaccreditation, and (3) discussions, separate from this study, about what hours the EHSL building should be open. We requested user feedback on hours through the EHSL blog, a comment box at entry/exit doors, and display signage with the blog URL. We were thoroughly surprised and grateful to receive over seventy responses. The majority of responders were medical students, and every respondent asked for the EHSL building to be open more hours. Unbeknownst to us, the medical student leadership created its own petition to gather comments supporting extended library hours. When presented with the results, the EHSL associate director for research and education, the deputy director, and executive director met with student leadership. In that meeting, we learned that many students do not feel they can study effectively in the adjacent HSEB, which was designed as a space for 24/7 use by students from all health sciences disciplines. They felt it was too crowded and did not provide them with quiet space for uninterrupted work where they could spread out their materials. The EHSL building filled that gap. We agreed that longer hours were desirable, but building security was an issue. We did not have the funds to ensure the safety of the building overnight. However, students' board scores are very important, especially to medical school administrators, and they were not satisfied with the existing building hours. Additionally, preparation for the LCME reaccreditation had begun, and student satisfaction is considered in the site review. The medical students were vocal about their desire for longer building hours with School of Medicine administration. These factors, in addition to an effort to increase security on the Health Campus, paved the way for budgetary approval for security equipment and a guard to keep the library building open 24/7.

FUTURE PLANS

As we mentioned in our discussion, the findings are based on small interview and survey sample sizes. To gain more information to inform our future actions, we will hold focus groups with different sets of user types (e.g., faculty, students) as well as different schools and departments. We realize that users have different expectations and space needs based on whether they are educating, conducting research, or providing clinical care, recognizing these are not discrete functions. They often happen simultaneously in one interaction.

We will continue to be a member of the Health Campus space transformation steering committee, where decisions are made about how information access can be integrated into the new buildings. The beauty of digital information is that it can be easily distributed, accessed, and applied 24/7. Unfortunately, librarian expertise has yet to be digitized in the same way as the content, so we need to monitor our scarce human resources and apply them in a diplomatic, yet useful, way. Pilot tests may be the answer to determine where librarians can contribute the most to the success of the University and its many personnel.

How we communicate with our users will be something we need to constantly assess as again, communication takes human and financial resources. More study on what venues are reaching our users needs to be done. Additionally, we could ask our users what we might do to make the EHSL or the librarians seem more approachable, to meet the needs of those who are hesitant to use the library or ask for help. Meanwhile, we continue to seek feedback from our users through monitoring hits and numbers of subscribers to our email lists and to our news outlets. As use of the physical building continues to evolve, we will seek creative ways to encourage engagement with the EHSL and to stay informed of the many ways we can help tour users.

As space becomes an increasingly precious campus commodity, libraries may not go away but may have space to offer should they remove their print collections. Libraries can transform to meet the needs and desires of users and leaders. We need to think creatively and be willing to test new models, as our dependency on the print collection declines. Additional studies would help the university to understand where it should invest its facility dollars to accelerate the success of the university.

NOTES

1. Christy Jarvis, Joan M. Gregory, and Jean P. Shipman, "Books to Bytes at the Speed of Light: A Rapid Health Sciences Collection Transformation," *Collection Management* 39, no. 2–3 (2014): 60–76, doi:10.1080/01462679.2014.910150.

2. Jean P. Shipman and Barbara A. Ulmer, eds., *Information and Innovation: A Natural Combination for Health Sciences Libraries,* A Medical Library Association Books Series (Lanham, MD: Rowman & Littlefield, 2017).

3. Susan D. Blum, *My Word! Plagiarism and College Culture* (Ithaca, NY: Cornell University Press, 2010).

4. Dorothy C. Holland and Margaret A. Eisenhart, *Educated in Romance: Women, Achievement, and College Culture* (Chicago, IL: University of Chicago Press, 1990), e-book.

5. Michael Mofffatt, *Coming of Age in New Jersey: College and American Culture* (New Brunswick, NJ: Rutgers University Press, 2000).

6. Richard O'Connor, "Seeing duPont within Sewanee and Student Life" (Task Force Final Report for the Jessie Ball duPont Library, Sewanee, TN, 2005). https://www.pdffiller.com/13341550—Seeing-duPont-within-Sewanee-and-Student-Life-Ringling-College.

7. Rebekah Nathan, *My Freshman Year: What a Professor Learned by Becoming a Student* (New York, NY: Penguin Books, 2014), e-book.

8. Kathrina Aben et al., "Ethnographic Research on College Schoolwork and Libraries: A Study Completed by Graduate Students in the Methods of Cultural Analysis (ANTH606) Department of Anthropology, University of Maryland" (Study Report, College Park, MD, 2011).

9. Henry D. Delcore, James Mullooly, and Michael Scroggins, "The Library Study at Fresno State" (Institute of Public Anthropology Publication, Fresno, CA, 2009), http://fresnostate.edu/socialsciences/anthropology/ipa/thelibrarystudy.html.

10. Lynda M. Duke and Andrew D. Asher, *College Libraries and Student Culture: What We Now Know* (Chicago, IL: American Library Association, 2012), e-book.

11. Nicole Hennig, et al. "User Needs Assessment of Information Seeking Activities of MIT Students—Spring 2006" (D-Space @ MIT Archived Report, Cambridge, MA, 2006), http://dspace.mit.edu/handle/1721.1/33456.

12. Patricia A. Steele, David Cronrath, Sandra Parsons Vicchio, and Nancy Fried Foster, *The Living Library: An Intellectual Ecosystem* (Chicago, IL: Association of College & Research Libraries, 2015).

13. Doug Suarez, "What Students Do When They Study in the Library: Using Ethnographic Methods to Observe Student Behavior," *Electronic Journal of Academic and Special Librarianship* 8, no. 3 (2007), http://southernlibrarianship. icaap.org/content/v08n03/suarez_d01.html.

14. Nancy Fried Foster, ed., *Studying Students: A Second Look* (Chicago, IL: Association of College & Research Libraries, 2013).

15. Nancy Fried et al., "Participatory Design of Purdue University's Active Learning Center Final Report" (Libraries Reports, West Lafayette, IN, 2013), http://docs.lib. purdue.edu/libreports/1.

16. Nancy Fried Foster and Susan Gibbons, eds., *Studying Students: The Undergraduate Research Project at the University of Rochester* (Chicago, IL: Association of College & Research Libraries, 2007), e-book.

17. Nancy Fried Foster and Susan Gibbons, "Understanding Faculty to Improve Content Recruitment for Institutional Repositories," *D-Lib Magazine* 11, no. 1 (2005), doi:10.1045/january2005-foster.

18. Jeanne Link and Jonna Peterson, "Replicating Rochester: Developing a Feasible Multi-Institution Study of User Information Needs in the Health Sciences" (Council

on Library and Information Resources Reports, Washington, DC), 2014, https://www.clir.org/wp-content/uploads/sites/6/pub161.pdf, 82–97.

19. Andrea B. Twiss-Brooks et al., "A Day in the Life of Third-Year Medical Students: Using an Ethnographic Method to Understand Information Seeking and Use," *Journal of the Medical Library Association* 105, no. 1 (2017): 12–19, doi:10.5195/jmla.2017.95.

20. Marcia Boosinger et al., "Reconfiguring Auburn University's Main Library for Engaged Active Student Learning" (Ithaka S+R Libraries & Scholarly Communications Research Report, New York, NY, 2016), doi: 10.18665/sr.284239.

21. Foster, "Participatory Design of Purdue University's."

22. Ann Medaille et al., "Exploring Group Study at the University of Nevada, Reno" (Ithaka S+R Libraries & Scholarly Communications Research Report, New York, NY, 2015), http://www.sr.ithaka.org/publications/exploring-group-study-at-the-university-of-nevada-reno/.

23. Montgomery College Libraries, "Montgomery College Libraries Ethnography Study: Home," Montgomery College Libraries, last updated June 13, 2017, http://libguides.montgomerycollege.edu/ethnographic.

3

Services and Space in Support of Innovation

Valrie Minson, Christine Driver Yip,
Sara Russell Gonzalez, Neelam Bharti,
and Adam Brown

In 2014, the University of Florida's (UF) Marston Science Library (MSL) transformed from a traditional, collection-centric library to a reinvigorated collaboration and learning hub. The science library quickly became a center point for the university with the inclusion of 3D printing, the MADE@UF lab (for mobile app development), visualization and conference room, and open floor seating in the new Collaboration Commons. Results have been very impressive with building occupancy statistics reaching 1.4 million annually. Marston's transformation of the physical space has been so successful that other UF libraries are following with similar renovations. This transition represents a redesign of a traditional library space and a step toward becoming the innovative library of the future and has changed the library's organizational culture and the responsibilities of the library staff. The success of these changes has also impacted nonlibrary buildings and areas around campus, creating a culture of public spaces as learning hubs. This chapter will highlight the impact of space renovation and service creation on the visibility of the library, the modification and enhancement of existing services, and transformation of the library as a major collaborator within the campus community. Data discussed will also include the results of a student technology and space survey that have informed the reshaping of our library service model.

INTRODUCTION

UF in Gainesville, Florida, is a comprehensive, public, land-grant institution with more than 50,000 students studying in more than 15 colleges, including a robust number of health science center colleges. In 2017, the U.S. News and World Report ranked UF tied for the ninth-best public university in the United States and forty-second among all national universities, public and private.[1] Within UF, the George A. Smathers Libraries include six library branches with two serving the sciences, namely the Health Science Center Library (HSCL) and the MSL. The HSCL serves the College of Dentistry, Medicine, Nursing, Pharmacy, Public Health and Health Professions, and Veterinary Medicine. MSL serves primarily the nonmedical sciences, but also health-related fields that include biology; biomedical engineering; family, youth, and community sciences; food science and human nutrition; microbiology and cell science; and nuclear and radiological engineering. Additionally, MSL has expertise in areas of informatics and geographic information systems (GIS), which overlap with all disciplines.

In 2013, in an effort to better meet the study needs of a large student body, UF administration requested that the Smathers Libraries identify spaces having the potential to transform into a collaborative study space for students. The libraries proposed the ground floor of MSL, which held only fifty study seats and housed compact shelving containing historical science journals and government documents, a Map & Imagery Library, and offices for staff. The total square footage of the MSL ground floor is comparable to another campus, nonlibrary space, Newell Hall, also considered by UF administration; however, this historic building required expensive asbestos remediation and other structural renovations such as the construction of elevators and bathrooms.

This opportunity to renovate the ground floor into a collision space—a space where students come together to share ideas, collaborate, and engage in serendipitous learning—was welcomed by library staff, although staff also expressed concern regarding important historical research collections moving off-site and becoming less discoverable. Moving the collections off-site was a shift in approach for our library, from collections to space and services, but an important step for meeting today's science and health science student community. Ultimately, due to the existing infrastructure of MSL, UF administration chose the MSL ground floor as the location of the new study area and funded a $5.5 million renovation that would create the MSL Collaboration Commons (CC) and transform MSL into a highly utilized student collision space.

RENOVATION

Prior to the renovation, the library received an average of 725,000 visitors per year in a building containing approximately 81,000 square feet. The ground floor, where the renovation was planned, is approximately 26,000 square feet (32 percent of the total square footage of the building), but provided limited seating (50 in all) and power outlets due to the housing of low-use materials. Within the entire library there were only 1,404 seats and 324 power outlets total.

In preparation for the renovations, the Map & Imagery Library and a portion of their collections were relocated to the Smathers Library, which houses the Special & Area Studies Collections. All other collections, including pre-1990 journals, government documents, and a portion of the map collection, were moved to an off-site shared storage facility. This required processing our collection, containing more than 200,000 items and 21,500 linear feet, in preparation for relocation to an off-site shared storage facility. The collection processing was completed in three phases over a four-month period and this effort laid the groundwork for the overall renovations to begin. The three phases included updating item records in the library catalog, selecting and relocating high use titles to the general circulating collection, and relocating low- or no-use materials to the off-site shared storage facility. Once collections were relocated, the compact shelving housing the materials were also removed from the ground floor. Beginning in March 2014, the construction crews began work, and six months later, by the beginning of fall semester 2014, the floor was open to students. The entire renovation team met weekly to accomplish the ambitious six-month construction goal. To provide some indication of the scope of the project, the planning team included representatives from UF's Design, Planning, & Construction unit, an architectural firm, a construction company, electricians, interior designers, UF information technology staff, a library associate dean responsible for all facilities, the library facilities head, and the chair of MSL.

The final renovation transformed the ground floor into two computer labs and 20 technology-rich study rooms, and included more than 1,700 power outlets and 700 seats in a wide variety of styles. Furniture styles included lounge chairs, sofas, two seater tables, four-seater tables, pinwheel carrels, and high and low top tables with an emphasis on allowing line of sight throughout the entire floor. Because of the large square footage of the floor, there are five different-colored way finder features that can assist students in locating their fellow students. Additionally, the libraries and University of Florida Information Technology (UFIT) unit created a new partnership as management of the computer labs shifted over to UFIT control. This new relationship was the first of several new collaborations developing from this renovation and the start of a highly productive service partnership.

NEW COLLABORATIONS AND SERVICE CHANGES

University of Florida Information Technology Partnership

From enhancement of existing services to the development of new services, the renovation opened up several opportunities for collaboration with other university entities and to expand existing library services in new directions. These opportunities included developing spaces for mobile application development (MADE@UF), data visualization, as well as 3D printing. The libraries have their own library information technology unit, separate from the campus-wide UFIT department. Many institutions have merged libraries and IT departments, but in cases where the units exist separately there is strong evidence that "collaboration between departments can enhance the value and visibility of libraries as well as open up new possibilities in sharing resources, reaching new patrons, and expanding services."[2] The libraries viewed the renovation as an excellent time to begin a collaborative partnership with UFIT, redirecting library IT efforts away from public printing and computing and refocusing on the libraries' core competencies in the area of innovative technology development. The renovation increased the overall number of public computers offered in MSL and transitioned to UFIT managed computers, scanners, and printers. Together, our respective units developed a memorandum of understanding and service-level agreement to establish the parameters and responsibilities of each unit. The libraries coordinate all building management issues, including facilities and maintenance support for meeting rooms and group study rooms, as well as oversight of the new study room reservation system. UFIT staff provide support services related to the technology, including maintenance and repair of computers, printers, plotter printers, and audio/visual (A/V) equipment. They also created a new help desk in the MSL CC space, which is staffed during open business hours. By shifting from library to UFIT managed computers, students have reported greater consistency of service, higher quality hardware, shorter computer loading times, and a larger breadth of support than what was previously provided by the libraries. This new collaborative support model also allows the libraries to explore new innovation and service changes that have direct impact on research and scholarship.

The collaboration between UFIT and MSL marked the first large-scale implementation of UFIT services in a non-UFIT space. From the UFIT perspective this large project arrived at an opportune time as UFIT was moving forward with centralizing campus IT resources and investigating services to non-UFIT departments and units. UFIT has a long tradition of learning technologies in the classroom and open spaces, which dovetailed nicely with the goals of the MSL CC space.

Both UFIT and MSL were able to play to their strengths and leverage existing services in new areas, as well as make new services available to the student body. In the new Collaboration Commons, UFIT provided A/V technology in the group study rooms, printing services (black and white, color, and large format plotting), open computers, and student staff to operate the space. The key to our success was early integration of UFIT and MSL staff in the planning process, and utilization of a UFIT core competency: their technical knowledge. Planning with all groups and vendor involvement the space would have been trapped in a renovation/adaption cycle. Instead, it was completed ahead of schedule, and allowed fine tuning of the final product. Another reason for the success was that all equipment was fully functional at the grand opening. The libraries hosted an opening showcase in August 2014 with the UF provost and president as speakers who actively demonstrated the equipment for attendees. All technology was interactive and ready for our students to use at the opening. Being ready for this showcase required significant resources from both UFIT and MSL staff, as in many cases what we were doing had not been done before at UF.

MSL also added twenty-one new group study rooms to the building, increasing from four (located on the second floor) to twenty-five study rooms. The new study rooms are a mixture of sizes and seating configuration, including "reading rooms" designed for two to four students with soft chairs and low tables and larger spaces holding six to fourteen students with conference tables. All study rooms have glass boards and a large monitor with AirMedia capability that allow students to wirelessly cast their laptops to the display. UFIT supports all the technologies provided in the study rooms.

Initially the study rooms used a reservation system connected to the library catalog. Students reserved the room, available in two-hour time windows, and checked out the key at the MSL service desk. Staff were responsible for ensuring that at least two patrons were present to check out the key. These procedures proved time-consuming for both patrons and staff since there was a wave of students returning and checking out keys every two hours. Often groups would stand in front of the desk while they waited for the previous group to return the key. Staff also had to keep the keys sorted since each of the twenty-five study rooms had a unique key.

Eventually this key system was untenable for staff and the library switched to using D!bs, Demco's room reservation system, that still gives students the option of two-hour time slots but now the rooms are unmediated. The room doors are unlocked and anyone can use an empty room until a patron with a reservation arrives. This has removed the patron rush at the desk and encourages full use of the rooms. Figure 3.1 shows the rapid increase in utilization of the D!bs reservation system from its introduction in fall 2014. The variability in usage is due to lower occupancy during the summer semester.

Out of this endeavor, UFIT created a standardization of service that served as a model for future enterprises. Moving forward, UFIT has worked further with the UF libraries along with other UF units to provide support services in both smaller and larger spaces. These range from small-scale renovations in two- to four-person study spaces to entire building remodels in UF's $15 million Newell Hall Learning Commons. All of those successes are based on the Collaboration Commons, whether in the types of study seating, technologies, or space design. The student feedback is overwhelmingly positive, and the usage figures have held steady at impressive numbers. Not only was it a success at opening, but it has continued and formed a tradition of excellence for the University of Florida community.

Visualization and Conference Room

The creation of computer labs was the shift of responsibilities from one UF unit to another, but the renovation also created the Visualization and Confer-

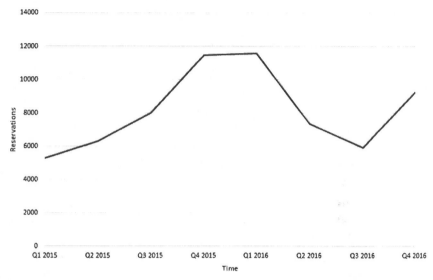

FIGURE 3.1
Line plot displaying reservations made using D!bs for MSL study rooms from January 2015 until the end of 2016.

ence Room. MSL provides a suite of spatial services and offers the expertise of a geographic information system (GIS) librarian. Individual graduate students without access to departmental labs needed a place to conduct spatial research as many of the GIS and Remote Sensing Labs on campus service the faculty and students within their departments. The Visualization and Conference Room comfortably holds forty-five seats and was created to facilitate data visualization for researchers with large, high-resolution datasets. A new room (L136) was partitioned from former staff space and installed with a Planar 3x3 panel 32 multitouch visualization wall, workstation, and multiple cameras and microphones for video conferencing. A power and data grid was placed in the floor and the furnishings are highly movable to allow for multiple use configurations. The instructor computer provided GIS, remote sensing, and photogrammetry software and is designed to support the creation and manipulation of spatial data. This space has improved the students' learning and collaboration experience and the faculty's capacity to create quality learning experiences.

Due to the specialized nature of the new conference room, the library decided to treat this room differently than other classroom, study, and meeting
spaces in the building. L136 was given a public calendar along with a reservation form for directly reserving the room for any type of use. Priority is given
to users who require the large visualization wall followed by video conferencing; however, there is no minimum number of patrons and the room can be
reserved for as long as needed. Thus, L136 has hosted single researchers who
wished to view large datasets on the wall, multiday conferences that were
streamed to remote sites, and student organization meetings that needed a
large space to accommodate their members.

This new Visualization and Conference room was part of the new collaboration with UFIT and its emerging technology and patron access model
presented several initial challenges. One difficulty was the realization that
most users were unfamiliar with how to operate the equipment and thus an
orientation and handbook to the room were developed. The orientation was
mandatory for patrons to attend before using the room for the first time.
Another challenge was internal ambiguity about which IT was responsible
for technical difficulties in the room. UFIT manages the equipment, however library staff were accustomed to contacting library IT for assistance and
there was initial confusion as to who was responsible for solving problems,
especially with time-sensitive dilemmas such as missing audio in a video conference. This was solved with additional communication and posting clear
signage directing users to contact UFIT with all room problems.

MADE@UF

Another new opportunity that arose from the renovation was a collaboration with UFIT to open a lab dedicated to mobile application development.
This space, termed MADE@UF for "Mobile Application Development Environment," provided a technical sandbox for students interested in exploring
mobile app development. The major objectives were to facilitate students
learning how to program Android and iOS apps individually or in groups,
testing apps on variety of devices, networking with other students, and finding mentors within the local tech community.

This new lab was another example of a partnership between the library
and UFIT where the library provided infrastructure, marketing, circulation
support, and coordinated workshops while UFIT managed the hardware

and software, and initially provided students to supervise MADE@UF. This emerging technology presented many challenges since technology use mandated development of a liability agreement in collaboration with UF general counsel, new software required a lengthy license review process, and it was difficult to recruit qualified and willing instructors to lead workshops for beginning students.

After the first year of operation, MADE@UF expanded to a new location in Infinity Hall, an off-campus residence hall with a mission to support the entrepreneurship activities of students. This new location expanded the collaboration to include the UF housing residence staff and IT. Infinity's MADE@UF was designed to be a twin of Marston's location, and staff duplicated procedures as much as possible for seamless student access.

Over time, new technology was added to MADE@UF that broadened the scope beyond mobile app development including Google Glasses and the Epson Moverio headsets. Students expressed enthusiasm for adding virtual reality devices to the lab, and this led to a new student technology fee grant to add Oculus Rift and Microsoft HoloLens headsets. In 2018, the lab is almost exclusively focused on virtual and augmented reality development. The UF VR student club holds regular meetings and a new interdisciplinary class, "VR for the Social Good," is tightly integrated with student teams utilizing the room and technology for their class projects. Putnam and Gonzalez provide more detail about the development and technology in MADE@UF in their article, "Getting Real in the Library: A Case Study at the University of Florida."[3]

IMPACTS ON THE LIBRARIES

In addition to the development of a new and multifaceted partnership with UFIT, the renovation directly impacted MSL in several ways. Impacts included a dramatic increase in occupancy each subsequent year; an increase in usage of 3D-printing services and paving the way for further expansion of services, a campus-wide conversation regarding which library should host 24/5 overnight hours, and continued prioritization of renovations.

Occupancy

Occupancy statistics have been the single-most valuable indicator of success. Occupancy numbers from before and after the renovation are included in the charts that follow. MSL experienced a 52 percent increase in occupancy

Table 3.1. Occupancy by semester, Marston Science Library—University of Florida

	2013 (Before renovation)	2014 (During renovation)	2015 (After renovation)
Spring	317,094	312,581	523,309
Summer	66,629	64,079	126,461
Fall	319,641	484,865	754,492

the fall semester immediately following the renovation in fall 2014 and a 67 percent increase in occupancy the following spring semester in spring 2015 (see tables 3.1 and 3.2). The increase in occupancy numbers clearly show the positive impact that the renovation had on our building usage. Note that an additional renovation to our second floor took place during the summer semester 2015, which accounts for some of the increase in occupancy during fall semester 2015.

The UF Libraries were interested in understanding whether the increases at MSL resulted in decreases at the other branch libraries. The other libraries during this same period did not experience a decline in occupancy, but in fact were stable or increasing in their own occupancy statistics. These statistics indicate that students were not necessarily shifting their library of choice, but rather the libraries were meeting an unmet need for additional study space within the campus environment.

3D Printing Services

The increase in 3D-printing requests is another indicator of success. Prior to the renovation in April 2014, MSL introduced a 3D-printing service with two printers located on the second floor. Library staff manage this service in which patrons submit an order for 3D printing either in person or online and, once paid and printed, the patron returns to MSL to pick up the completed

Table 3.2. Percent increase/decrease in occupancy by semester, Marston Science Library—University of Florida. Percentages are in comparison to previous year's spring/summer/fall semester

	2013–2014	2014–2015
Spring	−1%	67%
Summer	−4%	97%
Fall	52%	56%

order. (For more details about the service, see Gonzalez and Bennett.[4]) This service was featured during the first floor's opening event and underwent a sharp increase in usage correlated with the increase in library occupancy. Figure 3.2 illustrates the effect that this renovation had upon raising exposure to the new service. The columns show material in grams printed during these time periods, and the line illustrates the number of orders placed.

Due to the increase in usage, 3D printing expanded to two other campus libraries and MSL received a new technology grant to purchase additional equipment. New technology added to the service included the following:

- Printrbot Simple Metals: for staff workshops and outreach
- Printrbot Simple Plays: for circulation to students
- Fusion F306 single and dual extruder 3D printers
- Structure 3D scanners
- NextEngine 3D scanner and workstation

The growing strength of 3D printing services within the library resulted in UF Ambassador Tours, designed to showcase the campus services and ini-

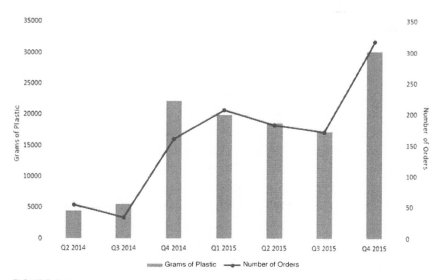

FIGURE 3.2

Usage statistics from MSL's 3D printing service between April 2014 and December 2015. The left axis shows grams printed and right axis the number of patron orders.

tiatives to prospective students with the overall goal of student recruitment, being re-routed to walk through MSL and stop in front of the 3D printers. Lastly, this success has also resulted in ongoing discussions about the creation of a centrally located, library-managed makerspace to be located in the Reitz Student Union building. While the makerspace may not become a reality, these discussions are indirectly stemming from the high-profile and overall success of the MSL 3D printing services.

Changes in Skills and Expectations

The success of a renovation can be expressed in terms of strong occupancy statistics or an increase in an already successful 3D printing program; however, another indicator of success can be in the less tangible changes in responsibilities or workload. For example, with the increase in 3D printing, one MSL staff position shifted from a collections (book binding) emphasis to managing the 3D print queue. Additionally, with greater visibility of spatial support services, the GIS Librarian now has a colleague providing informatics support services. Renovations offer new avenues for enhancing the ways libraries may connect users to the resources and increase the emphasis on user-centered service.

Overnight Hours

After completion of the renovation, the UF libraries shifted 24/5 overnight hours from Library West to MSL. The decision to shift locations was carefully considered and library administration took into account MSL's open floorplan, increased power and seating, and availability of the UFIT help desk. In order to accommodate the night hours, MSL hired two full-time employees and increased the number of custodial services. Students generally feel loyal to one particular library, and there was heavy discussion within social media and in email feedback about whether the shift was appropriate. In order to assess students' perception of the MSL's renovation and new 24/5 availability, an in-house survey was distributed to the library's overnight users. Out of twenty-six questions, sixteen questions were related to the renovation and Marston 24/5 services (see appendix). The purpose of this survey was to evaluate the students' need and library's space usage and included demographic questions and questions related to services and space at Marston. Some questions were multiple choice, while other were open-ended and required a written text response.

The survey was completed in 2016, from January 25–29 and February 2–26 during overnight hours between the hours of 1:00 a.m. and 8:00 a.m. More than half of the responses received were between 1:00 a.m. and 2:00 a.m. Results showed that Thursday was the most popular day and 1:00 a.m. to 2:00 a.m. was the most popular time. Most of the responders were UF undergraduate students (91.09 percent) and UF graduate students (6.93 percent). A very small percentage of the users were from Santa Fe College (0.99 percent), and others who also used the library overnight (figure 3.3). Most of the overnight users were from STEM departments, including students from the sciences, health sciences, engineering, liberal arts, accounting, and linguistics.

When surveyed about satisfaction with the services and meeting the students' needs, most students responded that they were satisfied with the services provided by the library and agreed that their needs were met. On a scale from one to five, MSL was rated five in opening hours, lighted area, personal safety, and cleanliness of the bathrooms and building (figure 3.4).

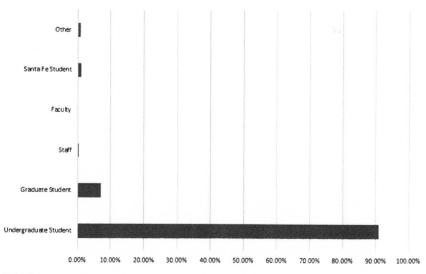

FIGURE 3.3
Status of the survey responders.

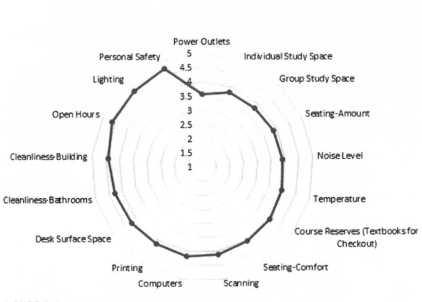

FIGURE 3.4
Students' satisfaction rating/score.

The most popular services and spaces for overnight users were the open study area (23.73 percent), Starbucks (21.42 percent), group study areas (16.22 percent), and study rooms (15.43 percent) (figure 3.5). The print and course reserve materials are the least used services by the students during overnight hours.

We were also interested in learning which library these overnight users utilized during the day. The majority of the overnight users were regular MSL users (71.77 percent), while 19.09 percent of the overnight students responded that they were regular Library West visitors. All others used other campus libraries during the daytime (figure 3.6).

When asked about the regular study area of choice, the respondents said that the open study area was the most commonly used. Study tables in the Collaboration Commons were the primary choice followed by the second- and third-floor open study tables. Study rooms in the Collaboration Com-

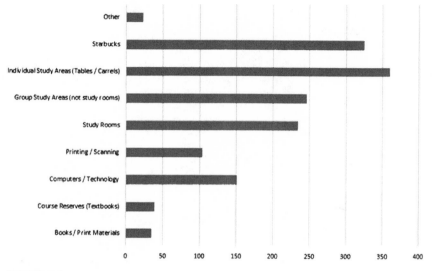

FIGURE 3.5
Services used by patrons during an overnight library visit.

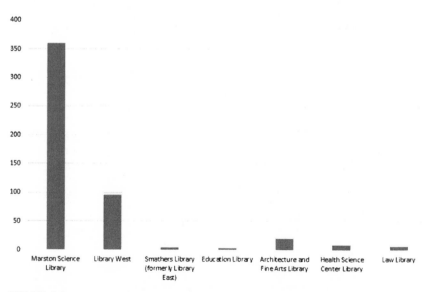

FIGURE 3.6
Libraries used by the responders during daytime hours.

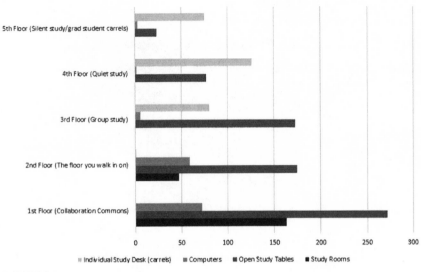

FIGURE 3.7
Spaces used most during overnight hours.

mons were commonly used (figure 3.7). Some students preferred the third-, fourth-, and fifth-floor quiet study spaces, which are individual study areas. The quiet study areas provide students with a traditional library experience.

The survey also highlighted that most of the responders were regular MSL users, with a majority of them visiting the library more than two to three times a week (78.7 percent). A small number of students used MSL once a week (8.97 percent), whereas the rest visit occasionally, from once a month to once a year (figure 3.8).

A majority of the overnight survey respondents used the library between 8:00 p.m. and 4:00 a.m. Respondents used the library in the daytime as well, but the trend showed a slow and gradual increase in user numbers during the library's usual day hours (8:00 a.m.–7:00 p.m.). After 7:00 p.m., there was a sharp increase in number of users, which stabilized around midnight, and started declining after 1:00 a.m. Many of users noted using the library from 11:00 p.m. to 1:00 a.m. (figure 3.9).

When asked if they visited MSL prior to the survey night, 91.36 percent responded that they had and 8.64 percent said that they were new to using the library during night hours. More than half (54.64 percent) of the respondents

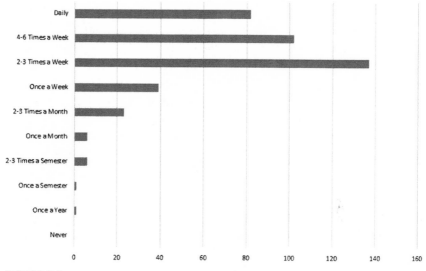

FIGURE 3.8
Frequency of MSL usage by patron.

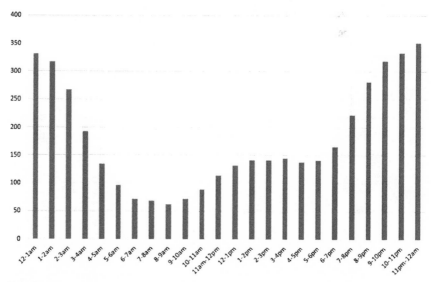

FIGURE 3.9
Use of the library during twenty-four hours by the survey respondents.

used Library West overnight during past semesters. When questioned about what they liked about MSL, an overwhelming number of students answered opening hours, closeness to the dorms and departments, amount of study space, security, technology access, and friendly people. Marston is centrally located close to the Student Nighttime Auxiliary Patrol designated pickup location, campus bus stop, many STEM departments, dorms, and other recreational facilities, which makes it even more accessible. When asked about what they would like to see changed or improved upon at Marston, many responders said they wanted more outlets on all floors, more collaborative desks, individual study spaces, and study rooms. More Mac computers, stronger Wi-Fi, warmer temperatures, and late-night food options were also recommended. Although MSL hosts a Starbucks inside the library, some users suggested having an additional food vending machine. One of the open-ended questions was "describe your ideal library," and it received 332 written responses. Some notable answers were "Marston," "collaboration commons with more outlets," "more aesthetic/cooler entry point," and "Marston plus napping pods." Due to extenuating circumstances, the location of overnight hours shifted back to Library West. Student government funded the overnight hours and had received negative feedback about the shift in location. In our experience, students have incredible loyalty to their subject library and are nervous of changing routines. Despite this decision, made outside our control, we have found the survey results an invaluable tool for guiding future improvements of MSL's building and services.

Prioritization of Renovations

Given the success of the MSL CC renovation, the libraries have continued to fund further renovations with the overall goal of providing additional study spaces for students. In 2015, the year following the initial renovation, MSL renovated the second floor and continued to see increases in the occupancy statistics. In 2018, MSL is continuing the renovations to include the third floor and beginning to plan renovations of the fourth and fifth silent study floors. These discussions have touched on the importance of grad-only areas, recharge/meditation spaces, and increased classroom and meeting spaces. We foresee that the renovation of a silent study floor may present different opportunities or challenges and encourage further library discussion about the careful balance of space and collections.

CONCLUSION

This chapter outlines many of the triumphs and trials of one successful building renovation. MSL continues to grapple with the balance of collections and study space and to explore a new vision for what makes a library in the digital age. A renovation of this type has the potential to create new partnerships, similar to the MADE@UF initiative, and to better meet the needs of the campus community. Renovations in other libraries or other academic buildings spurred the term "Marstonization" of a space. In the end, the Newell Hall renovation—considered by UF administration as a possible location at the time of the MSL renovation—was eventually also completed and "Marstonized." Newell Hall is a five-story building with the same square feet as the MSL CC project and yet the MSL space continues to have greater occupancy overall. The successes of the MSL CC project have revealed the role of the library in increasing campus-wide engagement that extends beyond becoming a perceived study hall. If you are given the opportunity and funds to renovate all or part of your library, there are a number of practical tips that may be helpful to consider:

- When planning the renovation, include students in the planning. We provided chair models with a whiteboard and asked students to pick the one that was most comfortable. We also queried students about the types of technology they needed.
- Explore partnerships, such as with individual colleges or campus IT, that help further the mission and goals of the library. Try to limit feelings of territorialism, but also write memorandum of understanding documents to help define the partnership and expectations.
- Consider your potential champions, such as student government, to help communicate changes and recognize that sometimes decisions are outside your ability to control.
- Document your success with stories. The dramatic increase in the number of students visiting MSL or utilizing 3D printing has developed into a "that time we succeeded" story that resonates with the campus community.
- Renovations have the potential to raise your profile within the campus community. You may be approached to host services that are a poor fit or coopt the space for a service with limited impact. The more successful or popular your renovation, the more likely students and student groups will

feel a sense of ownership and the stronger need for greater publicity in the planning and decision-making stages of future renovations.

- A successful renovation will task your infrastructure in ways you never thought possible. Custodial and facilities issues will increase. Some ways we have learned to manage the challenges have been to bolt down all furniture (moving furniture always ends up places we don't want it to go), provide power at each seat (to avoid power cords as obstacles), and avoid furniture with receptacles (they are garbage collectors).
- Accept that you will have issues along the way (such as selecting furniture that was a poor fit or you weren't successful in your publicity approach). Assess what parts of the process or renovation went awry and adjust as needed. Apply what you learned to future renovations.

Libraries have a responsibility to meet the needs of their student body and to explore possible partnerships and collaborations that meet the varied and complex needs of faculty, staff, and students. As physical collections become less central, libraries must have difficult conversations about the future of low- or no-use collections. Highly utilized spaces are not always the final goal, but can create opportunities to transform the library into a place where students can meet, share, and collaborate.

NOTES

1. U.S. News & World Report, "The 10 Best Public Universities in America," *U.S. News & World Report*, accessed February 19, 2018, https://www.usnews.com/best-colleges/rankings/national-universities/top-public.

2. Samuel King, Erica Cataldi-Roberts, and Erin Wentz, "Meeting at the Crossroads: Collaboration between Information Technology Departments and Health Sciences Libraries," *Journal of the Medical Library Association* 105, no. 1 (2017): 27, doi: 10.5195/jmla.2017.104.

3. Samuel R. Putnam and Sara Russell Gonzalez, "Getting Real in the Library: A Case Study at the University of Florida, *The Code4Lib Journal* 39 (2018), http://journal.code4lib.org/articles/13201.

4. Sara Russell Gonzalez and Denise Beaubien Bennett, "Planning and Implementing a 3D Printing Service in an Academic Library," *Issues in Science and Technology Librarianship* 78 (2014): 1–14, doi:10.5062/F4M043CC.

Rethink, Redo, Repurpose

Transforming the Library Space to Meet Clients' Needs

STEVO ROKSANDIC AND ALLISON ERLINGER

Iron rusts from disuse; water loses its purity from stagnation even so does inaction sap the vigor of the mind.

—*Leonardo da Vinci*

BACKGROUND

Mount Carmel Library services were established in 1921, and primarily served the information needs of both the professional medical staff of the Hawkes Hospital of Mount Carmel and faculty and students of the Mount Carmel School of Nursing. From its beginning, when it occupied only a single room, the library's multiphased expansion and growth mirrored that of both the hospital's services and its diverse academic entities. Today, Mount Carmel Health System (MCHS) is an integral part of the nationwide Trinity Health System and encompasses seven distinct operating sites in Central Ohio. The MCHS clinical staff, Mount Carmel College of Nursing (MCCN) students (totaling over 1,100), participants in the seven Graduate Medical Education (GME) residency programs, and regularly hosted medical students together form the largest academic health system within the Trinity Health network. The Mount Carmel Health Sciences Library (MCHSL) is positioned as an innovative organizational hub for information services, resources, and knowledge within MCHS. Over the last decade, we have embarked on a journey beyond the boundaries of traditional academic and medical library spaces and services, transforming physically to better meet the needs of local clients and extending virtual services to six corporate operating sites across three different states to support the educational and information needs of the larger Trinity Health System.

NEW LOCATION AND NEW LEADERSHIP

In 2006, I, Stevo, was appointed director of library services. At this time, I developed and disseminated a clear vision for the transformation of MCHSL services, resources, and spaces. Two years prior to this appointment, owing to the generosity of the MCHS community, donors, and the Mount Carmel Foundation, MCHSL had moved into a newly constructed Center for Learning and Education (CLE), occupying the third and fourth floors of the building. Under the direction of previous leadership, the design of this new library space had focused primarily on the display of print collections and implementation of new technologies. Neither alignment with the MCHS organizational vision and strategic plan nor the future growth of academic departments were taken into consideration in the initial planning and design of the new library space. The client groups—MCHS medical staff, GME personnel, and MCCN students and faculty—were not consulted about their needs in the design process.

The library actively reached out to all library stakeholders, familiarizing ourselves with the strategic plans of these primary client groups and assessing their unique needs for library services and support. This active approach paved the way for open discussion and the creation of new and relevant collaborative initiatives. These discussions and emerging plans focused on the adaptation of services to fit the evolving learning patterns of the large continuing education professional staff (physicians, nurses, pharmacists, and other clinical staff), diverse academic entities (MCCN, GME, medical students, Clinical Pastoral Care program, etc.), and other stakeholders, setting a new course in motion for ongoing collaboration and development in order to meet the identified information needs and optimize the usage of library services and newly created spaces.

LAYING THE FOUNDATION THROUGH ASSESSMENT

In order to bring this new collaborative vision to life, it was time for the library team to take a step back and complete fundamental assessments of the library, keeping in mind that any planned changes must ultimately contribute to the maximization of operational efficiency. An environmental scan, including internal and external SWOT analysis, and an evaluation of operational efficiency were successfully completed. With further consideration for the position of MCHSL within the corporate structure of MCHS and Trinity Health, library goals were aligned to organizational strategic initiatives, and the organization-wide culture of service excellence was applied.

The findings of these fundamental assessments were compiled, summarized, and then used to guide the creation of an action plan, which established priorities, identified areas in need for more focused assessment, and set goals that defined the library's future course and strategies—paving the way for its continuous revitalization. Upon completion of fundamental library assessments, the following steps were taken:

- Redefining the library's mission, vision, role, and purpose within MCHS.
- Changing the library's organizational and reporting structure.
- Assessing and evaluating technology resources.
- Evaluating operational functionality.
- Defining the engagement of library staff and their willingness to adapt and implement change.
- Understanding the library's financial capacity.
- Addressing the ability to execute marketing and outreach strategies.
- Analyzing the relationship between library staff and library users.

Completion of these steps resulted in collaborative initiatives with primary user groups and the exchange of ideas for the transformation of library space, services, and its role as a hub of academic and professional medical information. This process of increasingly focused assessment, collaboration, and redefinition of the library's structure and purpose positioned the plans for transformation at the intersection of user needs and available library resources.

Building on this foundation, and with a focus on the trends in the academic library industry, the transformation of a newly built, but structurally traditional, warehouse-like library into an innovative, user-centered physical and virtual space was underway. The already fixed brick and mortar limitations and boundaries of the library design were looked upon not just as a challenge, but as an inspiration and an opportunity for creativity, which, over the following decade, resulted in functional, imaginative, entrepreneurial, and innovative transformations. This course of action, change, and continuous transformations was inspired and led by a shared vision in a supportive, dedicated, and engaged team environment.

By sharing our experience with the transformation and repurposing of our library spaces, we hope to help prepare other medical and academic librarians to confidently plan and undertake their own process of continuous library renovation and revitalization. Our accomplishments may inspire others to identify and take advantage of opportunities and emerging ideas to rethink, redo, and repurpose library spaces to meet their clients' needs.

TRANSFORMATION IN ACTION

Study Space

The newly created library space was very large and open, lacking needed distinctions in space. Several areas were furnished with contemporary upholstered sofas and chairs, which quickly attracted the student population to socialize and engage in conversations, often getting rather loud. Many of these spaces were positioned very close to quiet study tables and carrels, as well as computer stations, creating mounting complaints from users who intended to work quietly in the library. In order to reduce such conflict and create a suitable environment for studying, a new furniture layout was created to distinguish casual social spaces from designated quiet study areas on both floors of the library.

It also quickly became apparent that a designated storage space had not been included in the design. The floor plan did, however, include four private study rooms and initially one of these was used as a much needed storage space. Meanwhile, the new larger library became the prime study destination for MCCN students who, at that time, did not have residential opportunities on campus. Aside from classrooms, their only other designated space was a combined dining and recreation room with television and gaming tables. Thus, a need was clearly identified for a functional study space, and the three existing private study rooms were not sufficient. Consequently, the room that was being used as storage of largely unused library artifacts was converted back into a study space, as it was originally designed to be. To solve the storage dilemma, the library worked with MCCN to establish a shared space located outside of the library. This shared space is still used today and over time the limited available storage space has helped to prevent the accumulation and long-term storage of unused and obsolete library materials.

The added study room was met with enthusiasm by our users, but demand for additional private study continued. As mobile technologies became more affordable and widespread, the use of hardwired library PC stations significantly decreased while the demand for the more private areas to work and study increased. Taking this into consideration, the library added free wireless Internet access. With that service available, at the suggestion of our users, the largest open area of the warehouse-like library fourth floor was redesigned, and three modular study rooms were added, allowing for additional private study space without having to change the architectural footprint of the library. In an effort to provide equal access to information via web and mobile technologies, the library also added ten laptops to the collection for

FIGURE 4.1
Fourth floor: Before.
Photo reprinted with the permission of Mount Carmel Health system Supervisor of Audiovisual services, Frank Shepherd

FIGURE 4.2
Fourth floor: After.
Photo reprinted with the permission of Mount Carmel Health system Supervisor of Audiovisual services,
Frank Shepherd

FIGURE 4.3
Fourth floor: After—Modular study rooms.
Photo reprinted with the permission of Mount Carmel Health system Supervisor of Audiovisual services,
Frank Shepherd

check-out and use in the library. Today, we have thirty-two portable devices in circulation and the laptops are by far the most checked-out items in our collection. These changes attracted more users to the library, and the study rooms became very popular. Initially all study rooms were available on a first-come, first-served basis, but in order to optimize usage and reduce conflict, we implemented an advanced online room reservation system, which was also very well received by our users.

With the expansion of private study areas and increased usage of mobile devices for study purposes, our users were spending larger amounts of time in the library and it became clear that one of the most strictly enforced library policies—the food and beverage policy—needed to be reassessed. At the time that the new library opened, only drinks with lids were allowed and all food was prohibited; users who were in violation of the policy were asked to leave the library. But in a time when coffee shops were becoming prime study destinations, this restrictive policy was driving away library users. The policy was revised to allow cold food and snacks in addition to drinks with lids. This, too, was a welcome change and once again, by listening to our users and accommodating their needs, we gained further trust and support.

Give to Gain

The initial reaction of library staff upon moving into the new library space was one of awe and celebration. The new library boasted large open spaces, modern and functional furniture, spacious study areas, ample natural light, an impressive view of the Columbus skyline, and a vast expanse of shelving units. The CLE building, in which the library is located, was constructed primarily to provide additional classroom space for MCCN and the basement, first, and second floors were largely dedicated to that purpose. Since 1990, when Mount Carmel School of Nursing transitioned into Mount Carmel College of Nursing, enrollment steadily grew and new degree programs were added. In 2006, MCCN planned to add a new bachelor of science in nursing program—the Second Degree Accelerated Program—in order to fast track a certain population of students in an effort to mitigate the growing nursing shortage. Great interest in this program resulted in the need for significantly larger class sizes at MCCN. This, in turn, demanded more classroom space that could not be accommodated in the design of the newly created CLE building.

Despite the increasing popularity and availability of our digital collection, particularly serials, MCHSL continued to maintain a very large print collection comprised primarily of bound serials following the move into the new space. The collection was not inventoried nor had a much-needed evaluation and weeding process taken place. Moreover, MCHSL is an established member of the Ohio Private Academic Libraries (OPAL) consortium, the Ohio Library and Information Network (OhioLINK), a consortium of Ohio's college and university libraries and the National Network of Libraries in Medicine (NNLM). We also have full access to the State Library of Ohio. All of these entities offer interlibrary loan and most have organized repository systems to keep necessary volumes of hard copy journal volumes for archival purposes.

We began to plan a major weeding project. Around the same time, the MCCN president and dean asked if it might be possible to repurpose at least one quarter of the library third floor to build a new classroom. The already planned evaluation and weeding project resulted in the elimination of more

FIGURE 4.4
Third floor: Before weeding and space reduction.
Photo reprinted with the permission of Mount Carmel Health system Supervisor of Audiovisual services, Frank Shepherd

FIGURE 4.5
Third floor: After weeding and space reduction.
Photo reprinted with the permission of Mount Carmel Health system Supervisor of Audiovisual services, Frank Shepherd

than 50 percent of the bound nursing serials collection and the ability to offer the now unoccupied space to MCCN for the construction of a new classroom. This was, of course, great news for MCCN leadership, and we viewed it as a win. The library was able to demonstrate a spirit of collaboration and dedication to user needs of all kinds, and the reduction in physical space served as an impetus for a renewed focus on building a web presence and joining other medical and academic libraries in the digital age. This was a first step toward the goal of establishing the library as an e-platform service.

Called "give to gain," this opportunity to build a classroom as an extension of the library strengthened our relationship with our primary user group, the MCCN students and faculty. This willingness to repurpose newly built and dedicated library space to meet their needs was warmly welcomed within our health system. Seeing the positive outcome of this initiative, we used it as a springboard to begin generating and evaluating new ideas to repurpose other areas in the library to support our continuously growing MCCN student, GME, and MCHS staff populations.

Our proactive engagement in providing additional learning environments, redesigning physical space, significantly improving our web presence, and streamlining electronic access to information had a very positive impact on not only MCCN students and faculty, but on our users in general. As we continuously evaluate and update our collections, and replace print with electronic materials (the MCHSL collection is now 92 percent electronic), our need for the ample shelving in the library has decreased, opening up additional space where we can meet our users' needs in innovative ways. For example, MCHSL collaborated with the hospital's patient education department to repurpose a portion of our space for the organization and storage of print educational materials that cannot be accessed online. Much like the construction of a classroom in the library, this change put library space to use in a way that has increased library support from one of our major user groups, in this case the hospital's clinical staff.

Creating Displays

The initial interior design of the new library space featured gray walls throughout, decorated with a variety of reproduction photographs and framed botanical prints. We could not understand why the brand-new health sciences library space featured primarily botanical prints, without any medical, nursing, or health-related themes and felt that the wall color and artwork detracted from the creation of a warm and inspiring learning environment.

It was also well known that, at the time, the MCCN archives collection containing artifacts of more than one hundred years of nursing education was located in the basement of the Marion Hall, a much older building to which the CLE provided supplemental space. Important historic documents, photographs, yearbooks, Mount Carmel School of Nursing uniforms, caps and pins, medical instruments, and other memorabilia were completely out of sight of both students and visitors. The majority of these materials was stored in closed drawers and file cabinets. A handful of showcases displayed historic uniforms, documents, and artifacts, but these were located in open areas without any security or physical protection. Furthermore, this more than one-hundred-year-old collection was lacking a complete inventory to properly track and provide information about the materials.

We often expressed our concerns about the ongoing care and maintenance of this important archival collection of the school of nursing. Beginning in

2006, we made several attempts to share with leaders of the MCCN Alumni Association our vision of cataloging and displaying the archival materials in the library. Unfortunately, a series of proposals for carrying this out in various ways was rejected. In sharp contrast to the reaction of the Alumni Association, however, the idea was welcomed and supported by MCCN leadership, and the majority of faculty, staff, and students.

Not wanting to let this historic collection fall by the wayside, we decided that a slower and more practical approach may be effective in persuading the MCCN Alumni Association. We took a step back from the idea of displaying the collection in the library and instead offered to provide support in professionally evaluating and inventorying the historic archive by engaging practicum students from the Kent State School of Library and Information Science who specialized in archival and historic document preservation. This offer was readily accepted by the MCCN Alumni Association. The project was then expanded with the creation of a searchable online portal of historic photographs of all graduating classes from the Mount Carmel School of Nursing, which was made accessible to all alumni. The successful completion of this project significantly changed the dynamics of the relationship between the library and the MCCN Alumni Association.

This set the stage for a renewed effort to make the vision of MCCN archival displays in the library a reality. We cleared obsolete and unused materials from an area on the third floor, removed the botanical prints from the walls, and painted them the signature Mount Carmel burgundy. The alumni leaders were then invited into this space where we shared the vision of creating murals with photographs and a timeline describing more than one hundred years of nursing education at MCHS. The most memorable moment was when we asked the alumni who were present to stand before the painted wall, hold each other's hands, close their eyes, and imagine the mural that would showcase this vast history and tradition. There was great hope that the alumni would soften their firm decision to not pursue the project, but instead, the hand chain dissolved and heavy sighs and suspicious looks created a somewhat uncomfortable and very disappointing feeling. Then the questions and concerns started to pour in: "We don't have money to do that!"; "How can we be sure that this idea will benefit our organization?"; "How long will it take to complete?"; "What will happen to all the displays if you leave MCHSL?" Although this was somewhat daunting, each question opened the door wider and created more opportunities to explore, discuss, share, plan, and propose a final project.

Despite an inauspicious beginning, this event turned a new page in the redesign of the new library space. In the following two years, supported by a generous grant from the Mount Carmel Foundation, we worked together with alumni leaders and the MCCN president and dean, under the championship of the MCCN director of development, to plan and execute the completion of both the wall mural and new appropriately protected and outstanding displays of the MCCN archival collection in the library space. Following the successful completion of this primary project, another wall display was installed above a section of study carrels, including a large-scale library logo across the wall and a framed portrait of Mother M. Constantine, Provincial Superior of the Sisters of the Holy Cross, and founder of Mount Carmel Health Sciences Library. These new displays both ensured the care and maintenance of the MCCN archival collection and added much needed curb appeal to the physical space of the library. Additionally, and perhaps most importantly for the

FIGURE 4.6
Third floor stacks: Before renovation.
Photo reprinted with the permission of Mount Carmel Health system Supervisor of Audiovisual services, Frank Shepherd

FIGURE 4.7
Third floor stacks: After renovation and addition of display cases.
Photo reprinted with the permission of Mount Carmel Health system Supervisor of Audiovisual services, Frank Shepherd

development of MCHSL, they emphasized the importance of the library as a key partner in nursing and education at MCHS.

Thanks to the tenacity and collaborative efforts of MCHSL, the Mount Carmel Foundation, and MCCN leaders and alumni, the third floor of the library received a complete makeover. This transformed space, now vibrant with murals, nursing artifacts, memorabilia, and displays, continues to inspire MCHSL users and visitors alike. Most important, by celebrating and honoring the traditions of nursing education and the history of MCCN, these displays have transformed the previously bland library into a colorful and inspiring learning environment. This space has become a top study location for our nursing students, who have expressed to us that it is much more inviting than other available areas on the campus. The library has also become a destination for visiting alumni, both on official tours and individually, who visit to view the history of college and discover photographs and memorabilia belonging to themselves or their relatives.

This project serves an excellent example of how patience, persistence, and determination can prevail. Through the establishment of mutual support and

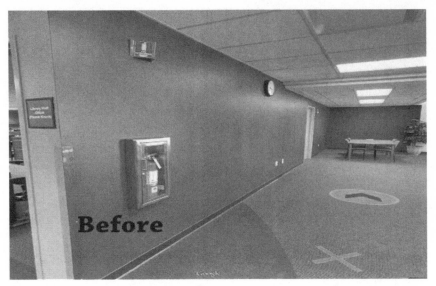

FIGURE 4.8

Third floor study space: Before renovation.

Photo reprinted with the permission of Mount Carmel Health system Supervisor of Audiovisual services,
Frank Shepherd

FIGURE 4.9

Third floor study space: After renovation and addition of wall mural.

Photo reprinted with the permission of Mount Carmel Health system Supervisor of Audiovisual services,
Frank Shepherd

FIGURE 4.10

Third floor: Study carrels.

Photo reprinted with the permission of Mount Carmel Health system Supervisor of Audiovisual services,
Frank Shepherd

FIGURE 4.11

Third floor: Study carrels with added design and logo.

Photo reprinted with the permission of Mount Carmel Health system Supervisor of Audiovisual services,
Frank Shepherd

FIGURE 4.12
MCHSL Libraries Transform marketing slide: All marketing slides were displayed on library TV screens.
Photo reprinted with the permission of Mount Carmel Health system Supervisor of Audiovisual services, Frank Shepherd

trust, collaborative hard work, and a commitment to succeed, the project was completed in 2014. This inspired transformation, merging past and present and celebrating the long history of MCCN and MCHSL, demonstrates how changes to the physical space can reinvigorate a study and learning environment.

Libraries Transform

Following the success of the third floor transformation, an energized and inspired MCHSL staff actively engaged in a search for ideas to further rethink, redo, and repurpose the library space based on our users' needs. Reaching out to our primary users and visitor populations—MCCN students, faculty, and staff—several new ideas and suggestions emerged. It was at this point that MCHSL joined ALA's Libraries Transform initiative, which, according to their website, is "designed to increase public awareness of the value, impact and services provided by libraries and library professionals."[1] In order to establish a solid foundation for this next phase of transformation, a new needs assessment was conducted, defining the role of MCHSL in its current state and time—the digital age. The results of the previous repurposing and transformation of the library space were evaluated, and goals and priorities were identified by exploring the following facets of the current state and future direction of MCHSL:

1. Identity: Who we are as an institution; the basis for teaching, learning, and research initiatives.

2. User needs: How we accommodate our unique user populations; must consider new information technologies and the ways in which our users access and interact with them.

3. Legacy: The institutional inheritance we will leave to future generations of staff and users; this should reflect the values, mission, and goals of the institution.

4. Tradition: The history of our institution—in the case of MCHSL, over 100 years in the making; this is the academic heart of the organizational community and should be reflected in the changes we make.

5. Scholarship: The academic facet of the institution, which develops and changes over time with the addition of new educational programs; the current state of scholarly activity should be considered when designing spaces and service points.

6. Empiricalness: How we leverage our observations and experiences with our users to drive pragmatic change; the identified needs of library users should be a primary factor in ongoing library transformation.

7. Sustainability: The consideration of long-term endurance in our choice of values and use of resources; human capital, financial capacity, and institutional support should be considered when planning new initiatives and changes.

8. Modality: How change will be affected in a practice sense; when planning for a transformation the specific methods and processes involved should be considered and planned in advance.

9. Spatiality: The available physical space we have to work with; it is not always possible to add space, so we should think creatively about how to use the space that is available to best fulfill the educational vision of the institution.

10. Flexibility: The willingness and ability to continue to adapt to evolving user needs over time; library transformations are never fully complete, we must remain ready to update and refresh our spaces and services to remain relevant to our users.

11. Finance: The budgetary resources at our disposal; transformations must be done within our means, and with consideration for ongoing costs; creativity is key and outside funding from institutional foundations and external grants should be sought out.

12. Vision: How we conceptualize the outcome of the transformation; this should be contemporary, imaginative, and entrepreneurial, incorporating the spirit of the institution and our users, while carefully weighing innovation with risk.

In addition to a formal needs assessment, we wanted to gain direct input from our library users. Rather than attempting to formally survey our user populations remotely, we brought them to us, in person, by hosting several informal social events offering free food, ice cream, and cookies during the busier hours of library operation. By creating these opportunities for our users to socialize in the library and directly engaging them in conversations about their library use and needs, we generated a host of new ideas and suggestions for further transforming the library. These new ideas, combined with the results of the needs assessment, directed a reevaluation of our services and a new phase of the library transformation.

This open and user-centered approach fostered the position of the library as a primary study and social destination, especially for the MCCN student population. But our assessments had identified additional unmet needs among a new generation of library users. Meeting them would require taking risks by stepping outside the bounds of traditional library roles and services. We were ready to meet this challenge and have now successfully implemented a number of innovative user-centered changes as part of our participation in the Libraries Transform initiative.

A large portion of the MCCN student body and MCHS nursing and professional staff is female and many of them have children. The relatively large population of MCCN students with infants and young children expressed a particular need for a private, clean, and easily accessible lactation space. MCHSL reached out to the MCCN school nurse and the hospital's lactation department in order to better understand what such a space would require. Library staff also exported and assessed usage data from the study room scheduling system in order to determine whether we could create a lactation space without detracting from our primary role as an academic library space. It was determined that the smallest study room, which also lacked windows, was being used very rarely in comparison to all of the others. The design of this room also made it an ideal lactation space due to its level of privacy. The MCHSL staff then collaborated with the MCHS lactation nurses to properly

FIGURE 4.13

Libraries Transform slide depicting mothers' room.

Photo reprinted with the permission of Mount Carmel Health system Supervisor of Audiovisual services, Frank Shepherd

design and professionally equip the space for this purpose. Through the creative use of space and existing resources we successfully transformed the little-used study room into a new fully equipped and very popular "Mothers' Room." Through this transformation we were able to expand our services to meet a demonstrated user need at no cost and in the space of only a few weeks.

Although MCHS and MCCN are Catholic institutions, the staff and student populations are quite religiously diverse and both institutions strive to embrace and support this diversity. At MCCN in particular, there is a large Muslim student population, who expressed a need for an appropriate and convenient space for prayer throughout the day. Engaging in open conversation with many of these students, we determined precisely what type of space was needed and when. Again, we turned to our room scheduling data in order

FIGURE 4.14

Libraries Transform slide depicting historic prayer and relaxation room.

Photo reprinted with the permission of Mount Carmel Health system Supervisor of Audiovisual services, Frank Shepherd

to determine the most efficient way to meet this need. It was determined that the historic reading room, which was already designed to be a quiet space, not conducive to group study, could easily be reserved at specified times throughout the day without disrupting the existing usage pattern. In the spirit of inclusivity and diversity, MCHSL staff established standing reservations of this room for prayer and/or meditation throughout the day. Again, by listening to our users and creatively leveraging our resources we successfully transformed the use of library space to meet a demonstrated need without altering structures or incurring costs.

Finally, taking into consideration both the current widespread digital landscape and the known MCCN curriculum, as well as our observations of how library spaces were being used on a daily basis, we transformed two general study/conference rooms into dedicated MCCN practice rooms: one primarily serving MCCN clinical faculty and students for their pre- and postclinical conferences and the other equipped with audio-visual equipment for video conferencing and presentation practice. In the interest of flexibility, both of

FIGURE 4.15
Standard conference room.
Photo reprinted with the permission of Mount Carmel Health system Supervisor of Audiovisual services, Frank Shepherd

FIGURE 4.16
A/V conference room.
Photo reprinted with the permission of Mount Carmel Health system Supervisor of Audiovisual services, Frank Shepherd

these spaces can still also be booked for group study, meetings, and so forth. The A/V conference room, which is the largest private space in the library, has also become a destination for MCCN reading groups to conduct formal discussions. In the case of these two spaces, very little physical change took place, but in the spirit of the Libraries Transform purpose to increase public awareness of our services, we strategically re-named them and encouraged our users to view and utilize them in innovative ways.

Inspired and encouraged by our participation in ALA's Libraries Transform initiative, and through the use of collaboration and two-way communication, we have engaged our users and found that they have become our best advocates and supporters. Guided by their needs, suggestions, and demands, we have already taken great strides in the ongoing transformation of our library space. Looking ahead, a plan is in place to remodel the former copy room, creating additional individual study rooms, a physical exam practice room, and a "Creative Station" with all of the necessary supplies for students to work on their projects and poster presentations. As we move forward, we will continue to observe and

engage our users to stay informed about their evolving needs and evaluate our
ability to meet them in new, transformative ways.

Digital Spaces

It is undeniable that the digital age has significantly impacted the evolution
of libraries. We are presently witnessing this evolution at MCHSL and working to stay abreast of new innovations and trends that significantly impact
the role of libraries and librarians, especially related to supporting information needs in medical and academic institutions. The concept of the library
as a center of information services continues to evolve: from the traditional
brick and mortar library, to a hybrid of physical and digital materials, and
ultimately to libraries as primarily digital learning spaces. Medical and health
sciences libraries are no less affected than other types of libraries in this evo-
lutionary transformation. The nature of our organization as a health system
that operates on multiple sites, and as an integral part of a national corporate
organization had already impelled us to embrace and continue to explore
these newer operational models. Moreover, MCCN's addition of new online
educational programs, and the fast-paced development of information and
learning technologies and communication platforms (especially in academic
medicine), have also encouraged this change.

MCHSL consistently transforms and changes its digital spaces by implementing new software and platforms as the need arises. Minor updates and
modifications to the library website that do not disrupt the way our users
interface with it are made continuously, often on a daily basis. A number of
larger scale targeted projects have also been completed over the last several
years: updating the website to be ADA compliant, adapting the language to
improve usability for the millennial student population, simplifying request
forms, and adding new self-directed learning modules for various resources
and databases. Focusing primarily on our most active user population—the
MCCN students—most of our digital transformations have been related to
the implementation of innovative information and learning technologies.

We have, however, also made changes in the tech realm to improve the experience of any user who enters the library. A book display located just inside
the entrance to the library, in view of library staff at the front desk, has been
repurposed as a stand for a mobile device charging station that we purchased
with the help of the Mount Carmel Foundation. Large television screens located throughout the library environment and rotating slides on the library

homepage serve as modern and efficient news and message boards to share the latest updates and announcements, and to market the transformations in our spaces and services. A recent Twitter post by one of our physicians is a great example of this marketing at work. The tweet (shown in figure 4.17) includes an image of one of our digital message boards advertising a newly implemented "text for quiet" initiative, harnessing digital technology to optimize the use of our physical space.

One of the most important transformations that MCHSL has undergone bridges the digital and physical worlds to meet the unique needs of our user population. MCHSL had two unstaffed satellite libraries at different MCHS operating sites, known previously as "Information Commons." Through the elimination of many outdated and little-used print resources and the addition of more computers and other technologies, these spaces were transformed into "Gateway Libraries" designed to optimize virtual services and support in a modern and comfortable space suitable for learning purposes. All of our MCHSL library locations have been made accessible to our users any time of day or night using an existing ID badge entry system, demonstrating our commitment to providing personalized support and services 24/7/365, based upon user request.

The successful transformation of our digital space also created opportunities to extend our services beyond MCHS, by providing virtual library support to five other hospitals within our parent corporation in three different states. In addition to providing complete virtual library support through a specially designed LibGuide for each hospital, we also assisted in redesigning their existing physical library spaces, creating opportunities to repurpose at least a portion of them to meet other institutional needs. With this successful transformation of services and access to information, we've gone on to develop a proposal for consolidation and centralization of all library services and support within our parent corporation. Our proposed idea to form a unified corporate library enterprise will create opportunities to further rethink, redo, and repurpose library spaces and transform services to meet clients' needs on a national scale.

We strongly believe that physical spaces will continue to play a vital role in libraries for years to come, however, it is undeniable that the continuing development of the digital age and information technology have already had a significant impact on the change and transformation of library spaces, demanding the agility, readiness, and active engagement of librarians. As the

Dr.Binay Eapen
@MedEdFanatic

Following

If you need to study and it's loud don't worry about it just send a text and problem solved .Thanks so much @MCHSLibrary.Now that's what I call innovative. #wellness #MedEd #MindfulMonday #patientsafety

Too much *NOISE* in the library to study effectively?

TEXT

(614) 541-2224

and Library Staff will assist you!

Text to SHHH

Available Mon. - Fri., 8am - 5pm
* Standard messaging rates apply.

3:06 PM - 29 Jan 2018 from Mount Carmel West Hospital

1 Retweet 2 Likes

Q 2   ⫝ 1   ♥ 2   ✉

Tweet your reply

Dr.Binay Eapen @MedEdFanatic · Jan 30

@normullibrarian @MCHSLibrary you guys are the best!! Plus such dedicated and caring people who are always helping and supporting medical education! #BestLibraryInOhio

Q   ⫝   ♥ 2   ✉

FIGURE 4.17

Tweet from an MCHS physician depicting TV screen as digital message board.
Photo reprinted with the permission of Mount Carmel Health system Supervisor of Audiovisual services, Frank Shepherd

FIGURE 4.18

Mount Carmel St. Anns: Before—Information Commons.
Photo reprinted with the permission of Mount Carmel Health system Supervisor of Audiovisual services, Frank Shepherd

FIGURE 4.19

Mount Carmel St. Anns: After—Gateway Library.
Photo reprinted with the permission of Mount Carmel Health system Supervisor of Audiovisual services, Frank Shepherd

previous examples suggest, physical and digital library spaces can no longer be considered in isolation from one another and it is up to librarians to employ innovative transformations to successfully bridge these two worlds in order to meet our users where they are.

CONCLUSION

Our experience serves as an example of the possibilities for successful transformation of any library, working primarily with only an open-minded staff and a brick and mortar inheritance. We learned that such challenges can be a path to frustration or to joy, depending on the approach one takes. We believe that the experiences of MCHSL can serve as an inspiration for successful and joyful library transformations. There is no better way to illustrate this than by sharing the positive results we are achieving through the ongoing transformation of our physical and digital spaces.

The key drivers of our success were the fundamental assessments of the library through environmental scanning and alignment to our organizational strategic initiatives. Readiness to accept change, visionary conceptual ideas, self-assurance, creativity, innovation, connectedness, patience, persistence, engagement of a trusting collaborative team, and a lot of energy were also vital ingredients in the recipe for our successful transformation. The most important lesson learned from our library space and services transformation is that in order to be successful the process should involve active participation from all stakeholders: users, information technologists, librarians, institutional leadership, library professional designers, finance organizations and staff, architects, and other specialty consultants.

Our take-away message can be simply summarized: by consciously observing and listening to your users and stakeholders, leveraging available resources, being ready to take risks, and having a devoted team, you can succeed in transforming your library and establishing it as not just relevant, but one of the key services in today's highly competitive medical and academic information services environments.

NOTE

1. American Library Association (ALA), "About," Libraries Transform: An Initiative of the American Library Association, accessed April 15, 2018, par.1, http://www.ilovelibraries.org/librariestransform/about.

II

WORKING IN UNIQUE SPACES

From There to Here to Virtual

Transformative Change at Chamberlain University

Lisa Blackwell

We've long believed that when the rate of change inside an institution becomes slower than the rate of change outside, the end is in sight.

—*General Electric Company*[1]

HISTORICAL BACKGROUND

For 113 years, the Deaconess College of Nursing in St. Louis, Missouri, produced diploma degreed nurses. In 1983, the college began offering baccalaureate degree (BSN) programs. Fast forward seventeen years, and with a nod to the evolving educational needs of nurses, the online RN to BSN degree completion option was launched. In 2005, Adtalem Global Education (formerly DeVry Education Group) acquired Deaconess and changed the name to Chamberlain College of Nursing.[2] Near constant growth and expansion of both physical and virtual Chamberlain programs have presented unique challenges as well as opportunities to create innovative library operations. Following the 2005 acquisition, the Chamberlain College of Nursing continued to draw upon the resources of the Forest Park Hospital Library, which historically supported both the Deaconess College of Nursing and the hospital's Family Practice Residency. Ownership of the library collection was permanently transferred to Chamberlain College of Nursing the following year and the first Chamberlain librarian was hired.

Valerie Meyer MLS, RN, pioneered the role of a nursing subject specialist librarian at Chamberlain. She managed the transition of the Forest Park
Hospital Library collection to Chamberlain including the physical relocation
from the hospital location in 2009 to the newly built St. Louis campus library.
With help from the Chamberlain marketing department, Valerie also developed a separate library webpage for the Chamberlain library. Chamberlain
students could now seek assistance from a librarian skilled in nursing librarianship as well as locate appropriate library resources online.

During the next few years, the Chamberlain library's physical collection
remained small as did the initial set of nursing specific online resources. The
online library resources were initially provided through existing DeVry University library contracts amended to include access by Chamberlain students.
A clear imperative to add more library resources to support a nursing curriculum led to the formation of a national library committee in 2008. In addition, as new Chamberlain campuses began to be planned, Valerie was charged
with creating an opening-day print collection for the libraries. Setting up
initial campus libraries became another task on her list of responsibilities as
a solo librarian serving a geographically expanding school with a growing
student population.

Valerie also recognized the necessity of providing an interlibrary loan
mechanism to share copies of articles and chapters from the print collection
held by the St. Louis library. She planned and implemented an article request
email service for Chamberlain patrons. After an intense project to integrate
Chamberlain patron accounts into Voyager, lending and borrowing of the
print resources of the collections of both schools was also enabled between
campuses. Valerie's accomplishments within two short years laid the foundation for the Chamberlain library to thrive and evolve to meet changing circumstances. She continues to serve as a Chamberlain librarian, albeit working
virtually, with her unique knowledge about where Chamberlain began and
how history continues to inform the mission of the school within the context
of constant change.

The year 2007 continues to be regarded as a defining period for Chamberlain. The first campus beyond St. Louis was launched in Columbus, Ohio. It
was established as a co-location with an existing DeVry University campus.
As a convenient and cost-saving strategy, many of the earliest Chamberlain
College of Nursing campuses were established as co-locations with DeVry

University campuses. Each of the existing DeVry University campuses had a library and a DeVry librarian employed onsite. An operational decision was made that co-located campuses would enter into service level agreements that expanded the responsibilities of the DeVry librarian to include providing services to Chamberlain nursing students. The DeVry librarians continued to report to the DeVry campus administration on campus. Service level agreements were tailored to specific campus conditions and thus not standardized. Unfortunately, this meant that the number of nursing specific resources in the library collection and specialized librarian services available varied by campus. This variance inevitably led to some inconsistencies in expectations for library supports for Chamberlain students, clearly not an ideal situation.

The relationship between DeVry and Chamberlain library services was also complicated from the beginning by the academic arrangement between the schools. On co-located campuses most Chamberlain students would take required courses in the hard sciences and liberal arts if offered through the existing DeVry University curriculum. Students enrolled in DeVry managed courses would be utilizing the library resources purchased by both schools to support that curriculum. What began as a cost-efficient way to share resources so that neither school would need to duplicate purchases of expensive library resources became much more complicated as print resources were steadily replaced by online resources. Sharing licensed resources requires a completely different approach than simply sharing resources owned in a campus collection. Within a short period of time, a reexamination of this shared operating structure would become inevitable, driven in part by changing institutional priorities and divergent paths chosen by both DeVry and Chamberlain.

Eight additional campuses were opened between 2008 and early 2012. Chamberlain also added the master of science in nursing (MSN) degree online in 2009. Consequently, the growth of the on-campus and online student populations rapidly expanded and with that came increased demand for information resources and services. The addition of an exclusively online graduate degree program provided further urgency for the development of a robust collection of digital resources and virtual reference services.

It is within the context of all that had transpired that I was hired as the first library director for Chamberlain at the national level in the spring of 2012. I reported to the vice president of academic affairs with the explicit mandate to guide library operations that would better serve the needs of Chamberlain. I spent time visiting each campus to meet the librarians serving Chamberlain students. In addition to Valerie, who served the St. Louis campus, Chamberlain librarians had been hired for the Indianapolis, Indiana; Jacksonville, Florida; and Atlanta, Georgia, campuses in response to state specific accreditation requirements. The eight additional campuses that were added between 2007 and 2012 already employed DeVry University librarians who were also serving Chamberlain students.

The initial three months of travel to our campuses led to the next steps toward understanding my role as a leader within Chamberlain. Chamberlain began to build a new campus in Cleveland, Ohio. The campus would not be a co-location and would require building a library from scratch prior to opening. As the new national library director, it would be my responsibility to successfully build a campus library that met accreditation requirements. The logistics of planning and acquiring the collection for that library served as my initiation into being an integrated member of a new campus project. It provided me with an opportunity to observe and participate in the operational decision making processes for a new campus such as space allocation, staffing proposals, budget parameters, and the demands and requirements posed by several accrediting organizations. In short, the successful launch of a new campus is a delicate coordination led by a team of individuals representing many departments who must collectively respond to a multitude of internal and external requirements.

Over the ensuing several months leading to the campus launch, I began to understand the rationale that determines how a campus budget is designed and operationalized. Each campus is budgeted in such a way that student enrollment plays a significant role in determining available funds for everything from classroom seating to administrative staff. The reality that I faced was that a librarian hired to report on site at opening was not always feasible if other means to provide services and resources could be utilized. The seeds for my envisioning a radical change in how library services would be structured for Chamberlain began to develop during subsequent months. This chapter will address the transition of staffing, resources, and services from a physical campus-based library operation to a cohesive, primarily virtual, enterprise-wide operational infrastructure at Chamberlain University.

REWRITING THE TEMPLATE

A variety of considerations needed to be addressed before a viable proposal to fundamentally alter the traditional structural and operational model for Chamberlain libraries could be proposed. Program developments went beyond a steady rate of opening new campuses across the country. They accelerated the increasingly urgent need to find a better way to equitably deliver library services and resources to all Chamberlain students. The successful launch of a fully online program was the MSN degree in 2009. Library resources and services delivered in completely campus-based environments were clearly not going to adequately meet the needs of an entire population of students who would likely never step onto a physical campus. Furthermore, the depth of the resource collections required by advanced degree students and faculty scholars would no longer be sufficient if offered primarily in print and dependent on using resources housed on a campus.

The complexity of the regulatory landscape must also be considered before planning any significant operational changes. Chamberlain is accredited by the Higher Learning Commission (HLC) at the institutional level. All nursing programs are accredited by the Commission on Collegiate Nursing Education (CCNE). However, by 2012, Chamberlain had established campuses in nine states. Within each state a Chamberlain program is accredited by the state specific Board of Nursing (BON). The Higher Education Board (HEB) regulations for the specific state also apply and those can vary widely in requirements. A thorough grasp of the requirements mandated by each regulatory agency means that any proposals regarding library materials, formats, physical space characteristics, staffing, collection size, accessibility, and so on are critically scrutinized. Failure to fully meet any of the requirements for library services, resources, and contributions to the institutional mission presents a tangible risk to successful accreditation or reaccreditation. Any substantial change in library operations, while arguably essential, is therefore not undertaken lightly. Also worth acknowledgment is that libraries are expensive investments. Libraries as we have historically built them will be considered expendable if they no longer meet identified needs and requirements.

The expectations that students have for what libraries offer also continues to evolve. Students in all types of higher education programs are increasingly also distance-education students who attend classes online, participate in both synchronous and asynchronous virtual discussions, meet with professors in virtual offices, and utilize the library frequently, or exclusively, online and often during nights and weekends. When a place is designated as a "classroom," is it necessarily a room in a building? Might it instead exist in a virtual room hosted by a web domain? The iconic image of a room with rows and rows of desks facing an instructor has faded, although what that image symbolizes remains. The same might be said for the ingrained image of the library. In higher education it is often portrayed as the physical and symbolic center of the institution. A grand façade and impressive shelves filled with books are a tribute to the fundamental role that the archived knowledge contained within a curated collection of artifacts plays in educating students and scholars. What happens to the definition and/or meaning of "library" when the building doesn't matter because people are occupying other spaces? Is "library" a building or place, a type of space, or a collection of resources? Could it be that a library is also subject to the rule that "form ever follows function?"[3] If so, then library presence need not be defined by space on a campus.

Let's flesh out more of the context in which the Chamberlain library presence exists. The Chamberlain University College of Nursing offers a uniquely defining element of the pre-licensure student experience. Each campus includes a center for academic success (CAS). Dedicated resources to help students to be successful in their studies and licensure examinations are available during all hours that students are on campus. Mentors, faculty, and peers frequent the CAS, building a culture of Chamberlain Care that permeates the Chamberlain experience.[4] Copies of textbooks, the presence of nursing tutors, group study spaces, and quiet study rooms are some of the standard resources to be found in a campus CAS. Up until recently, the CAS and the library on each campus served some complementary needs while duplicating a large number of expensive resources, such as print books. What has always been shared by both Chamberlain librarians and CAS team members is a passion for helping students be successful scholars. Both strive to provide the best possible resources to facilitate student learning. Historically, each department occupied separate physical spaces, managed resource acquisitions independently, and were viewed as functionally separate operations. Real estate on a campus is expensive as are print resources. Not unexpectedly, both operations are regularly scrutinized to attempt to minimize underutilization or unnecessary duplication of expenses. It was inevitable that sooner or later the question would arise about whether one or the other space might be sacrificed without harming student success, scholarly endeavors, or campus operations. If the library were to be absorbed or dismantled, how would users discover and access library resources and services as required by standards for higher education institutions and accreditation requirements?

I steadily considered these questions while Chamberlain continued to build and launch eighteen campuses in nine additional states. Of those campuses, eight were built as co-located campuses with existing DeVry University campuses and thus included libraries and librarians in place. Just four of the stand-alone campuses were required by a regulatory body to hire a librarian prior to opening (although all locations were required to offer library services as well as some materials in print). The six remaining campuses hired managers for their centers for academic success. Those managers were tasked with providing additional support for students while preparing for their NCLEX-RN exams. They were also expected to assist students with library-related questions and refer them appropriately to a Chamberlain librarian on another campus. The acquisition of many additional e-resources, and the OCLC QuestionPoint online chat service Chamberlain shared with DeVry provided an operational arrangement to meet many student needs. However, immediate library assistance at the point of need on librarian-less campuses was far from ideal. Circulation of campus-based print collections plummeted, a fact which, when combined with online resource usage statistics, provided ongoing evidence that students often preferred online resources. The question that emerged was that as students increasingly embraced digital environments, would the library remain an indispensable part of their academic experience? If so, how could library availability become as discoverable and resources (including the services of librarians) be as accessible if offered primarily online? To answer these questions, the importance of a library website that operates as the virtual "front door" cannot be underestimated.

Early on at Chamberlain, I became aware of a great deal of dissatisfaction regarding the utility of the Chamberlain library website. It was very far from being viewed as a welcoming entry point to the resources of the academic library. The lack of visibility was compounded by the failure to provide easy access to library resources and detailed information about how to contact a librarian for assistance. That dissatisfaction only grew as the number of resources available in e-format expanded and students expressed frustration in trying to find and access them. Access was hindered by a poor search interface and the outdated OPAC used, Voyager. Further complicating the issue was that Chamberlain continued the DeVry University legacy model of relying on the already stretched resources of a marketing team to manage the library webpage. The page was sporadically updated and primarily served to remind students that a library existed on their campuses. The demand to dramatically expand access to library resources and services to a growing population of distance education students drove an exploration of and a subsequent proposal to obtain a library specific platform on which to house and develop a robust online library.

The Springshare platform was identified as an affordable, cloud-based solution designed for libraries and featuring an unparalleled ease of use and uncomplicated adaptation. We chose Springshare to host our new library website and signed a contract in late 2013. During the following months, Chamberlain librarians worked together to learn to use the platform to build a new library website. Deployment of this new website in June 2014, opened the doors to building user satisfaction with accessing and utilizing what the library had to offer. The real work of re-envisioning and rebuilding the Chamberlain library presence had begun.

BUILDING THE MAP

By the fall of 2014, after planning and building five campus library spaces and collections in five separate states, acquiring and implementing the Springshare platform, and forging some productive connections with internal stakeholders, I was prepared to pitch a new leadership vision for the future of Chamberlain library operations. A primary goal was to reshape the library operations model to better meet the needs of the entire student population, maximize the value of expensive library e-resource investments, and maintain lean, identical collections of essential print materials on all campuses. To maximize investment in e-resources, a new technical infrastructure would need to be selected and a discovery interface with a robust link resolver would be required. The flexibility of LibGuides offered by the Springshare platform, had already inspired a vision to create resources linked to the library website that we would call "Course Guides." These would link supplementary library resources and services seamlessly to specific courses and assignments within the online learning management system (LMS) used by all Chamberlain students. Librarians would partner with faculty course developers to ensure that library resources would be highlighted to complement course learning objectives.

One paradigm change integral to the plan was the proposal to centralize the library operational structure, including the financial management and librarian reporting structure. Centralizing the library budget at a national level would concretely eliminate disparities in campus level expenditures for library collections and services. The largest portion of the global library resources budget could advantageously be weighted to favor e-resource acquisitions. This had the added attraction of securing uninterrupted access to library resources for all of Chamberlain. It would also mean that Chamberlain librarians, who already served students both on and off campus, were appropriately aligned under academics and not operations. Another desirable outcome would be that librarian salaries would be equitably funded by the entire student population and thus ease the financial burden placed on campus operations under the existing reporting structure.

Another positive change that emerged was that the steady growth in the population of Chamberlain distance education students enrolled in the graduate programs provided an acceptable business rationale for hiring a librarian whose virtual role would match that of a virtual population of students. The librarian in this role would be primarily assigned to serving the population of graduate students. Susan Bridgers, a graduate of North Carolina Central University, the first entirely online master of library science program in the country, accepted the position in early 2015. She became the first member of what would eventually become the Chamberlain national team of remote librarians. Susan steadily built the template for how an entirely remote librarian demonstrates excellence in providing professional information services that best meet the needs of students who are engaged in pursuing advanced degrees as distance education students.

Shortly after Susan joined the team, Valerie was chosen to transition to virtual library services, making her the second member of the national team of librarians aligned under academics. Susan and Valerie quickly demonstrated that serving as virtual librarians advanced the visibility and accessibility of the library for Chamberlain students. Quite simply, instead of spending time on tasks such as assisting with copy machines, they found that 100 percent of their energies were concentrated on information literacy activities. As the library virtual presence continued to grow, the requests for librarian assistance from students steadily climbed as evidenced by chat, email, and telephone inquiries regardless whether the student was campus based or enrolled online.

Springshare announced the launch of v.2 while the librarians were building the initial guides. Springshare encourage libraries to transition to v.2 as soon as possible to take advantage of a multitude of enhanced features. Eventual transition for subscribers was not optional since v.1 would be retired within two years. We made the decision to migrate to v.2 at the end of June 2015, before beginning the next academic cycle to ensure the least disruption should the website require any downtime during the transition. In the end the transition was seamless and well worth the early adoption. Springshare's excellent support for our implementation led directly to our decision to embrace their entire suite of applications. Text messaging, LibChat services, virtual office hours scheduled through integrated calendar features—we implemented them all over the following months. Interactions with our students and faculty stakeholders increased immediately and continue to climb.

Working towards a technical infrastructure for the library that would foster discoverability we planned to take advantage of an offer from EBSCO to allow us to pilot the EBSCO Discovery Service (EDS), their proprietary web-scale discovery service.[5] Our users would, theoretically, be able to use a single search box to search for resources available from the vendors, aggregators, and publishers from which we held subscriptions or licenses. Implementing the EDS was not easy and there were some unpleasant downsides. A later 2016 study by California librarians compared the commercial discovery interfaces most commonly considered by libraries searching for a comprehensive solution.[6] The study uncovered limitations in all of the products, including EDS. We can confirm that the most frequent frustrations that we've experienced after implementing EDS are not unique: uneven indexing of content from non-EBSCO databases, unexpected link resolver failures, and downtime for maintenance that can be unpredictable and/or inconvenient. However, having EDS does satisfy many of our users, particularly those users who are not engaged in comprehensive literature reviews or reliant on a source that is not working well with EDS.[7]

The question of what cataloging system to choose to replace Voyager still remained. One non-negotiable characteristic was that the system be completely cloud based. Plans were well underway to transition most, if not all Chamberlain librarians to remote status. It would have been foolish to invest in a machine-based system that would require internal IT support. There was some thought given to whether or not a catalog was truly necessary if we were planning to eliminate most print materials, including any circulation. However, detailed review of several state higher education board accreditation statutes revealed that some still specified that library collections be traditionally cataloged.

During the time that we were evaluating systems, OCLC Worldshare Management Services (WMS) offered the cataloging solution that we identified as best meeting our requirements. Additional features available through the integrated platform were also very appealing. WMS includes a federated search to uncover both locally indexed resources as well as resources indexed by libraries around the globe. The facilitated integration of an interlibrary loan technology, Illiad, and an integrated license manager option were solutions that we had also been considering. That we already utilized EZproxy meant that authenticating our users into proprietary content could be simplified by transferring oversight to OCLC rather than manipulating EZproxy on our local servers. Negotiations with OCLC began in earnest in fall of 2015.

Meanwhile, the comprehensive transitional proposal for Chamberlain library operations and services had been approved by administration. The timeline to fully transition librarians to a national, centralized reporting structure and to move them into remote worker status was set for July 2016. A new human resources job description was created and campus leaders were engaged in confidential conversation to plan the least disruptive transition for campus operations and services provided by librarians. The optimal time to announce the plan publicly was agreed as not more than two months prior to the June transition. During implementation the campus library spaces would be merged with the CAS spaces to create a multipurpose learning commons. However, during December 2015, preliminary plans were shared by DeVry University leaders regarding planned changes in their own library operations. This unexpected overlap of significant changes for both schools played a pivotal role in accelerating the Chamberlain timeline.

The planned DeVry University operational changes would alter the campus structure and space utilization. The impact on Chamberlain co-located campuses would also be significant. The DeVry plan included a strategic workforce reorganization that would commence in March 2016. Part of the strategic plan included creation of a much smaller team of remote librarians who would serve DeVry students virtually. The campus libraries were to be dismantled and space reconfigured as an open "learning commons." Each DeVry librarian would be invited to apply for one of the five newly created positions. A public announcement of the planned changes would be made during the last week of February 2016, and DeVry owned libraries would close the following month.

Dramatic changes made to operational infrastructures in complex organizations can be exceedingly disruptive. Chamberlain leaders decided to share the operational redesign quietly with Chamberlain stakeholders to initiate a change process that would be deemed positive rather than negative. With respect to Chamberlain, the highest priority would be to provide uninterrupted excellence in library services for our students. The Chamberlain team of librarians was much smaller and therefore would not be reduced. Rather, librarians would have an opportunity to accept transition to the newly defined remote position and with that to a new reporting structure. All seven of the Chamberlain librarians agreed to the transition immediately. As of March 2016, shared library operations were discontinued. Library services were continued but as complementary rather than combined to ensure that students from both schools retained uninterrupted library services. An additional step was added to the Chamberlain transition plan. Oversight of library services for all Chamberlain campuses, included the nine existing co-located locations was divided amongst the Chamberlain librarians. A key piece of the strategic response was an operational requirement that Chamberlain librarians schedule campus site visits at least once per term and more often if needed. There could be no doubt about continuity of services from librarians for students on campuses.

Almost immediately there were several pressing tasks following separation of service operations. All of the Chamberlain campus collection materials that had previously been circulated were recoded as reserves and were no longer available off location. One positive benefit was that it provided a convenient opportunity to weed the collections and plan for standardized campus collection inventories. The search interface for Voyager was removed from the library website. Chamberlain librarians were removed from the QuestionPoint chat service schedule, and the Chamberlain chat service began operating via LibChat, already in place on the Springshare platform.

To free up physical space to create an expanded CAS/Learning Commons on campus, the St. Louis archival collection of books and bound journal volumes began to be heavily weeded. Resources available online were eliminated. A list of journal titles was identified for purchase of the archives online which would also free up campus space. Print books of historical value were placed in secure locations. The Chamberlain library collection was completely reenvisioned as a minimally archival, immediately relevant, fully online collection meant to serve the educational needs of students and faculty engaged in advancing the nursing profession.

The contract with OCLC to implement WMS was finalized in October 2016. Chamberlain was added to the cohort of institutions that were slated to build out their deployment during the assigned six-month project period (January–June 2017) per the terms of the contract. The Illiad project would commence following completion of the WMS project in July 2017. A contract with the Copyright Clearance Center would be negotiated in tandem with the Illiad project. The migration to the OCLC cloud-hosted EZproxy was added to our internal information technology team project and slated for August 2017.

It is important to note that the infrastructure changes for Chamberlain University extended far beyond the library during the years leading up to the transformation of library operations and services. In parallel with the negotiations for WMS, the academic technologies department at Adtalem finalized a contract for a new LMS to replace the Pearson eCollege system that was being retired. A decision made to adopt Cisco WebEx as the standard web-based meeting technology available to all students as well as employees enabled a multitude of creative options for connecting with students to offer on-demand library services. These are just a few of the most significant technologies adopted internally that would be engineered to work together seamlessly for academic operations to advance as planned.

The Canvas LMS contract was completed and the project team planned to launch Canvas for the July 2017 academic session. On the library's side, Springshare v.2 now included an LTI application to embed library resources into Canvas that we planned to deploy during the autumn break. To throw another complicated project into the mix, Adtalem technology teams were in the midst of rolling out a single-sign on mechanism (OKTA) that would allow a streamlined experience within Canvas when accessing a variety of licensed resources with separate authentication requirements. The Chamberlain roll-out was planned to take place in stages, although we later discovered that enabling library access through OKTA was scheduled last. Until authentication into the library EZproxy could be enabled in OKTA, users would continue to be forced to login to the library resources both inside and outside of Canvas with a separate set of credentials. This would continue to be a major source of confusion and frustration during the months leading up to the October OKTA integration deployment for the library.

Despite the highly anticipated advances in technology applications across many areas of educational support, all projects were initiated during the same period of time. In retrospect it might have been acknowledged that a strong possibility for a perfect storm of complications existed. Probably the final piece was the launch of the first program for the Chamberlain University College of Health Professions. The first class of students enrolled in the MPH program also launched in July 2017. One of the most important priorities at the institutional level is to ensure that students have the best possible experience with the online learning environment. Stakes are particularly high when launching a new online program where the student experience can make or break the success of the program. Fortuitously for the Chamberlain library, students found that our librarians were easily accessible, needed resources were easy to find and access through library course guides, and firmly established relationships between the MPH faculty and Chamberlain librarians meant that any issues related to library services for students were quickly resolved.

Over the course of the summer of 2017, the librarians struggled to deploy the public search box attached to WMS. It was less than successful. The students were accustomed to immediate displays of search results identical to what they experienced using the EDS search box. They were frustrated by being presented with a new way of searching without warning and with no explanation as to why. It certainly didn't help that they were rapidly becoming accustomed to the single sign-on experience in Canvas in which the library was not yet enabled. With overwhelmingly negative feedback greeting the WMS search interface, we restored the original EDS search box and conducted a root cause analysis. As a growing university with a significantly expanding research population, the imperative to add access to resources worldwide will only increase. WMS provides a federated search interface to meet that need so what we found during our analysis has implications for the relaunch:

- Users like the familiarity of an existing library website. Surprise improvements that change the look and feel of a website aren't eagerly embraced.
- Response times matter. When searching for online resources, "good enough" is often viewed through the lens of speed of return.
- Usability testing prior to launching a redesign provides opportunities to leverage the user perspective to build satisfaction with the end product.
- Adequate time to market and prepare users for a website redesign must be part of the project planning. The more that stakeholders understand the "why" of changes made and how they are beneficial, the greater the odds of acceptance.
- Identifying problematic issues with the product that cannot be adjusted on the user side allows time to craft a work-around solution. Documenting the issues in detail provides evidence to push the vendor to make needed changes.

Librarians continued to use, test, and improve the WMS interface internally. The consensus emerged that WMS does offer superior search results and can be customized in ways that dramatically change search speeds. It offers much better support for interlibrary loan activities. In retrospect, planning to go live with WMS without adequately considering the other technology changes that would impact students was perhaps the biggest mistake leading to a negative outcome.

Moving forward, in spite of turmoil and frustration, projects were successfully completed during the summer and fall of 2017. Successfully transitioning EZproxy to a cloud solution and connecting our users to resources through OKTA single-sign on led to dramatic improvements in user satisfaction and steadily climbing higher levels of user engagement with library resources. In December, the Illiad implementation and training was complete and launched in January 2018. It has been a complete success and appropriate usage is increasing. The Springshare LTI that enables library links directly into Canvas was launched in December 2017 as well. Usage statistics tracked on library links within Canvas are exciting. Also due to embedding chat links into courses within Canvas the number of reference transactions through the service continues to escalate.

A formal project team consisting of the technology team of librarians, Adtalem IT solutions analysts, marketing partners, and OCLC support teams was created in November 2017. User testing of the new WMS search box is underway. A decision has been made to provide two search boxes on the library homepage. A search box for WMS would be added while the original EDS search box would remain with slight adjustments made to address some coding conflicts created by attempting to link specific EBSCO databases to both search engines. Usability testing of a page where both boxes are visible will be conducted with student and faculty volunteers during February and March 2018, after which any recommended adjustments will be made. Marketing will be creating announcements and providing informational verbiage to be posted within Canvas classrooms prior to the launch of the enhanced library homepage in late June 2018.

At the same time, we are already preparing for the future evolution of the library. Building a library website at the speed at which we did so over the past three years means that we now must reexamine design and consider changes or enhancements to continuously build a better presence. By applying web design best practices and accessibility standards while re-evaluating the virtual presence of the library, we continue the systematic evaluation of our library services. Steadily analyzing the vast amount of data that we can mine through LibInsight and LibAnalytics via the Springshare platform provides powerful tools for assessing value. Overlaying Google Analytics to build a library operations dashboard pushes us further toward effectively using evidence to make operational decisions. Done with deliberate intention, robust analyses will drive decisions regarding resource investment, staffing, and service schedules.

THE JOURNEY CONTINUES

Given that so many changes have happened within Chamberlain as a whole as well as to Chamberlain library services specifically, it should come as no surprise that we are in the midst of planning more transformation over the next fiscal year. Our technical services librarians have completed a formal analysis of the library website's accessibility. Google analytics applied to our website show that user access via mobile platforms is outpacing desktop access. Our population of students with English language challenges is growing as is the number of nontraditional students facing other limitations. As library users and their preferred behaviors shift, an agile library environment must be purposefully created to retain relevancy. And it is our users as well as our administrative leaders who determine what is or is not relevant to what they wish to achieve.

Students at Chamberlain, like all students in higher education, rely on the tools that their schools provide to access, comprehend, and apply resources that successfully lead to attaining academic, scholarly, and career aspirations. Our specific transformation of library services, while necessarily unique to a national organization, should, I hope, provide useful examples of effective transition management in libraries as well as some lessons on potential pitfalls. The responsibility to shape our library presence, resources, and services to best meet the needs of our students where, when, and how they choose to access the library rests with a team of stakeholders led by our librarians. My professional journey as a Chamberlain library director has taught me to expect detours and challenges on the way to a chosen destination. I've learned to be flexible, getting somewhere is rarely in a straight line. How we get somewhere is often more transformational than arriving at the destination, as many times upon arrival we immediately realize that another destination lies ahead. Librarians do not ask themselves often enough if a transformative path is the only route to the same destination that our users intend to go.

NOTES

1. General Electric Company, "GE Annual Report" (Annual Report, Fairfield, CT, 2000), 4, http://www.ge.com/annual00/download/images/GEannual00.pdf.

2. Chamberlain University, "Our History and Heritage," Chamberlain University, accessed March 23, 2018, http://www.chamberlain.edu/about/history.

3. Louis H. Sullivan, "The Tall Office Building Artistically Considered," *Lippincott's Monthly Magazine*, 339 (1896): 408, https://archive.org/details/tallofficebuildi00sull.

4. Susan L. Groenwald, *Designing and Creating a Culture of Care for Students and Faculty: The Chamberlain University College of Nursing Model* (Philadelphia: Wolters Kluwer, 2018).

5. Marshall Breeding, "Relationship with Discovery," *Library Technology Reports* 51, no. 4 (2015): 22–25, https://journals.ala.org/index.php/ltr/article/view/5688.

6. Council of Chief Librarians Electronic Access and Resources Committee, "Discovery Comparison," Review Document, s.n., 2016, https://cclibrarians.org/sites/default/files/reviews/Documents/DiscoveryComparisonCCLEAR16.pdf.

7. Council of Chief Librarians, "Discovery."

6

Showing Leadership in Virtual Library Spaces

HELEN-ANN BROWN EPSTEIN

Regardless of the configuration of a library space, effective information professionals demonstrate leadership by leading themselves or empowering others to follow the fundamental tenets of asking what "needs to be done."[1] Considering "what's right for the enterprise," developing realistic action plans, taking "responsibility for decisions" and communicating them, and always focusing on opportunities, not problems, are the true signs of a strong leader.[2] In physical or virtual library spaces, effective information professionals and their staff embrace these principles with energy, tenacity, and enthusiasm.

In addition to energy and enthusiasm, the virtual library leader in particular must possess the personal cognitive skills necessary to lead in a virtual space. They must ready their teams and themselves to face the dynamic and unpredictable challenges of the digital world. They must be attentive and able to focus and manage thoughts and emotions. The big picture must be clear to them. A library leader needs to analyze problems and find creative solutions. They should not be afraid to use their intuition and go with a gut feeling. Finally, they should communicate well and inspire others.

You will notice the term "customer" in this chapter instead of "user." As you know, librarianship is a service industry, and libraries, especially in hospitals, may not always embrace the concept that they should be run like a business. However, the Joint Commission standards for hospitals no longer mention the necessity of having a library. Therefore, without this business acumen, at the first sign of the hospital's revenue declining the librarian may be laid off and the library closed. In my library's virtual space, especially when a first impression is made without face-to-face contact, I employ a customer service standard that focuses on patrons as customers, not just users of the service. This demonstrates the library's services worth to customers who I hope will go on to bring repeat business and advertise on behalf of the library.

As a solo hospital librarian, I manage the virtual library at Virtua Health, one of New Jersey's largest, nonprofit health systems with over 9,000 potential customers. Within this position I apply energy, excitement, and enthusiasm; years of experience managing a hospital library; and clinical outreach in the hospital of an academic medical center library. I hold a second master's degree in organizational dynamics from the University of Pennsylvania with coursework that has led me to understand that a solo librarian of a virtual library, or any librarian for that matter, needs to lead themselves. If you cannot lead yourself, it will be difficult to lead and influence others.

Virtual library spaces were first called digital libraries. Today they come in many forms. Most, if not all health sciences libraries have a website where customers can access resources, services, and speak to library staff via email, chat, or services such as WebEx or Skype. Other virtual spaces take it a step further with no physical library space and only an office where either the solo librarian, such as myself, works. Such librarians may never meet their customers in person, while others will still have the ability to meet customers and stakeholders through institutional and sometimes library-specific events and activities. Within my position, I am able to have face-to-face interactions with customers by visiting them during routine and scheduled visits. They can also visit my office.

This chapter explores successful leadership skills and teamwork with a focus on virtual library spaces based on research and practical experience. First, I will further discuss perspectives on virtual library spaces and my experience leading a virtual library. I'll then look at the different types of leadership qualities and styles as outlined by experts including Warren Bennis, William Morton Marston, and John R. Stoker and how they relate to leading virtual library spaces including leading oneself, leading staff, and leading the library and its customers. Lastly, I will take a look at leaders as managers and the business of leading.

VIRTUAL LIBRARY SPACES

Robert Braude wrote in as early as 1999 in the *Bulletin of the Medical Library Association* (MLA), that a library was known "as a place and as the interface between the scholar, and the information the scholar needed."[3] He discussed the importance of libraries connecting people to information regardless of whether it be print or electronic. Braude emphasized that print information is really just one kind of container and electronic is a different kind of container.[4] Scott Plutchak in his Janet Doe Lecture at the Annual Meeting of the MLA in 2011 noted that in the digital age, librarians "are more necessary than ever in helping" customers in their communities navigate the increasingly complex information space such as those evolving electronic containers Braude spoke to.[5, 6] Scott believed that the great age of physical libraries was coming to an end, but the great age of librarians was just beginning.

Some may view virtual libraries as impersonal, isolated, inaccessible thoughts in cold storage containers. Knowing however that Virtua's well-designed virtual library website would be attractive, easy to use, and a welcoming environment for patient care, education, and research, this was not a concern at Virtua Health. In a virtual library, the website is the library space. It must be easily accessible onsite or remotely. The design may need to start with the parent organization's webpage layout but can then be customized, especially for access to information resources.

Virtual libraries are self-service. There is usually no one person to meet and greet the user upon accessing the site, although many libraries have an automated invitation to chat. Some libraries have found sister libraries in other time zones to collaborate with to provide twenty-four-hour chat service. In my time at Cornell Medicine in New York City, we worked with our sister school in Qatar to provide chat when we were closed and vice versa. Most important, the number one priority of the virtual library site should be that customers are successful in finding what they need.

For customers' ease of use, the Virtua library's intranet-based site with rolling banner of announcements at the top has links to our e-journal and e-book collections and point of care tools for medicine and nursing (see figure 6.1). The Virtua Button brings literature to customer's fingertips with links to full text of individual papers or an interlibrary loan form within the bibliographic databases. My InfoBasket at the bottom of the page, inspired by colleagues at Vanderbilt University Medical Center, welcomes customers

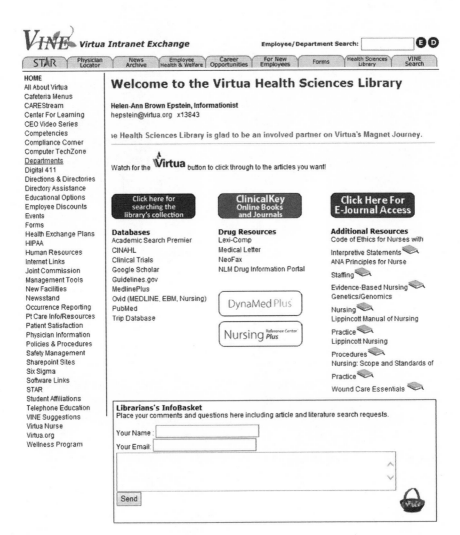

FIGURE 6.1
Virtua library site.

and offers space to explain their information needs. The site looks high tech and is streamlined and organized—nothing akin to a cold storage container.

Virtual library customers demand the same, if not more, service as they would from a physical library. Virtual libraries must look for new ways to meet customer needs. Take for instance, the former ability of customers to browse the shelves and serendipitously discover a valuable article. Virtual libraries today can provide such capabilities through resources like Browzine, which displays covers of the library's journal holdings. Browzine can also bring the latest tables of contents to one's fingertips. Keeping a customer up-to-the-minute in their specialty is a valuable library service.

As early as 2009, Michael Homan's Doe Lecture at the Annual Meeting of the MLA reflected on the impact of the evolving digital ecology on the information professional as an expert "intermediary and knowledge coach."[7] He concluded that librarian-mediated services linking knowledge and critical decision-making have become more valuable than ever as technology continues to reshape an increasingly complex knowledge environment.

Virtual libraries depend on powerful technology and it is the expert librarian, who makes sense out of competing systems, resources, and priorities and provides the essential link to information, knowledge, and decision making for their customers. The information professional is the quality filter for customers. Experienced knowledge coaches marry librarian expertise with high-tech and soft-touch personalized service, to create a winning combination.

Virtua is a three-hospital health system. The Virtua virtual library allows me to provide soft touch personalized service through my clinical rounding schedule. Monday takes me to one hospital's ICU. Tuesday, I am at a second hospital's ICU and a cardiology unit. Wednesday, I visit a third hospital including two medical/surgical floors. Thursday is catch-up day in my office. Friday I return to the third hospital to round in the NICU and pediatrics. I take information requests, but more important, perceive the information needs of the interprofessional teams. I quality filter the literature for a handful of topics and push them to the team members before the end of the day. I have been welcomed to the teams and considered an asset.

Leading the virtual library effectively with a positive attitude, energy, ambition, and authenticity is imperative. I am transparent, own my mistakes, and listen well. As a clinical librarian I perceive and anticipate information needs. I am eager to learn new things and share my knowledge with others. I communicate well and draw people together to achieve. My purpose focuses on being a fiscally responsible, passionate instrument of service and contribution. I strive to be an effective leader that walks the walk and talks the talk.

In virtual library spaces, the information delivered to a customer most often precedes meeting the librarian behind the website. Customers, however, need to positively picture the face behind the product. They need to sense the expertise and energy. The My InfoBasket feature of the Virtua Library website welcomes information requests. These are completed in a timely manner and material is pushed to the requester. In 2017, I filled almost 1,000 such requests, out of 9,000 potential customers, for either literature searches or acquiring articles through interlibrary loan. Requests came from new and repeat customers. When customers and I finally meet, it is an opportunity for both me and for them to see the person behind the virtual library transaction. They always have praise for the service they have received. As I am the library's ambassador, I am responsible for library marketing and promotion, however customers are themselves one of my top promoters.

Lecturer Jean-Claude Guédon of the Université de Montréal delivered a Leiter Lecture at the National Library of Medicine in 1999 entitled, "The Digital Library: An Oxymoron." He eloquently said librarians of virtual libraries might well discover that they have reempowered institutions if they place human interaction at the heart of their operations.[8] In other words, rather than envisioning themselves as knowledge bankers sitting on treasure vaults of knowledge, they should see themselves as an essential part of these communities and not as external repositories of knowledge. I myself am a member of an Institutional Review Board (IRB), Patient Education Committee, Nursing Research Council, Magnet Champion, welcomed visitor to Shared Governance Council meetings and was in on the ground floor planning for a Center for Precision Medicine. Participating in these activities gives me a sense of customer's needs and wants from both a service and collection perspective. However, information gleaned from formal needs assessments, usability studies, or the occasional popup snapshot survey are other methods I use to check the pulse of the library's success. Smart librarians incorporate customer suggestions and feedback. I always close emails with "send comments and questions my way."

LEADERSHIP

Types of Leaders

Self-Leaders

A solo virtual librarian needs to lead themselves and their library on a daily basis. Ken Blanchard and Susan Fowler, in their book entitled, *Self Leadership and the One Minute Manager,* state that empowered self-leaders are the key to organizational success and outline three primary fundamental principles needed for self-leadership. The first is that assumed constraints need to be challenged. The second is that points of power—knowledge power, personal power, relationship power, task power, and position power are activated. Lastly, the self-leader gets what is needed to succeed. Shortcomings are assessed and support is sought. [9] Successful leaders with strong interpersonal business skills create safe environments for the practice and possibility of making mistakes without financial or social consequences. Organizations led by empowered self-leaders are customer driven, cost effective, innovative, and flexible.[10]

As Virtua's informationist, I am a member of the clinical learning team, a team of empowered self-leaders. I report directly to a doctor of nursing practice who is the assistant vice president of clinical learning and academic affiliations. Other highly credentialed nurses oversee continuing education, nursing research, evidence-based practice, and clinical excellence. A PhD engineer oversees the clinical research efforts. The rest of the clinical learning team handles Virtua's clinical affiliations and coordinates the IRBs. My team members offer a profound amount of support and an environment in which I thrive. I offer the same support to them. Our work contributes a great deal to Virtua's success.

Warren Bennis, the well-known guru on leadership, suggests that the first step to take in becoming a leader is to learn to know yourself, realize your strengths, and nurture them. He outlines six personal qualities of a leader. The first is integrity. One should align words and actions with inner values to establish trust that leads to admiration and copying of actions. The second quality is dedication, being committed to quality and excellence. Bennis puts magnanimity third, reminding us one needs to give credit where credit is due. Humility is fourth, being able to apologize and be gracious. Robert Braude, a leader in the health sciences library world and mentor of mine, would say, a bit of tasteful self-promotion is really okay, and I agree, if done modestly. The information professional should take the opportunity to explain their special skills and use their honorifics if others do. My colleagues in the nursing world have many honorifics after their names. I proudly display AHIP, the credentialing from the Academy of Health Information Professionals of the MLA, and FMLA, designating my fellowship in the Medical Library Association at the end of my signature. Bennis lists openness and creativity as the final two qualities of a leader. One should listen well to all ideas and viewpoints and consider alternatives, even those way, way outside the box. My supervisor gives points for good intention and welcomes all ideas to offer our services in a more creative way.[11]

As the solo librarian for Virtua, all employees are the library's customers. I want to serve all of them. Sometimes it takes some creativity to demonstrate this. Virtua is on the Magnet journey, the seal of approval of quality nursing care. As a Memorial Magnet Champion, I pushed the coffee cart one Magnet Monday as we traveled the floors handing out cookies and asking questions about Magnet. Also, as Magnet Champion, I acted in our Magnet video playing one of the Magnet appraisers. I catch and am the co-manager of the winning Virtua softball team. I represent the clinical learning team on the local employee change team (LECT), a group always looking to make the Virtua experience better for customers and staff. I put myself out into the Virtua community building connections that undoubtedly have impacted the success of the Virtua library.

Authentic Leaders

Warren Bennis has also addressed the qualities of an authentic leader. He places integrity as being the most important characteristic of such leaders and adds that great leaders cultivate a culture of candor always speaking truth to power. Authentic leaders create a collaborative environment bringing the best out of each employee.[12] In a later publication, he continues his thoughts on competencies of leaders. He looks at authentic leaders as those who pay attention to directions, goals, and outcomes. They empower their workforce with pace and energy, creating an atmosphere of challenges, excitement, and fun.[13]

Authentic leaders are particularly important in virtual library's, where leaders must exercise e-leadership on a daily basis. Avolio and colleagues note that as virtual technologies become increasingly prevalent, and there is an increased susceptibility for deception, it is not unexpected that customers, staff, and other leaders may not be willing to follow a library leader if they are unsure of their authenticity.[14] The authors provide methods by which such leaders can demonstrate their authenticity such as by transmitting their positivity online.[15] In a virtual library setting this could be done via a blog, email, or forum such as LibAnswers, a Springshare product that allows customers to ask questions and library staff to reply in a forum like manner. Customers and staff then receive and interpret the leader's positivity and authenticity and they themselves go on to transmit the resulting effects. "The original source of positivity may then spread or 'go viral' in some cases, while in others be mitigated depending on whether constituents believe the leader's authenticity and message."[16]

Hogan Leadership Profiles

Companies worldwide, since 1987, have hired Hogan Assessments Systems, Inc. for personality assessment. They work with human resource departments, applying their extensive research, to help find the best person for an initial hire or the best person for promotion within the company. The Hogan Assessments Systems website outlines six leadership profiles that can be used to determine both your own and your employees' leadership styles.

1. *The Thought Leader* is a visionary. They are optimistic that they will find a better way to manage issues, but they may not always be practical.
2. *The Process Leader* is disciplined and gets things done. They feel that there is a place for everything and everything needs to be in place. They lead by the notion that structured order brings success. However, the Process Leader, insisting on having all the facts before moving forward, may stall progress. If they over structure they may also stifle creativity.
3. *The Data Leader* lives by numbers, metrics, and quantifiable goals. At times, however, they may over analyze. Their numbers should be supplemented with qualitative and subjective data.
4. *The Results Leader* loves to win! They are motivated, ambitious, self-starting, outspoken hard workers. They demand a lot from their team and supply them with a game plan for success. Results Leaders know their team and the team knows what to expect. Such leaders should use caution not to exercise too much ambition.
5. *The Social Leader* is democratic and wants to have all team members on-board to make decisions. Their team is loyal. The Social Leader, however, may make decisions slowly as a result of wanting to hear each team member's opinion before drawing conclusions.
6. *The People Leader* is a warm, compassionate, well-loved, thoughtful communicator that wants to maintain strong relationships. For them conflict

is to be avoided, agreements are mutual, and workers are friends. Sometimes these leaders need to remember to focus on facts and data versus solely on their people.[17]

Knowing what type of Hogan leader you are can benefit your ability to lead in a variety of virtual library spaces. For example, if you are a People Leader working virtually with both your staff and customers, you should look for ways to interact with them that play to your strengths, such as research consultations via virtual meeting software, videoconferencing monthly meetings, or simply picking up the phone versus sending an email message. A Process Leader leading a virtual library space should take pride in their knack for structure but should be aware of the fact that how they think things should be structured, such as on their library website, isn't necessarily how their staff or customers interact with information online. The Results Leader, particularly, a solo virtual library leader, should assess what "winning" looks like in their library space. If it's not how many people are coming in the library, what does success look like?

DISC Personality Types

Besides demonstrating power and confidence, a leader should also exude caring and empathy, especially to their staff.[18] A strong leader is warm, appreciative, respectful, and a good listener with a sincere interest in staff well-being. They take the time for each employee, regardless how busy they may be. A strong leader is as passionate about staff professional development as they are about their own. True leaders create the right conditions for individual persons within an organization to thrive. They build a platform for others' success. True leaders listen to feedback and modify the environment. Worker contributions and successes are recognized, rewarded, and thanked.

In the 1920s, William Moulton Marston from Harvard created the DISC personality types to understand people and their personalities and therefore build stronger relationships to solve conflicts. The DISC behavior assessment focuses on four behavioral traits: dominance, inducement, submission, and compliance. Results of staff profiles can be used as a tool to organize a work environment that appreciates reactions and understands behavior to predict successful workflow. Most people have a combination of at least one major and one minor personality type.

Birds represent the personality types. The eagle represents dominance. Results are achieved quickly and efficiently. These are bold, strong-willed, forceful leaders. The parrot represents influence. Such leaders are outgoing, optimistic, enthusiastic, inspirational, energetic, interactive, and hardworking morale boosters who like to have fun. The dove represents steadiness and being even tempered. These leaders are accommodating, consistent, patient, tactful, even-paced, and thorough. They usually remain neutral and want to create harmonious collaboration. The owl represents conscientiousness. These leaders are analytical, reserved, precise, private, systematic, and inquisitive. They have a zest for details and ask why often as they may work behind the scenes. They sort out complex problems.[19]

The clinical learning team at Virtua completed the DISC assessment. I am a combination parrot and dove. My parrot qualities of being outgoing, optimistic, enthusiastic, energetic, and hardworking brings me success as a solo hospital librarian by practicing clinical outreach with a most ambitious rounding schedule and sitting on hospital-wide committees. The dove characteristics of being accommodating, consistent, and thorough also contribute to my success to listen carefully and provide quality evidence based information in a timely manner. If given the opportunity to hire library staff, I have considered whether I should hire the same combination as myself or complementary types. There are advantages and disadvantages of either combination.

Certainly the bold, strong-willed, forceful dominating characteristic of the eagle that achieves quick and efficient results is an asset to any library leader. Sometimes administrative decisions must be made quickly. In these times of staying-the-same budget dollars or cutting the budget, an eagle personality could be called on to demonstrate resource stewardship to justify library acquisitions. The library leader may call on eagle characteristics to also plan strategically and defend additional staff. An owl characteristic of being systematic and sorting out complex problems is an advantage for a virtual librarian. These attributes could aid in the organization of the webpage design to make it easy to navigate. Precision analysis helps when anticipating all pathways that a customer could take when using the virtual library.

ASSESSING THE QUALITY OF LEADERSHIP

John R. Stoker, an experienced consultant in organizational development, poses eight questions for one to assess the quality of their leadership.

1. Do you seek feedback from those with whom you work?
2. Do you have foresight to anticipate what is needed and take the initiative to accomplish your goals?
3. Do you make decisions and stay committed to them?
4. Do you make course corrections when things don't go well?
5. When you give directions, do you take the time to explain why?
6. Do you recognize those who work hard and do a good job?
7. Do you make things harder than they need to be?
8. Do you take the time to enjoy the adventure?[20]

These questions are meant to inspire leaders to be visionaries who are thoughtful, caring, and encouraging to enjoy their work and are comfortable with taking mistakes and learning from them. These questions could easily be applied to assess the quality of a virtual library leader. Take for instance question one, feedback should be sought not just by the staff you lead but also from customers. Questions three and four are very important when it comes to developing and maintaining a library website. You want to be able to commit to the site's layout and not change access points to resources confusing patrons. At the same time, however, you need to know when it's time to course correct. Question five can be used to assess your success when leading users and staff at a distance. You might understand why you've directed a user to interlibrary loan or asked a staff member to begin using a particular software but users and staff benefit from the reason behind it. Providing a reason strengthens learning opportunities, uptake, and retention.

LEADERS AS MANAGERS

Library leaders are also library managers. Joyce Backus, of the National Library of Medicine, participated on a panel in a 2012 symposium at the Annual Meeting of the MLA entitled, "Managing and Revitalizing Your Career as a Medical Librarian," and outlined six skills a library leader needs to navigate complex organizations. This first is to aspire. One should find role models and emulate their behavior and professionalism. The second is to listen to one's own instincts as well as to colleagues, supervisors, and coworkers. Experimentation is the third skill. New ideas should be tried with little fear of failing. Fourth, one should find the balance within them and within the organization. One needs a strong, solid foundation on which to thrive and experiment. This is particularly important in an exclusively virtual library setting where many leaders are navigating such waters for the first time and often alone. One must manage their own reputation and career to align with their personal values and goals. The fifth skill is keeping the perspective that a job is a job and your own personal importance is imperative. Lastly is being humble. One should always give credit where credit is due.[21] For example, in instances where staff are working at a distance from each other, the leader should find methods to give credit privately and publicly in front of the team. This could be by group emails and teleconference or video conferenced staff meetings. The leader could also nominate the team or staff for organizational awards. With careful planning, the team can meet in person for special events, like a holiday celebration or an annual meeting, providing leaders with opportunity to praise and provide credit to their team.

THE BUSINESS OF LEADING

Librarians have been encouraged to run their libraries like a business with an entrepreneurial spirit that drives them to success despite any obstacle. Such an approach is thought to help them gain a sense of excitement from challenges they face. This advice was delivered throughout a four-part CE class offered through the MidAtlantic Region of the National Network of Libraries of Medicine. Claire Joseph and I presented the fourth segment on proving your worth and proving your value. The session was then published in the *Journal of Hospital Librarianship*.[22] A successful library leader makes sure everyone in the institution knows there is a library and its location and web address. It cannot be assumed that all administration and staff know about the library's programs and services particularly in institutions where the library is exclusively virtual or is not in a central location. A good leader asks customers about their information needs and seeks out those who do not use the library.

Katherine Stemmer Frumento, a leader in hospital librarianship, has also suggested the library should be run like one's own personal business.[23] The work really does revolve around attracting and keeping customers. Flexible planning should be employed to prepare for unplanned opportunities as they arise. However, one must be able to say no with an explanation. It is impossible to be all things to all customers. Librarians do not necessarily sell products; however, they engage in non-sales selling. Daniel Pink, in his book, *To Sell is Human,* writes that about 40 percent of employees work is devoted to the non-sales selling skills of persuading, influencing, and convincing others.[24] A library leader's elevator speech is a non-selling sales pitch. It is a form of promotion that should be focused, thought provoking, memorable, and kept to no more than thirty seconds. This requires memorizing and practicing it in advance. It can highlight the library staff or the benefits of a particular library resource. This is particularly important to those leading virtual library spaces that may get very limited opportunity for face time with users, prospective users, and stakeholders. The rolling banner at the top of the library website is like an elevator speech, promoting a particular event, like National Medical Librarians Month in October or a trial of a particular resource, like Browzine or tastefully mentioning accolades the library and its staff have received. Information on elevator speeches with sample speeches can be found on online through resources such as the American Library Association, *Library Journal,* and more.

CONCLUSION

Libraries are service enterprises and must be run by ethical leaders. An article by M. J. Tooey and Gretchen Arnold published in the *Journal of the Medical Library Association* in 2014 reported the results of a survey of the Association of Academic Health Science Libraries (AAHSL) directors about ethics. The number one goal was that the director be honest and treat others with "respect and fairness."[25] They need to realize the power they have over others and that all must be treated with civility and honor without bias. The director must "talk the talk and walk the walk," leading themselves and their staffs.[26]

Regardless of the library venue in which they work, the successful library leader is aware of their personality characteristics and works to enrich them. The successful virtual library leader is always considerate of the fact that they do not have the luxury of face to face interactions with customers and staff. Though they may have leadership attributes they are used to employing in nonvirtual circumstances, these may not directly translate to a virtual setting. They continually are acquiring new skills to practice their trade effectively and efficiently. True leaders create the right conditions for individual persons within an organization to thrive. Energy they radiate inspires and drives the team. They take care of themselves and their team to build a platform, virtual or physical for success.

NOTES

1. Peter F. Drucker, "What Makes an Effective Executive," *Harvard Business Review* 82, no. 6 (2004): par. 2, https://hbr.org/2004/06/what-makes-an-effective-executive.

2. Drucker, "What Makes an Effective Executive," par. 2.

3. Robert M. Braude, "Virtual of Actual: The Term Library is Enough," *Bulletin of the Medical Library Association* 87 no. 1 (1999): 86, https://www.ncbi.nlm.nih.gov/pmc/articles/PMC226533/.

4. Braude, "Virtual of Actual," 87.

5. Scott T. Plutchak, "Breaking the Barriers of Time and Space: The Dawning of the Great Age of Librarians," *Journal of the Medical Library Association* 100, no. 1 (2012): 10, doi: 10.3163/1536-5050.100.1.004.

6. Braude, "Virtual of Actual," 87.

7. Michael J. Homan, "Eyes on the Prize: Reflections on the Impact of the Evolving Digital Ecology on the Librarian as Expert Intermediary and Knowledge Coach, 1969–2009," *Journal of the Medical Library Association* 98, no. 1 (2010): 55. doi: 10.3163/1536-5050.98.1.016.

8. Jean-Claude Guédon, "The Digital Library: An Oxymoron?" *Bulletin of the Medical Library Association* 87, no. 1 (1999): 9, https://www.ncbi.nlm.nih.gov/pmc/articles/PMC226505/.

9. Ken Blanchard and Susan Fowler, *Self Leadership and the One-Minute Manager Revised Edition: Gain the Mindset and Skillset for Getting What You Need to Succeed* (New York: William Morrow, 2017).

10. Orrin Woodward, "Warren Bennis Six Personal Qualities of Leadership," *Orrin Woodward on LIFE & Leadership,* April 18, 2008, http://orrinwoodwardblog.com/2008/04/18/warren-bennis-six-personal-qualities-of-leadership/.

11. Woodward, "Warren Bennis Six."

12. Warren Bennis, "Authentic Leaders Engage More in Creative Collaboration," *Leadership Excellence Essentials* 23, no. 8 (2006): 3–4.

13. Warren Bennis, "Leadership Competencies," *Leadership Excellence Essentials* 27, no. 2 (2010): 20.

14. Bruce J. Avolio, John J. Soski, Surinder S. Kahai, and Bradford Baker, "E-Leadership: Re-Examining Transformations in Leadership Source

and Transmission," *Leadership Quarterly* 14 (2014): 111, doi: 10.1016/j. leaqua.2013.11.003.

15. Avolio et al., "E-Leadership: Re-Examining Transformations," 108.

16. Avolio et al., "E-Leadership: Re-Examining Transformations," 108.

17. Hogan, "Leader Focus," Hogan, accessed April 16, 2018, www.hoganleaderfocus. com.

18. Scott Mautz, "8 Powerful Ways to Lead from the Heart: Here's How to Roll Up Your Sleeves and Wear Your Heart on Them," *Leadership Excellence Essentials* 34, no. 11 (2017): 5, https://www.hr.com/en/magazines/leadership_excellence_ essentials/november_2017_leadership.

19. Merrick Rosenberg, "Which Bird Are You? Taking Flight with the DISC Styles," Training: The Source for Professional Development, last modified September 10, 2014, https://trainingmag.com/which-bird-are-you-taking-flight-disc-styles.

20. John R. Stoker, "Leadership Lessons from the River of No Return-8 Questions to Assess the Qualifications of Your Leadership," *Leadership Excellence Essentials* 34, no. 11 (2017): 6–7, https://www.hr.com/en/magazines/leadership_excellence_ essentials/november_2017_leadership.

21. Tanya P. Bardyn, Elizabeth Atcheson, Colleen Cuddy, and Gerald J. Perry, "Managing and Revitalizing Your Career as a Medical Librarian: A Symposium Report," *Journal of Hospital Librarianship* 13, no. 3 (2013): 224–25, doi:10.1080/153 23269.2013.798770.

22. Claire Joseph and Helen-Ann Brown Epstein, "Proving Your Worth/Adding to Your Value," *Journal of Hospital Librarianship* 14, no. 1 (2014): 69–79, doi: 10.1080/15323269.2014.860842.

23. Bardyn et al., "Managing and Revitalizing Your Career as a Medical Librarian," 225.

24. Daniel H. Pink, *To Sell Is Human: The Surprising Truth about Moving Others,* e-book (New York: Riverhead Books, 2013), 107.

25. Mary Joan Tooey and Gretchen N. Arnold, "The Impact of Institutional Ethics on Academic Health Sciences Library Leadership: A Survey of Academic Health Sciences Library Directors," *Journal of the Medical Library Association* 102, no. 4 (2014): 244, doi: 10.3163/1536-5050.102.4.005.

26. Tooey et al., "The Impact of Institutional Ethics," 245.

Reimagining Special Collections Spaces

Esther Carrigan and Nancy Burford

This chapter explores the renovation of a special collections space in an academic health sciences library. It draws relevant concepts from academic libraries into the health sciences concept and also generalizes to increase applicability to specialized health sciences environments such as association or hospital libraries. The goals for this chapter are to provide some of the most relevant global issues influencing the local decision to renovate a special collections space as well as the local factors involved, and to give concrete (no pun intended) examples and illustrations of renovation details, including practical advice. Chapter content and sections include Special Collections in Health Sciences Libraries; Why Consider a Special Collections Renovation; A Case Study in Special Collections Renovation: The Texas A&M Medical Sciences Library Experience; and Post-Project Evaluation and Reflections, Advice, and Best Practices.

SPECIAL COLLECTIONS IN HEALTH SCIENCES LIBRARIES

Special collections in health sciences libraries share many common attributes with their academic counterparts. They typically consist of rare and historical books, manuscripts, and often, the archives chronicling the parent institution. Many special collections began with the gift of materials from donors, perhaps even an entire personal library. Some of the earliest-founded universities and medical schools in the United States have the finest and most extensive special collections simply by virtue of being in existence long enough for the contemporary books from previous centuries to become part of their historical collections. In health sciences, where currency is tantamount, reviewing collection materials and moving earlier editions of classics can provide an ongoing supply of additions to the historical collections. But most health sciences special collections have a defined collection scope and cut-off date, for example, items must be published pre–World War I to be included. A library with an active donor or endowment program that supports ongoing additions to the collection, or one with significant parent institutional growth or changes, can be faced with the challenge of providing adequate physical and environmental space for these special materials.

WHY CONSIDER A SPECIAL COLLECTIONS RENOVATION?

As is evidenced by the existence of this volume, library spaces have been greatly impacted by changes coming from a variety of sources in the information and education worlds. One of the most impactful in terms of health sciences library space has been the profound change in the concept and nature of library collections that was triggered by the emergence and proliferation of online resources. The usual chain of events has been replacement of print with electronic, the reduction or elimination of ongoing print purchases, and the removal of little-used or redundant print volumes. These collection changes resulted in major declines in the collection footprint in libraries and the redefinition of collection spaces into a variety of user spaces.

Alongside the redefinition of library spaces triggered by the proliferation of electronic resources has been a developing recognition of the importance of special and unique content in research library collections, including in the health sciences—the nonmainstream content that is important to individual libraries' constituencies. Licensing of electronic resources through package and publisher deals has resulted in a substantial degree of homogeneity of content across research and health sciences libraries. Library reputations have long been built on the general collection size and on the breadth and depth of their rare and special materials. These two elements, comprehensive collections along with scarce or unique items, remain the primary measures of quality to many.[1] Another validation of the importance of unique library collections is the leadership role taken by the Center for Research Libraries in their recent initiatives to support scholarly resource preservation and access.[2] Following this lead, many of these unique materials are being included in digitization projects to preserve the intellectual and artistic content and to deliver and share that content over the web without damaging or risking the original and increasing the visibility of these materials.

Much has been written about library efforts to intellectually highlight and preserve this special material and to develop specialized services to leverage unique content. There is also growing published and anecdotal evidence that the physical space and environment provided for these special collections can be a positive factor in the competition to recruit potential students and faculty. Campus and library tours that effectively showcase unique and rare special collections materials can impress visitors, enhance the reputation of the library and parent institution, and help distinguish the library among research libraries and the institution from its competitors.[3] Special collections can also be an effective tool in campus development, fund-raising, and alumni relations.[4]

It is generally acknowledged that these unique or special materials have historically been managed outside the mainstream of library bibliographic control and access tools, limiting the awareness of many users to their presence in the library and their potential value to scholarship. Increased efforts continue to more completely describe and distinguish these often rare and unique items and to include them in standard discovery tools. But these special collections have also often been housed in less than optimal physical spaces from both an environmental and visibility perspective.

Several physical factors can influence the decision to renovate a special collections area. One of the most common is that the collection simply outgrows its allotted space. The specialized temperature and humidity requirements of such materials make the option of off-site storage more limited and expensive for them, although that can be part of renovation planning. As the collection grows, proper space for the use of the materials also grows, as does the ready availability of qualified staff to assist users with these materials. A slight variation on the collection growth factor is that changes in the types of materials included in the special collection may require additional or different housing. Libraries may also be faced with the need to provide better environmental control for the special collections space or to provide better security for the collection, or both. Older buildings are inherently an environmental challenge for both collections and users. The expansion of higher education facilities that blossomed in the decades following World War II produced many campus library buildings that are still in use today. The heightened environmental needs of special collections can be especially challenging for the infrastructure of an older facility.

One other factor that influences the renovation decision is a strategic one—the desire to more effectively showcase the collection by updating the space to intentionally create a particular atmosphere for the space that supports the new vision for the collection and its space, or by relocating the entire special collections space within the library. Given the potential positive impacts mentioned above, as well as the reputation-enhancing potential for both the library and parent institution, a well-designed and well-placed special collections space can be an integral and important part of a library "facility strategic plan."

As many libraries are reimagining their spaces, a number of design considerations have emerged with a consistency that suggests they could be considered trends. The service satisfaction dimension, the "library as place," which is integral to the LibQUAL+® survey places an emphasis on library spaces from a user perspective.[5] This perspective raises questions about the needs for collaborative spaces, individual study spaces, research and educational support services space, technology, power and connectivity capabilities and distribution, and specialized services space. Above all, it underscores the need for stakeholder input in planning renovations. While these trends come from general library renovations, the principles and user input elements can contribute much to the planning of a special collection renovation.

A CASE STUDY IN SPECIAL COLLECTIONS RENOVATION: THE TEXAS A&M MEDICAL SCIENCES LIBRARY EXPERIENCE

The Medical Sciences Library at Texas A&M University is one of five campus libraries under the umbrella of the university libraries. It began as the Veterinary Library, formally established in 1949 and housed in the College of Veterinary Medicine. Its name was changed to the Veterinary Medical Library in 1968, and it became the Medical Sciences Library (MSL) in 1974, with a mandate to serve the new College of Medicine as well as the College of Veterinary Medicine. Responsibility to serve the College of Agriculture and Life Sciences programs was added in 2000. The Texas A&M Health Science Center developed over the next decades and now includes professional schools of dentistry, medicine, nursing, pharmacy, public health, and an institute of biosciences and technology.

In 1985, the MSL moved into its new free-standing building, connected to the College of Veterinary Medicine by a tunnel under the highway and connected to the College of Medicine by a covered walkway. Its special collection encompasses the archives chronicling both the College of Veterinary Medicine and the Texas A&M Health Science Center, and a historical collection primarily focused on veterinary medicine, having begun as the library for the veterinary program which began at Texas A&M shortly after the university was established in 1876.

Local Decision Factors

The local decision to totally reimagine the special collections space was influenced not only by global trends in repurposing library spaces, but also by the vision of the Texas A&M University Libraries. The vision and mission statements of the libraries supported, encouraged, and inspired this renovation:

> The University Libraries will be the indispensable hub of discovery, learning & creativity at Texas A&M University.
> The Pillars of this vision will be:
>
> - A distinguished Collection of information resources unbounded by place and preserved for future generations;
> - A suite of robust Services and a Team exceeding customer expectations;
> - An inspirational Environment that delights and invites use;
> - And an Organizational Culture celebrated for its trust, openness to risk and strengthened by its collaboration and diversity.[5]

It speaks to the importance of collections "unbounded by place and preserved for future generations" and an "inspirational environment that delights and invites use."

Another local factor in this decision was the priority given by the University Libraries to renovate and reimagine library spaces, resulting in a progression of renovation projects over the past several years. At the Medical Sciences Library, these included a renovation of the first floor public space, the Graduate and Professional Students Zone (a 24/7 card access area that does not allow undergraduate student entry), the second floor public space (reduction of open stacks footprint by 50 percent), and most recently, the special collections area. All of the general public space renovations were guided by user input gathered from comments made in the LibQUAL+® customer satisfaction surveys conducted usually every two years at Texas A&M, suggestion box submissions, suggestions made on library white-boards for renovation of specific areas of the library, and comments made to staff at the service desk. LibQUAL+® survey responses also provided indications of the importance and value users placed on the "library as place." Sifting through this input revealed themes that also had relevance for the special collections renovation: increase electrical power outlets, increase wireless network access, provide more whiteboards, provide more tables and seats for quiet study, and provide furniture that is flexible and can be configured by users. The overarching lesson learned from earlier renovations was to create spaces that were flexible and could serve multiple purposes as the best approach to try to meet the needs of a changing campus and user population.

The existing special collections space could not adequately house the current number or types of historical and archival materials much less provide space for anticipated collection growth. It was part of the original Medical Sciences Library building construction, dating to the early 1980s. Although a pleasant space, its functional limitations and inadequacies came largely from the attempt to match its finishes and furnishings with the rest of the new library building. The scale and immovable qualities of the furnishings seemed more appropriate for a hotel seminar room than for a special collections area. The space did not offer space, security, or the environment truly appropriate for historical materials. The entry was dim, uninviting, and partially blocked by a massive black reception desk with a tall counter facing the entry doors. Little could be done to change the original placement of furniture to expand potential uses of the space.

Goals for the Renovation

Developing goals for the renovation project proved very helpful in communicating with the renovation project team and in guiding choices to be made as the vision of the space and actual plans began to take shape. Goals for the renovation were to

- Create a space to showcase the historical collections and encourage their use, while providing a secure collection space with optimal environmental control.
- Provide a museum space to display and highlight collection items, including the significant nontextual based artifacts.
- Create a space that provides flexibility in the effective display of the works of art included in the historical collection.
- Create a flexible space that can be open and available for quiet study, meetings, and special events.
- Create a space that employs technology and modern design techniques to tie the historical collection to the present, to promote and emphasize the continuing relevancy of historical materials.
- Create an aesthetically pleasing space in which the structural design and furnishings exude an atmosphere of quality and speak to visitors and potential donors of the commitment and pride of Texas A&M in those collections.
- Create a space that can be open to student use to raise their awareness and pique their interest in the historical collections.
- Create a space that supports and facilitates scholarship and a research service for the historical collections, including adequate, well-designed reading room.

Budget

Guided by the goals for the project, it became clear to all involved that the flexibility to support multiple diverse functions, the integration of technology, and the successful creation of the desired ambience for the renovated spaces would drive up the renovation budget. Funds were set aside for a number of years until the desired funding level for the project budget was achieved: one million dollars. Although specific costs for a renovation would be dependent on a number of local factors, presenting general expense categories for a particular project can be usal for comparisons, extrapolations, and estimates of funding levels required for other projects. The categories for the MSL expenditures are grouped by the separate vendors to whom payment was made.

For the MSL Special Collection renovation, construction costs were the single largest expenditure, covering numerous project components and representing 45 percent of renovation costs. This included actual demolition/construction costs for work such as eliminating several small rooms, creating connections between adjacent rooms to form a special collections suite, construction of the glass-enclosed collections vault, and the redesign of the entrance to the area. Construction costs also included all electrical work and fixtures, additional enhanced heating/ventilation and air-conditioning equipment/installation, enhanced security for the spaces, and all networking costs. Furniture and furnishings comprised the next largest expenditure group, totaling 40 percent of the renovation costs. This category of expenses included all tables, chairs, shelving, specialized work tables/cabinets, reading room tables, back-lit display wall units to decorate the spaces between collection shelves in the glass vault with images from collection materials, and six museum-quality exhibit cases. Only 6 percent of renovation costs were spent on carpeting and floor coverings for the space. A mere 5 percent was required to cover all architectural work to translate the vision into a space plan for the redesign, engineer-enhanced environmental systems, and provide all construction documents. The inspections and facilities project management required by Texas A&M represented 3 percent of the renovation costs. Networking and data management expenses to support card-reader access capabilities required 1 percent of the total project expenditures. Figure 7.1. summarizes the categories of renovation expenses.

Chronicling the MSL Renovation

The original design and construction of the special collections suite was a generously sized space, close to 3,400 square feet, covering about one sixth of the second floor. There was one large open room with stacks and tables, one private office, one workroom with running water, and five private study carrels. The library director at the time of construction had a vision of building an ethnic medicine collection, with the office and workroom for staff and study carrels for visiting scholars.

The furnishings of the room were typical of the 1980s, heavy, and for the most part, immovable. Three double-sided free-standing ranges of shallow shelving in golden oak and single-sided, glass-fronted oak shelves the length of one wall was thought to be adequate for the collection, along with a pair of large oak map cases and another wall with tall and deep oak cabinets for other storage. The environmental controls for the space were part of the

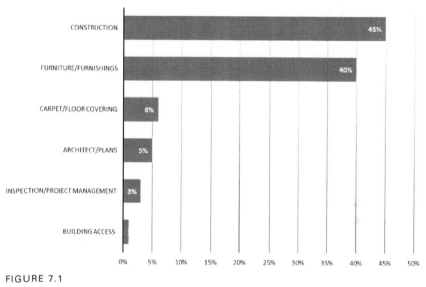

FIGURE 7.1
MSL special collection renovation expenses.

whole building system; no provision was made for additional HVAC to keep the temperature and humidity controlled appropriately for special collections materials. The lighting was standard fluorescent, and the suite had two large ten-foot square windows facing southeast with no overhang to ward off the heat and light; aluminum blinds provided the only protection from UV exposure. The only design or construction decision made for the suite that made it remotely appropriate as a special collections area was the inclusion of a halon fire suppression system.

A small ethnic medicine collection was donated by a faculty member, but no active purchasing occurred to build a collection of distinction. With the departure of that director a few short years after we occupied the new library building, that collection was recognized as not needing the protection of a locked room and moved into the general circulating collection by 1995. By that time, the halon system had been removed and the room used more as a second staff conference room. The oldest three to four hundred books in the collection, the original late-nineteenth and early-twentieth-century circulating collection of the veterinary library along with three historical works, had been in limbo for a number of years, stored in boxes or on shelves in our

The renovation team worked well together. The architect took care of the engineering consultants needed as well as the construction drawings. The contractor had a team for demolition, framing, Sheetrock, and paint and was responsible for subcontractors for electrical and HVAC work. The university project manager was responsible for fire suppression and health and safety, as well as communications. The interior design team was responsible for supplying flooring, furnishings, and shelving. The curator was the library project manager, a logical choice as the person most concerned with both the collection and the presentation of materials within the new space.

The strongest key to the success of the project was attention to detail and communication with everyone right from the beginning, and that was the curator's job. Every part of the construction drawings needed to be examined, and questions asked, such as where did we need additional power and where would we need network cables. The architect needed to be told what power we needed for the new wall-hung exhibit cases and what type of outlet boxes. The electricians needed to be shown how high to install the exhibit outlets. The framer needed to be told where we needed additional support for larger power boxes for transformers for lighted fabric panels. Daily check-ins with the contracting crews was a necessity to keep on top of questions to avoid problems. Even with that we discovered that the housekeeping outlets in the vault were wired to the lighted panels and could not be used unless those were turned on; the separation of these power outlets was not specified in the electrical drawings.

We would need to complete the renovation in two phases because we had no secure, environmentally safe place for the collection other than the old computer room. Because of the additional framing to securely support the glass walls, and the manufacturing time for the glass itself, four months were allocated to complete the new glass vault. With the installation of newly ordered shelving, the collection could be moved into the newly built and secured space and the second phase of renovation of the computer suite easily completed in four weeks. Our initial timeline was to have everything completed by the 2016 fall semester.

First, there were delays with the glass; panels of four-by-nine feet by one half inch must be specially manufactured, and the local glass company forgot to order it. Then, the flooring installers had not previously worked with the specified hard surface flooring for the new vault and installed it badly; it had to be removed and a special tool ordered to weld the seams properly. The new shelving arrived on schedule, but the matte finish selected was not what was delivered; all of the shelving parts felt gritty as if they were coated with sandpaper. All of it had to be remanufactured with a delay of two months. The nine-foot-tall glass door to the new vault arrived a half inch too long and had to be remade.

Once the new glass vault was secure, three months later than the initial timeline, library staff shifted the collection within two days, but the university facilities staff weren't available for breaking down the old shelving in the computer room. Eager to begin demolition, one of the contractor's team and the curator took them apart and the rest of the construction team carried them downstairs to the staging area. Once the computer suite was empty, the team removed the old raised floor to discover a high-voltage power box that was not on the original building plans. It took a few days for the electricians to trace it, disconnect it, and remove it.

During the second-phase demolition, the contractor discovered that the floor was off-level in the second-floor landing. It fell from the midpoint of the entry to two inches lower near the original computer suite doors; when that point was leveled to the exterior wall, it was three inches off. This affected the look of the entry doors that had been installed level, but the base was almost an inch off the floor on one side. It would also affect the solid floor that was being installed to replace the original raised floor. Another fix was needed before flooring was laid in the entry and exhibit area, another week's delay to float it out before the flooring contractor could finish their work.

After all the delays, we finally had a post-punch-list inspection four months later than initially estimated. One year after the renovation started, we had an official opening.

Table 7.1. Estimated project timeline

Predesign phase	1 month (Paperwork filed and project team set up)
Design phase	3 months
Demolition	1 month
Construction	5 months
Furnishings	3 months
Cleanup and inspections	1 month

Putting all the phases together into a timeline may prove a useful predictor for other projects. Some of the phases may take place simultaneously, like furniture and construction. This estimated timeline includes delays.

Before and After Space Comparisons

We began with a collection space of 735 shelf-feet of 10-inches-deep unsecured oak shelving, a third of which was behind glass with fluorescent lights at top of each section. There were two ten-drawer wooden map cabinets, seven deep-wooden cabinets, and ten three-drawer wooden horizontal file cabinets. The lighting was fluorescent lighting and the space under building temperature control, with no humidity control. We tried to avoid using the oak storage cabinets for special collections because of the acidity of the oak. Our renovation created two card-access collection spaces, with 1,666 shelf-feet of 12-inches-deep steel shelving, 44 shelves of 16-inches-deep x 35 inches-wide shelves for flat storage of folios, and two ten-drawer steel flat files for prints and broadsides. All lighting is LED and we have two separate Liebert systems to maintain air-conditioning, temperature, and humidity control suitable for preservation of materials in both vaults.

Creating an exhibit space that would be an immediate wow-factor upon entering the space was a key element in our vision for the renovated space. It was a major transformation. We began with exhibit cases that had poor to no lighting and easily broken or bypassed locks. There was poor mobility around the cases for handicap access and the space was shared with a large, immovable L-shaped sofa and reception desk. Specifically, we had two flat exhibit cases, 48 inches x 30 inches x 8 inches with no lighting, flimsy locks, and the floor of the case standing 30 inches from floor. Even worse were the five glass vitrines, 18 inches x 18 inches x 72 inches, with halogen lighting, and locks secured with hex bolts from the exterior. The postrenovation space provides museum-quality half-inch laminated glass and steel cases with dimmable, positional LED lights, desiccant trays to control humidity, and high security locks with additional cams; wall-hung cases at appropriate height for handicap access and space to maneuver through exhibit area. The space is shared with low, movable benches. We now have three wall-hung glass and steel exhibit cases 30 inches wide x 20 inches deep x 48 inches high, one wall-hung glass and steel exhibit case, 48 inches wide x 20 inches deep x 48 inches high, one wall-hung glass and steel exhibit case, 60 inches wide x 20 inches deep x 48 inches high, and one free-standing glass and steel exhibit case, 72 inches long x 36 inches wide x 11 inches high, with inset steel base raising the case floor up to 29 inches from floor.

Another element in our vision was to create flexible, multifunction space for people so that we could increase the overall use of the space. We began with much of the space taken up with immovable furnishings including free-standing book ranges, a bank of tall cabinets, another of four-foot-tall cabinets, a reception desk, a sofa, and one single-person office with chair.

There were a total of forty-two seats in the room, including those isolated in the office and the reception area. In addition, there were five study carrels that were never used as originally intended. In the main area, seating included one twelve-foot marble conference table with twelve leather Charles Pollock executive chairs, four 3 feet x 5 feet oak study tables with sixteen Marcel Breuer Cesca-style upholstered armchairs. Lounge seating was provided by eight low, leather Knoll Pfister lounge chairs and one six-seat low, leather Knoll Pfister L-shaped sofa. The lounge chairs were lower to the floor and didn't lend themselves to interaction with the other chairs. Electrical power was limited to wall outlets. Key elements in the renovation of people spaces were flexible, configurable furnishings, increased seating capacity, and much more available power. The renovated open people area has little fixed furniture; there is one round adjustable-height table built around a structural column. The space can be configured for a wide array of purposes: lecture, workshop, quiet study, reception. There are currently a total of sixty-eight possible seats in a variety of styles: fifty folding, nesting, wheeled chairs with flexible backs and upholstered seats; ten arc-shaped, leather, wheeled lounge chairs; and two four-seat benches in the exhibit area (one has small tables between seats). Additional seating is possible. Tables are configurable in a variety of shapes: ten rectangular, wheeled, folding and nesting tables, 59 inches χ 29.5 inches; eight half-round, wheeled, folding and nesting tables, 59 inches χ 29.5 inches; four "kite," wheeled, folding and nesting tables, 29.5 inches; and three reception-height, rectangular, wheeled, folding and nesting tables. Additional power is provided with floor plugs and electrical towers that can be plugged into the floor plugs that add six additional electrical outlets and six USB power outlets.

Square footage of the space was increased from 3,388 square feet to 4,453 square feet, over a 30 percent increase.

Table 7.2. Before and after renovation comparisons

Before	After
Square footage: 3,388 sq. ft.	*Square footage: 4,453 sq. ft.*

Collection space
- Shelf-feet total of 735' of 10" deep unsecured oak shelving
- Two 10-drawer wooden map cabinets
- Seven deep wooden cabinets
- 10 three-drawer wooden horizontal files
- Fluorescent lighting
- Building temperature control, no humidity control

Exhibit space
- Bad to no lighting in the cases with easily broken or opened locks
- Poor mobility around cases for handicap access
- Two flat exhibit cases, 48" x 30" x 8" with no lighting, flimsy locks, with floor of case 30" from floor
- Five glass vitrines, 18" x 18" x 72", halogen lighting, locks secured with hex bolts from exterior

People space
- Primarily immovable furnishings: free-standing book ranges, a large marble conference table, a bank of tall cabinets, another of 4' cabinets, a reception desk and sofa
- Total of thirty-six seats
- Five study carrels, used for storage
- Electrical power limited to wall outlets
- One 12' marble conference table
- Four 3' x 5' oak study tables
- Eight low, leather, Knoll Pfister lounge chairs
- One six-seat low, leather, Knoll Pfister L-shaped sofa
- One reception desk with chair
- One single-person office with chair

Collection space
- Increased by 125 percent
- In two card-access spaces, 1,666 shelf-feet of 12" deep steel shelving, 44 shelves of 16" deep for flat storage of folios, 20 flat drawers for flat materials
- Two 10-drawer steel flat files for prints and broadsides
- LED lighting
- Separate Liebert air-conditioning, temperature and humidity controlled for preservation of materials

Exhibit space
- Museum-quality ½" laminated glass and steel cases with dimmable, positional LED lights, desiccant trays to control humidity, and high security locks with additional cams
- Five wall-hung cases at appropriate height for handicap access and space to maneuver through exhibit area; space shared with low, movable benches
- One free-standing glass and steel exhibit case, 72"x 36"x 11"

People space
- Little fixed furniture with one round table built around a structural column
- Configurable space for a wide array of purposes: lecture, workshop, quiet study, reception
- Total of sixty-eight seats
- Additional power through floor plugs and electrical towers that can be plugged into the floor plugs to add six additional electrical outlets and six USB power outlets
- Primarily wheeled, folding and nesting tables in a variety of shapes
- Reception-height wheeled, folding and nesting tables
- Benches in exhibit area

POST-PROJECT EVALUATION, REFLECTIONS, ADVICE, AND BEST PRACTICES

Since the renovation was completed only a year ago, this will be a preliminary assessment of the project and initial reflections. The advice and best practices, since they stem from the renovation experience, should be more complete and hopefully, useful to other projects.

It seems reasonable to start with reviewing the project goals as an assessment and reflection tool for the project results. Goals for the renovation that were definitely accomplished were:

- Creation of space to showcase the historical collections and encourage their use, while providing a secure collection space with optimal environmental control
- Creation of a flexible space that is open and available for quiet study, meetings, and special events
- Creation of an aesthetically pleasing space in which the structural design and furnishings exude an atmosphere of quality and speak to visitors and potential donors of the commitment and pride of Texas A&M in those collections
- Creation of a space that is open to student use
- Creation a space that supports and facilitates scholarship and a research service for the historical collections, including adequate, well-designed reading room

Selected comments from visitors and users of the space underscore our accomplishment of the above goals. Comments from attendees at the opening included the following: "This library is a window, a window overlooking a landscape of veterinary literature. What you have achieved is magnificent," and, "The exhibit space is fabulous." Comments from an individual who reserved the space: "This space was perfect for our workshop." There are still a couple project goals that remain to be accomplished. Purchase of gallery rails is underway so that we can meet the goal to "create a space that provides flexibility in the effective display of the works of art included in the historical collection." The most challenging goal still to be met fully is to "create a space that employs technology and modern design techniques to tie the historical collection to the present, to promote and emphasize the continuing relevancy of historical materials." We have partially met the goal through the modern design and sleek look of the space and its furnishings. We used the Texas A&M color palette (maroon and white) in the space to connect to the strong sense of institutional traditions and pride. We are still hoping to install the most advanced technology component—an interactive wall, with computer-driven content which will use technology to provide tours, educational sessions, and online exhibits and to explicate collection materials while they can remain in the collection vaults.

Lessons Learned, Renovation Advice, and Best Practices

In an effort to match the A&M color palette and achieve the most striking and rich finishings, we chose "custom" tabletops rather than the surfaces provided by the manufacturer. This wasn't the wisest decision and created challenges for proper surface installation. The custom surfaces are proving a challenge to match, now that we can see the need for more tables.

We also tried to emphasize the gray and maroon combination. The selected maroon leather turned out to lack the color intensity we were seeking. All gray leather would have been a better choice rather than the rose-colored "maroon" leather.

The custom backlit panel frames which were planned as an accent to a central column within the room simply could not be mounted on the column as planned.

Based on our experience with this renovation, we offer this advice and suggested best practices:

- Visit other libraries with special collections and museums to gather ideas and help develop your vision. Take pictures!
- Create goals for your project, prioritize them, and share them with your renovation team.
- Provide established recommendations for specialized environmental requirements and keep them handy during the project.
- Use your renovation progress meetings to make certain all on the project team (architects, contractors, and designers) are on the same page concerning project specifics. Don't assume they are communicating outside of the regular meetings.
- Take detailed notes during your renovation progress meetings; you will definitely refer to them. If key renovation members are absent, make sure

they are sent notes from the meeting. Not everyone will be able to attend all meetings.

- Get to know the project functional managers, visit the work area, and monitor progress or problems.
- Provide regular renovation progress updates for all library staff, preferably in a venue where they can ask questions. Whenever possible and appropriate, involve them in the project.
- Get the largest color and fabric swatches that you can before making choices. Consider even ordering a single sample item of furniture to evaluate.
- Ask questions early and never assume!
- When you see something that doesn't look right, say something, sooner than later.
- Plan on delays!

Successful renovation projects depend primarily on careful planning. The cultivation and encouragement of a well-coordinated project team, followed by countless hours from a library project manager who pays careful attention to detail and questions any deviations from the plan can ensure the greatest success in the implementation of the plan. It is a real boon if the library project manager has solid knowledge of the library facility and knows something about building and construction processes. Most important though, is the plan. The wisdom of Benjamin Franklin offers this advice, well-suited to renovation projects: "By failing to prepare, you are preparing to fail."

Undertaking the renovation of a special collections space is daunting. In our virtual information world there are those who will question the wisdom of such a venture. Michael Gorman effectively counters this notion with these words: "What is the alternative to the bleak vision of the virtual library advocates? I believe the answer lies in exactly the opposite direction—in expanding the role of the library as place, not in abolishing that public place."[11] In a nutshell, the best advice we can offer for those contemplating a special collections renovation is create a vision for transforming the space, develop goals to guide your plan, and follow the plan.

We did not include pictures of the finished spaces in this chapter, but images are available at http://hdl.handle.net/1969.1/166340.

NOTES

1. Dan Hazen, "Rethinking Research Library Collections: A Policy Framework for Straitened Times, and Beyond," *Library Resources & Technical Services* 54, no. 2 (2010): 13, https://dash.harvard.edu/handle/1/4111039.

2. Bernard F. Reilly Jr., "The Future of Cooperative Collections and Repositories," *Library Management* 34, no. 4/5 (2013): 342–51, doi: 10.1108/01435121311328681.

3. Maggie Gallup Koop, "Academic Libraries, Institutional Missions, and New Student Recruitment: A Case Study," *Reference Services Review* 41, no. 2 (2013): 192–200, doi: 10.1108/00907321311326192.

4. Jennifer M. Welch, Susan D. Hoffius, and E. Brooke Fox, "Archives, Accessibility and Advocacy: A Case Study of Strategies for Creating and Maintaining Relevance," *Journal of the Medical Library Association* 99, no. 1 (2011): 60, doi: 10.3163/1536-5050.99.1.010.

5. Texas A&M University Libraries, "How We Build Our World Class Collections," Texas A&M University Libraries, accessed January 19, 2018, https://library.tamu.edu/research/how_build.html.

6. Association of Research Libraries, "LibQUAL+®" Association of Research Libraries, accessed February 8, 2018, http://www.arl.org/focus-areas/statistics-assessment/libqual#.WnyzYU3rvIU.

7. Michele F. Pacifico, ed., *Archival and Special Collections Facilities: Guidelines for Archivists, Librarians, Architects and Engineers* (Chicago: American Library Association, 2009).

8. National Archives and Record Administration, "TIP 13: Using Technology to Safeguard Archival Holdings" (Specifications and Research Document, College Park, MD, 1997), https://www.archives.gov/files/preservation/technical/tip13.pdf.

9. Sarah S. Wagner, "Published Environmental Standards" (Standards Document, Washington, DC, 2011), http://siarchives.si.edu/sites/default/files/pdfs/SummaryStorageStandards_0.pdf.

10. Texas Historical Commission, "Basic Guidelines for the Preservation of Historical Artifacts," Guideline, Austin, TX, 2013, http://www.thc.texas.gov/public/upload/publications/Basic%20Guidelines%20for%20the%20Preservation%20of%20historic%20artifacts%202013.pdf.

11. Michael Gorman, *Our Enduring Values: Librarianship in the 21st Century* (Chicago: American Library Association, 2000), 46.

III

LIBRARY SPACES
WORKING WITH
WHAT THEY'VE GOT

How One Library Streamlined, Slimmed Down, and Became More Efficient after Losing 50 Percent of Their Space

JESSICA DECARO AND SHANNON BUTCHECK

INTRODUCTION

On the morning of January 26, 2015, the interim director of the Cleveland Health Sciences Library (CHSL) at Case Western Reserve University (CWRU or Case) answered an urgent summons to meet with the assistant dean of the School of Medicine. She learned that administration had had to make difficult decisions regarding the Health Center Library. At that meeting, the interim director discovered that due to the addition of the new physician assistant tract, which was starting in July, as well as looming accreditation requirements and space constraints related to both issues, the School of Medicine administration realized a need for more collaborative and study space. The one location on the south side of campus that had a large enough space to accommodate all of the needs of the school was the second floor of the library. It had been decided that the entire upper floor of the Health Center Library would be reallocated into a collaborative education/study space. The interim director was instructed to devise a plan to immediately remove all of the materials on the second floor and was initially given the timeline of the end of March (sixty days) to have this completed. Additionally, she learned that many of the logistics were still unknown and that the details would be determined as the project was underway.

Though the news was a surprise, the sense of urgency conveyed was well understood. It didn't matter why or that many questions would need to be addressed, the reality was that our new directive, our library's prime objective, was to move the approximately 100,000 books, bound journals, theses, indexes, and abstracts from the second floor of the library and incorporate these materials into the remaining library space as soon as humanly possible.

Our 2015 library consolidation project consisted of three distinct parts:

- the rush to empty the second floor
- creating order from chaos (making the library functional and efficient)
- tweaking the finished product

During this project, the staff of the Cleveland Health Sciences Library came together as a team, had great ideas, made many time consuming mistakes, and learned a great deal about project management and library spaces.

BACKGROUND

The Cleveland Health Sciences Library was established in 1965 and was initially housed in a building named the Allen Memorial Medical Library. By 1970, the Allen resources were outgrowing the library space at the decades-old building and it was agreed that a second branch of the library would be built and housed on the south side of campus where the Schools of Medicine, Dental Medicine, and Nursing are located. This new library, named the Health Center Library (HCL), was built within the School of Medicine and located in the Robbins Building. The HCL housed the new print monographs and serials created after 1970. It was decided that each branch would have an overall different scope of objectives and distinct collections.

Please note that the majority of measurements provided in this chapter are presented in Net Assignable Square Footage (NASF). NASF is defined as "the sum of all areas on all floors of a building assigned to, or available for assignment to, an occupant or specific use."[1]

The Allen is the headquarters of the Cleveland Medical Library Association, 19,376 NASF, serves the clinicians of university hospitals, contains a vast collection dedicated to the history of medicine, medical, and biological theses and dissertations, as well as a repository of journals primarily printed before 1969 and medical texts dating back to the fourteenth century.

The Health Center Library (HCL) serves the information needs of the faculty, students, and staff engaged in health sciences education and research at Case. At that point, the two floor, 33,812 NASF HCL housed the print journal collection from 1970 to the present, as well as monographs dating from 1920, health and basic sciences dissertations and theses, a robust collection of course reserves, a large reference collection, a wide collection of print original abstracts and indexes such as Index Medicus, MeSH, and Chemistry Abstracts, and other publications from the CWRU community.

LOGISTICS

Before the reduction in space, the HCL's first floor reading room contained print journals from 1980 to present, the substantial reference collection, and the reserve collection.

The second floor of the HCL held the theses and dissertations, the abstracts and indexes, the print journals from 1970 to 1980, and the circulating collection of monographs. This represented about 100,000 print resources.

Connecting the two floors is a large, concrete staircase, featured prominently in front of the circulation/reference desk. An elevator connects the two floors. These two features played a role in the reconfiguration logistics.

The HCL's employee-access-only technical services department is a private 14,000 NASF area, which takes up approximately a fourth of the entire first floor of the library. Around the perimeter of this space are six open-cubicle office spaces and two enclosed offices. This space, which was renovated in 2002–2003, had seen no major changes other than a gradual shrinking of staff. As a result, the technical services area had become inefficiently utilized as attrition and retirement had eliminated positions, and the prevalence of electronic journals decreased the need for replacement staff. It had, over time, become rather a wasteland of retired librarian detritus. The interior of this large room was a maze of shelving, discarded papers, desks, old bookshelves, unused or outdated library furniture, unused, redundant or donated books that the library had neither recycled or cataloged, items that had been weeded but not discarded, never cataloged monographs, files and card catalogs, and old office/ electronic equipment. There were duplicate monographs back from the 1800s, A/V equipment, old microfiche, redundant government publications, and a variety of materials no longer compatible with modern technology.

While technical services presented another challenge to overcome, to be fair, we were ripe for renovation and rejuvenation. It was unlikely to have ever changed unless a big project was imposed upon us. Losing the second floor created chaos and an enormous amount of work, but it ultimately made the Health Center Library more efficient and forced us to streamline services and resources while best utilizing our space.

THE RUSH

Immediately after the January 26 meeting with administration, the interim director of the CHSL shared the news with the staff. Initially, there were many questions raised that didn't have solid answers from administration. While that was sorted, internally, we broke the project into several parts:

Manpower:

- How would the materials on the second floor be moved?
- Would we use movers?
- Would we use library staff?
- Would we use student workers?
- Who would be paying for moving expenses?

Location:

- Where would the materials go?
- What would go to the Allen?
- What would go to the reading room on the first floor of the HCL?
- Where would those materials be shelved?
- Was there sufficient shelving space on the first floor to accommodate new materials?
- What materials would go into technical services?
- What provisions would we need to make best use of technical services?
- Would materials be housed off site?
- If off site, where would that be and which company?
- Who would pay for off-site storage since that would be a long-term cost?

Materials:

- What materials could be discarded?
- What materials could be deduplicated?

- What materials needed repair?
- What materials needed to be electronically replaced?
- What materials needed to be physically replaced?
- What materials had historical value, for CWRU, for posterity?
- What materials must be kept?
- What materials could be stored in technical services or another location?
- What materials needed to be accessible to our patrons?

Logistics and timeline:

- When did materials need to be out of the second floor space?
- When would we move materials earmarked to be moved elsewhere?
- In what order do would things need to be moved?
- What needed to happen before materials could be moved?
- What did we need to be able to move materials?

We made quite a few mistakes during this portion of the project. We started without a comprehensive project management plan in place and without a full understanding of the entirety of our space considerations. What we did have was a sense of urgency that would not allow for delays. To add to the confusion, a preexisting journal shifting project was underway and mostly completed at the HCL. This project entailed moving the print journals, dated 1970 to 1980, from the second floor down to the first floor with the intention that all journals would be housed on the first floor of the library and all books on the second floor. This would have freed up space on the second floor for more monographs had the project not been preempted. This preexisting project added another layer of disruption to the new project. Blending the remaining print journals into the whole of the collection added another twist to planning and logistics.

We determined quickly that we needed to accomplish a number of goals before items could be removed from the second floor. Because we didn't initially have answers about whether the resources would be stored on site or off site, long term or short term, who would pay for that service if we ended up with off-site storage, and space considerations such as access to the second floor, we prioritized that we should focus on the redistribution of library materials. This included what collections were most valuable, what space was premium, what could be removed from the collection, and what could not.

In the first four to six weeks, librarians were tasked with identifying select collections to bring down to the first floor reading room. Since we were unsure how much of the second floor materials would end up in storage, and how much money would be available to redistribute the resources, these collections were determined to be the most valuable to our patrons and had the highest usage. Collections identified were educational support dating from 2010 to 2015, the nursing theorists, the local collections (authored by persons from CWRU), notable historical authors, as well as indexes and abstracts that were not available online electronically.

We were directed to pull these collections from the shelves upstairs and made space for them by tightly consolidating the reference collection, which was originally spread out over a set of ninety-eight shelves. We minimized the space used by reference materials to a few dozen shelves, which freed up space for our newest materials. This task was valuable in that we made sure that those collections were identified and preserved carefully. The downside was that we didn't know where we were putting these collections and ended up repeatedly moving thousands of monographs. In the case of the most recent materials, we initially brought 2,500 monographs downstairs. We then extended the date range from 2010, to 2007 to the present because we found we had extra shelf space in the designated area. This meant that we had to comb through the entire collection, again, and spend more time shifting and integrating the 2007–2009 monographs into the "new titles" shelving. In total, more than 3,000 monographs were moved downstairs and moved again as we realized they were in the way where we had put them. And eventually, a third time and fourth time as we reintegrated them into the entire collection before moving them (again) to their "final" homes.

In the beginning weeks of the project, we also moved the history of medicine collection and the medical and biological sciences theses and dissertations to the Allen Library as those more closely reflected the collections in that building. Several collections of abstracts and indexes are only available in print and we wanted to keep them on campus. These were moved to the Allen as well. Abstracts and indexes of which we had multiple copies, such as Index Medicus, or items that are available online were withdrawn from the collection and recycled.

The electronic resources and bibliographic control librarian generated a shelf list for deduping the monograph collection. Three librarians, several support staff, and multitudes of student workers combed through the entire monograph collection identifying thousands of duplicates. These duplications sometimes represented multiple copies at the HCL, and sometimes were duplicated in other campus libraries. The deduping process required comparing the physical items and discarding the most-worn copies (in the case of multiples housed at HCL).

Initially, as we combed through the collection, we pulled duplicate copies off the shelves, but very quickly found that this caused a backlog of books, which then needed to be withdrawn from the catalog. Initially, we didn't have enough staff withdrawing titles from the catalog to keep up with the physical aspect of the weeding process. Learning to withdraw the books from the catalog required training and this took time. As the books piled up, we ran out of carts, which then stalled, moving titles down to the first floor. It was then that we started turning the identified duplicates on their sides, while still leaving them in place on the shelf. This made them visually identifiable without moving thousands of books multiple times.

Weeding, deduping, and discarding all of the duplicate or extraneous print materials was time consuming and physically laborious. The team, led by two of the librarian staff, combed through the collection, removed the identified books from upstairs, carted them, brought them downstairs, and then individually remove each item from the catalog. Finally, the discarded books were recycled.

In most cases when books are deaccessioned, a cataloger removes the item from the catalog, stamps the book as withdrawn, and physically discards the material. Because so many books were being removed, the cataloger could not possibly process and withdraw them all in the short time frame. Hiring a temporary contract cataloger to help was suggested at some point, but because of the time crunch, we felt they would take too long to train. The electronic resources and bibliographic control librarian, two additional librarians, and one staff member who had ILS authorizations due to previous cataloging experience were tasked to deaccession the items. The electronic resources and bibliographic control librarian created a document with specific directions for the team. Directions included confirming through the catalog that the item was a duplicate before actually deaccessioning and double-checking that the item wasn't signed from the author.

We had a number of challenges getting recycling bins and boxes to be able to discard or move the mass of materials. We could fill multiple recycling bins with books in a matter of hours, but then stalled out waiting for them to be emptied and returned the next day. One of the custodial staff was injured by an overfilled recycling bin, which was both unfortunate for her, and it taught us to be more careful about overfilling bins. Not filling the bins completely also slowed the process. We needed more bins emptied more frequently. We had to reuse the boxes we were provided with, so we'd fill them with items being sent to the Allen, label them carefully, send them in small batches moved by student workers, emptied them to appropriate locations there, then the boxes were folded and brought back to HCL.

In retrospect, jumping into the project without a carefully constructed plan in place caused us to work harder than necessary and we ended up repeatedly moving the monographs and journals. By initially pruning the collection of extraneous, duplicated items, we were left with a well-organized and more streamlined collection with zero lost content, which was the most important standard we held.

At about week five, the School of Medicine brought in a vendor who proposed off-site storage with great features and services, but ultimately they were deemed too expensive to sustain. Our library director was able to discern shelf space needs and we creatively planned as to how to best utilize the space that we had. The School of Medicine agreed to pay for movers to break down and relocate the emptied shelving downstairs, as well as to haul a truckload of books and other materials over to the Allen. It was after these decisions were made that we started clearing out technical services to make space available for storage and shelving.

Initially, all of the furniture in technical services was either broken down and recycled, moved into a campus repository for office furniture or if unusable, discarded. The old wooden card catalog was removed. A cabinet that held an ancient copy of a shelf list was discarded. Computers, printers, A/V equipment, and so forth found new homes or were discarded. We ended up saving a few existing sets of wooden and metal shelving. A floor plan for the entire first floor was developed for shelving that would be brought down from the second floor and added to both technical services and the reading room. In the reading room, we were able to identify underutilized space and planned to add 280 shelves. In technical services, we planned to add 765 shelves to the newly cleaned and open space. Once we determined how many shelves could be added to the first floor, we could better determine the course of action needed to bring the monograph and journals remaining on the second floor down to the first.

One challenge we had to work through was emptying the upstairs shelves enough to make available the shelving for moving; an entire bay of shelves had to be cleared before any shelving could be broken down, moved, and reassembled in its final position. The scope of coordinating moving approximately 100,000 monographs and journals while keeping them in order was interesting. On several occasions, the movers were due to arrive and we found ourselves rushing to consolidate a hundred shelves of monographs from one bay earmarked to be broken down to the next bay over. Eventually, we emptied enough shelving so that the empty shelves were then freed to be removed from the second floor and set up downstairs.

Two things happened at this point. That preexisting project integrating the 1970–1980 journals down to the first floor reading room was resumed by one staff member and a team of student workers, while another staff member and a separate team of student workers began bringing the monographs downstairs to the technical services area. We were increasingly under pressure to get the second floor emptied so that construction could begin upstairs; the deadline for completion of the construction upstairs was by the start of the school year on July 1. Our deadline to have all library materials removed from the second floor was eventually extended by the School of Medicine for the end of April. With approximately six weeks left until our deadline, we assessed that there was enough shelving open and free to bring the print collection downstairs to the empty shelving in technical services.

Per general library practice, removing public access to the bulk of the print monographs is a bad idea but we were bound by circumstance to do what needed to be done. We filled nearly every square inch of space in technical services with our entire collection of monographs. Even the offices of our employees were filled. At the very end of the relocation, we ran out of shelving space. The last cart of books brought down was left next to its shelved neighbors. There was no more room.

We officially finished bringing all library resources down from the second floor two weeks earlier than our established deadline. With the upstairs empty

FIGURE 8.1
Second floor shelving: Before.
Kathleen Blazar, Interim Director of the Cleveland Health Science Library

FIGURE 8.2
Second floor shelving: After.
Kathleen Blazar, Interim Director of the Cleveland Health Science Library

of the library's property, the movers were quickly scheduled to break down the remaining upstairs shelves, which were recycled. Finally, access to the second floor from within the library was blocked. The door at the top of the steps was locked and the elevator disabled. The Health Center library was one single floor of chaos.

CREATING ORDER FROM CHAOS

The Health Center Library staff had a meeting in early May 2015, soon after the second floor was officially closed. We did it: the rush was done! While we were relieved to finally be out of the second floor, we now had an equally draining assignment ahead of us: cleaning up the chaos of the first floor and finding permanent homes for our resources. While we had a good idea of where items were, another staff meeting was needed on how to move forward and return the library to a functional space, where resources were easily browsable and accessible.

The first thing on everyone's mind was how to put the library back together. Books and journals were shelved, but the urgent deadline to vacate the second floor had created temporary (and sometimes unexpected) homes for most items: reference shelved in employees' offices, books and theses shelved in the unbrowsable technical services office, and so forth. The first floor (technical services included) clearly needed to be reorganized, which created questions such as these:

- Where should the theses permanently go?
- Where should the reference collection permanently go?
- How do we decide what goes into technical services?
- What goes into the reading room?
- What should the floorplan be in technical services?
- What should the reading room floor plan look like?
- Would part of technical services be browsable and open to the public?
- What manpower is available?
- What are the financial considerations?
- Do we have the manpower/resources to create what we want (or is it easier/ efficient to leave some things as they are now and just catalog them appropriately)?
- Who would do what?

THE WHO AND WHERE

The first decision we made was who would do what. We could not ask a student worker to "sort it out" and organize the library back together. Hiring commercial movers was not a realistic option either, as decisions would need to be made as we were physically reorganizing and shifting. It would have been expensive and time consuming to work with professional movers while still making decisions and planning. In the end, we decided that two or three librarians, one library assistant, and as many student workers as we could afford from our existing annual budget would have to get their hands dirty and physically reorganize the library materials.

The student workers' help was incredibly important. While we were not provided extra money for additional student salaries, we were able to schedule student workers an additional twenty to forty hours a week with the current student budget. To reduce fatigue and injury (and possible boredom), we scheduled the students to work in pairs of two-hour increments, sometimes one group of students in the morning and another group in the afternoon. Student workers were a huge part of the success of this project; without their help, we would not have completed our vision.

Next, before anything was physically moved again, we needed to engage in strategic planning to minimize effort and stress. We had to decide where materials would be permanently housed. We divided this issue into small pieces, starting with the smaller collections first, such as the audiovisual (A/V) and local history resources. A/V resources were already moved into an unused office in technical services and were in the process of being withdrawn by the interim director. The library's historical materials were not affected by the move, as they remained in locked cabinets in the reading room and the local subject collections remained where they always have in the technical services office.

Deciding where to house the theses and dissertations, monographs, and journals took a bit more planning. At this point in the process, circulating books and many journals were temporarily shelved in technical services in chunks and sections. Although frustrating, everything was still findable, which resulted in one suggestion: leave the books that were already shelved in the technical services office where they were, change their location status in the catalog, and then staff from circulation and/or reference could retrieve the items. Another suggestion was to shelve only the newest books (2007–

present) in the reading room, since they were the most used and leave the remaining books published prior to 2008 in technical services. In both these scenarios, the books placed in technical services would not be browsable; however they would still be findable in the catalog. We quickly decided that this would create more problems, since everything wasn't in one spot, which was confusing to the patrons, student workers, and staff. It also created more work for the staff who had to go on a scavenger hunt to find something. It was decided that all circulating monographs would be housed in the reading room.

Additionally, browsablity was an important factor when determining where the theses and dissertations would be permanently housed. The Health Sciences Library has over 4,400 heavily used volumes of theses and dissertations. We hold two copies: one is noncirculating and the second copy is circulating. In the initial phase of this project, the medical and biological theses had been moved to the Allen Medical Library, leaving the dental and nursing theses in technical services. This meant that patrons would have to go to the circulation desk, ask to browse the theses, and the circulation employee would walk them back into technical services. We also didn't have the manpower to watch the patron after being shown to the theses section. This scenario was deemed unworkable, as there were several employees who were uncomfortable to find unsupervised patrons in the technical services office. We decided to move the theses out into the reading room with the all the monographs so that they were easily findable and browsable.

Like the theses and dissertations, we had temporarily shelved the reference collection in technical services and in a reference librarian's office. While occasionally utilized (unlike the monographs or theses), we felt it was best that reference remain in the reading room for easy access. By chance, we had created a little corner nook just right for this collection when we had moved shelving from the second floor to the first floor. This corner nook created enough space for the reference and oversized books and was out of the way from the more heavily used items but was still easily accessible to patrons.

Deciding where the journals should go was problematic. The entire journal collection simply would not fit in the remaining reading room space after the monographs, theses, and reference items were shelved. Some journals needed to be shelved in technical services. But we debated about which journals should be in the reading room and which should be in technical services. One suggestion was to shelve journals that we had only in print out in the reading room and journals we held in both print and online in the technical services office. That way if a patron was looking for a journal, we could direct them to the online version. Early in the discussion, it was agreed that this would be the most efficient and easy way to proceed with the journals.

However, this created an additional hurdle. Most of our journals have transitioned to the online version over the years, which meant we could not possibly fit all journals that were both print and online into technical services, we had to pick specific titles. It was decided that the journal titles with the largest run would be shelved in technical services.

THE HOW

Now that we decided on the who and the where, we had to decide how the transition would physically take place. Clear leadership was extremely important during this phase, because goals would change daily due to the multiple shifting projects. In order to avoid confusion and inconsistencies, we decided that one of the librarians should create clear daily plans. The daily plan would list which specific titles would be moved that particular day, where it would be moved to, and in what order it would be shelved. Book trucks would be numbered one to twelve, librarians would physically shelve the items in the correct order on the book trucks, and then sort the trucks into numerical order. Once the student workers came in, they would report to the librarian, who would explain the goals of the day and then start to shelve, beginning with truck number one and ending with truck number twelve.

Staff decided that we would start moving the smaller collections to the reading room first beginning with reference, then the theses and dissertations, then monographs, and then the journals. Reference was easy since all we did was find and shelve all the reference books onto a book truck, organize them by call number, and then have a student shelve them in the newly created reference section.

The health sciences theses and dissertations are cataloged alphabetically by author's last name, so transferring the theses from the technical services office to the reading room moved quickly and easily. The theses were already in correct order in the technical services area, so the student workers simply transferred the theses from the technical services office shelving to a book truck and then out into the reading room, allowing for a quarter shelf for future growth.

Next, we shelved the monographs. We still had to make some room for all the books, which required us to shift the journals "back" simultaneously. This part of the renovation was like a puzzle piece because not only were there multiple shifting projects taking place, but in the urgency of relocating, chunks of books were either out of order or had been grouped into a smaller collection and had to be reintegrated into the larger collection. Every day, a librarian would find the next books within the NLM classification sequence and shelve them on the book truck in the correct order. Just like the journals, we would fill up twelve book trucks at a time and the students would shelve the books into the reading room, leaving a quarter of a shelf empty for future books), and starting with book truck one. This process took a few months to sort out since we had to reshift books and the journals several times.

The last of the puzzle piece was the journals. The journals were complicated for several reasons. Due to multiple shifts, many of the journals were out of order, and we had to find and recombine them before shelving them in their permanent home. Unlike monographs, journals are shelved alphabetically, and we had difficulties when a journal title had a small run, a title change, or simply being too thin that they would go unnoticed in the chaos we had created. We didn't want to miss them now, only to have to reshift later to fit them in.

To make things easier, we created a shelf-list of journals A–Z from the ILS, printed, and bound it into a binder. Using this binder, librarians organized the journals in the correct order onto book trucks and numbered the trucks one through twelve, just like with the books. The student workers would then check in with the librarians, the librarians would tell them where to start shelving, and then the students would start shelving the book trucks. We left space for growth for the few journals we still receive in print.

We still had to decide which of the print plus online titles would be shelved in technical services. The easiest way to determine these specific journals was by figuring out which journals we had the most volumes of. To figure this out, a librarian simply walked through the journal stacks and noted which journal series had ten or more shelves. For example: *Biochemistry, Science, Blood, Genetics*, and so forth. Those notes were searched in the catalog to verify online access, and then were printed in a list and handed to a student worker to load onto a book truck. Once a truck was loaded, the students were directed where to shelve those journals in the technical services office. Roughly 22,000 journal volumes be would be transferred to the technical services area.

TWEAKING THE FINISHED PRODUCT

Inventory

Finally, in October 2015, everything was in place and we were done with shifting. The theses, books, reference, and journals were in their final home and it was time for the entire staff to take a break. After the holidays, we discovered that many of the books were enough out of order to warrant a complete shelf-check or what we called an "inventory." Using the ILS, a shelf list of the monographs was created and imported into an Excel worksheet with the following values: call number, author, title. Once this Excel sheet was sorted into alphabetical order using the call numbers, a fourth column was created titled Notes. Here, students could leave questions or notes about missing items. The entire inventory list was printed and put into three large binders. When students arrived for their shifts, they would check in and grab the binder, and go line by line making sure what was on the shelf matched what the shelf list said.

At the time, doing an inventory seemed like a pesky step to finish off what had already been a draining project. However, performing this inventory was incredibly helpful as it did four unexpected things other than showing what was out of order and in what order it should be shelved. It showed the following:

- What was missing.
- What was marked missing but was actually on the shelf.
- What items belonged to other campus libraries that were accidentally shelved at the HCL.
- Coding mistakes such as location, missing barcodes, call numbers, etc.

After the inventory was completed in April 2016, the binders were stored back in technical services in the cataloger's office. Remarkably, the binders are still used at times when looking for lost items.

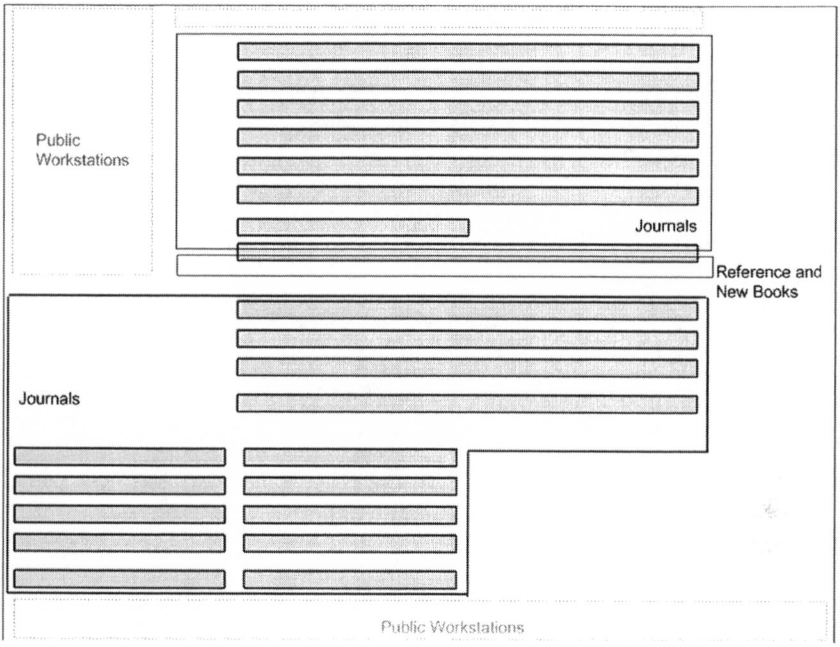

FIGURE 8.3
First floor reading room: Before.

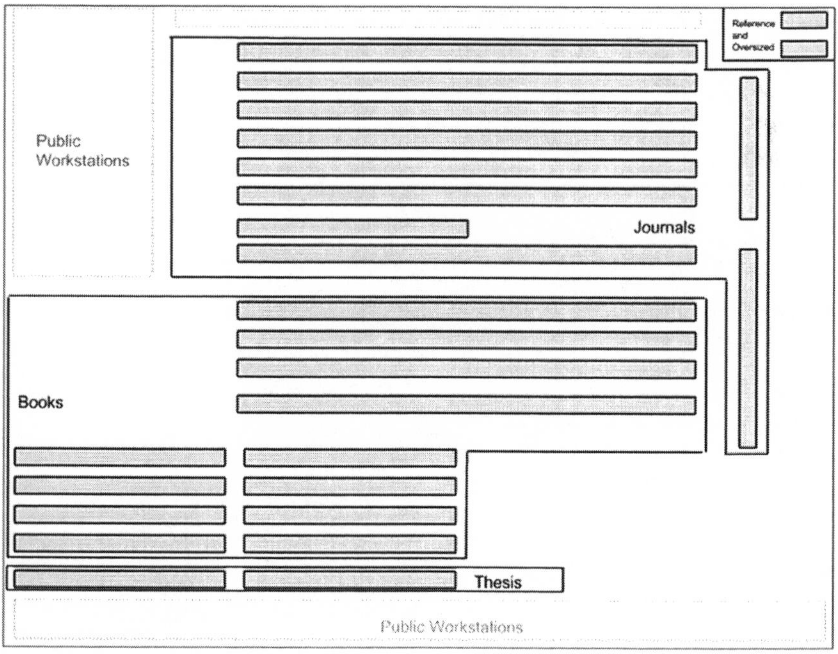

FIGURE 8.4
First floor reading room: After.

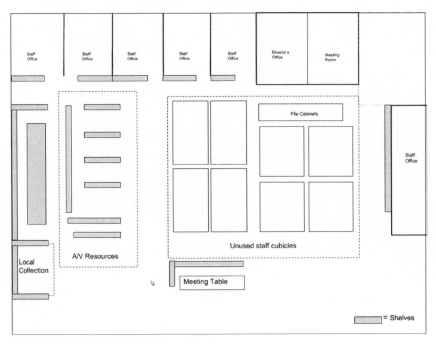

FIGURE 8.5
Technical Services: Before.

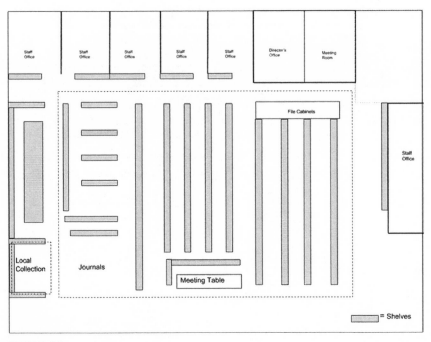

FIGURE 8.6
Technical Services: After.

THINGS WE DID RIGHT AND THEIR CONSEQUENCES/BENEFITS

After all was said and done, the library lost approximately 13,000 square feet of space, seven study rooms, one classroom, most A/V materials, and over 3,000 shelves. Although this project was a stressful and exhausting experience, losing half of our library made the library stronger and better in unexpected ways. Foremost, it forced us to streamline our collection in several ways. First, it required us to organize by deduplication. Previously, duplication normally occurred due to usage. With many books available online today, keeping duplicates is unnecessary and takes away precious shelf space for newer materials. By deduping, we were able to keep the content and stay committed to developing our print collection. Additionally, leaving a quarter of the shelves empty for future growth also reiterates our plan to grow and expand print resources to support both research and curriculum needs.

A second way we streamlined was through decluttering and purging what wasn't needed, which had held us back from our true potential. Many libraries have a backlog of things to catalog or unused items taking up space. Why we hold on to these things varies: maybe we feel it will be useful or used later? Or maybe those unused things aren't bothering anyone, and therefore are not a priority for weeding? In our case, we had a backlog shelf of items we would catalog someday and we had ignored old furniture and equipment that we would walk past to get to something else of importance. Attrition had added to the cavalier indifference since we were all busy, but this project superseded our everyday tasks, ultimately to our benefit. Decluttering also forced us to make better use of the space, which increased findability.

A third benefit to streamlining was that the experience helped us understand our own collection better. In the beginning, we knew the HCL could not hold all the books that would be redistributed from the second floor and that the Allen library would have to absorb some of the materials. After looking over the collection development plan of each location, there were books shelved at the HCL that made more sense at the Allen. Although there will inevitably be overlaps between the Allen library and HCL library, unifying Allen-specific books created a more robust and concentrated collection.

A fourth way we streamlined was through simplifying the floor plan in both the reading room and technical services. While the original floor plan made sense when it was created, separating collections by date and centuries does not work in today's academic environment. The new floor plan makes browsing and finding easier.

Lastly, the experience also forced some staff to step into leadership roles. The leaders of this project learned to work with the administration and the facilities department by operating within the bureaucratic nature of a large institution. They also gained experience in project management, space planning, and collaboration. Additionally, we learned through trial and error how to lead student workers.

TAKEAWAYS

- Take the time to plan, thus saving labor, time, and money.
- Prioritize your collection needs to determine your mission.
- Leave room to grow in the future.
- Engage in good communication.
- Empower staff to contribute to decision making.

NOTE

1. National Center for Education Statistics, "3.2.2 Net Assignable Area (Net Assignable Square Feet-NASF)," National Center for Education Statistics, accessed March 23, 2018, https://nces.ed.gov/pubs2006/ficm/content.asp?ContentType=Section&chapter=3&section=2&subsection=2.

Surviving Tight Budgets and Proving Value Added in Library Spaces

MARGARET HOOGLAND

INTRODUCTION

In the late 1990s and early 2000s, many health sciences libraries were built or renovated at universities and hospitals throughout the United States. In fact, in 1999, new construction projects occurred in half of the submitted projects outlined in "Health Sciences Library Building Projects, 1998 Survey."[1] By 2011, many library directors focused only on working with existing spaces. The high cost of building new libraries is often the determining factor for making renovations instead.[2]

Managing the space of the library and providing adequate staffing are a challenge, particularly when the budget is tight. Librarians are not the only people struggling to adapt. In fact, community members are now rethinking what the library provides. For instance, if something is available via Google, does it make sense for someone to consult with the library? The answer is yes, but it would behoove our profession to strive toward making the digital library approachable, comfortable, and easily accessible for all patrons.[3] Distance students are adjusting to not only a new way of learning but also a different way of accessing information. Not all libraries in academic environments are able to adequately support distance programs. Online learning is a perfect way for people to take classes, who work full-time, or live abroad, but it introduces new challenges for the libraries and librarians supporting this community. Faculty and students, who are instructing or enrolled in online schools and programs, frequently struggle with technology and this increases the workload of librarians supporting these programs. It is inherently challenging to balance all these demands, but it also provides a great opportunity to learn and to develop new skills.[4]

The changes in how our patrons are completing course work and research has trickled down to impact library sciences at the professional education level. In 1988, Toni Carbo, who served as the dean for the University of Pittsburgh Library and Information Science School (LIS), met with the dean of the Syracuse University LIS and the Dean of Drexel University LIS. People called the group the "Gang of Three," and by 2003, it expanded to ten schools and included faculty specializing in LIS, informatics, and computer science. By 2005, the group had expanded to include more than twenty-seven participants and changed its name to the iCaucus. Group members met annually to discuss relevant issues, improve content of the LIS and iSchools, exchange research ideas, and debate the benefits and pitfalls of changing programs. It also provided time to engage in professional development activities and to consider the requirements for faculty members.[5]

Students enrolled in LIS programs continue to take a standard set of core courses. Depending on the school, it could be anywhere from three to five courses. In 2018, students would now be likely to enroll in an information organization course (see table 9.2) and learn about the Dublin Core methods for cataloging digital books instead of the more traditional cataloging methods (i.e., the Library of Congress and The National Library of Medicine) and accepted standards for cataloging (i.e., AACR2). Although the content of such courses focuses more on linguistics, coding, and relational databases, the role of the cataloger continues to be important for making content easily accessible and searchable via online, not paper, library catalogs.[6]

These evolving roles have impacted who does what in the modern library. Paraprofessionals, instead of professionals with a master's or doctorate degree, now staff the desk and answer questions pertaining to updating library account information, renewing books, picking up books obtained from other libraries via interlibrary loan, and checking out headphones, computers, or books available on reserve. In the contemporary library systems, librarians manage information library systems and work with emerging technology librarians to connect applications (apps) to the discovery tools and virtual reference services (i.e., instant messaging) to all databases and online journal systems, such as EBSCO Full Text Finder, maintained by the library.[7]

This chapter addresses how libraries and librarians continue to provide excellent support on increasingly tight budgets and even contribute value added to their communities. First, we describe trends and technology in library spaces as indicators and predictors of where libraries and their spaces are headed. Second, we look at retooling and rethinking librarians' roles and the library space in response to these trends and technology. Last, we look at professional development options, library programs, and new hires and examine whether future and practicing librarians are being prepared for the transitional library setting.

TRENDS AND TECHNOLOGY IN LIBRARY SPACES

Libraries, required to provide data on how patrons use online journals and databases, are focusing on assessment of services and Strengths, Weaknesses, Opportunities, and Threats (SWOT) analyses to create and implement strategic plans. Once created, however, many libraries continue to make decisions without considering the patron's perspective, collected data on journal and database use, or even the strategic plan itself.[8, 9] Data-driven decision making, particularly in libraries supporting researchers, is similar to evidenced-based decision making by health care providers. It is something every library should use to guide their planning. Faculty and administrators, when presented with statistics and examples of research resulting from using databases, are usually more open to supporting renewals and new initiatives.[10] This section focuses on current trends, supported by published literature, on how libraries are working in virtual spaces, managing and reorganizing the physical spaces of libraries, developing programs to support data management, and adjusting to primarily digital rather than print collections.

The Virtual Space

Emails and submitting questions via instant messaging systems are the primary ways patrons communicate with libraries today.[11] Librarians, working with students and faculty in remote or off campus locations, are using web conferencing systems, such as Zoom or Free Conference Call, or collaborative document software such as Google Docs or One Drive to support patrons with searching databases or to work on collaborative projects. Faculty use both tools to enhance lecture quality and to facilitate creating and sub-mitting group assignments.[12] Other librarians, supporting primarily hybrid (online and face-to-face programs) are doing so directly within the Learning Management Systems (LMS). If libraries do not have staff to manage such services, they could work with instructors to include a link within the LMS to the library website contact page or course specific pages maintained by librarians on Google Sites or LibGuides.[13,14] It should be considered that patrons, not just students enrolled in hybrid or online classes, often first go to Google, Google Scholar, or point of care products not to the library website or librarians for answers to their questions. Libraries are using products, such as Discovery Tools, to meet the challenges presented by these behaviors. Within the virtual space, the library and library website are frequently the least appealing option. To change this perception, libraries need to put the equal or greater effort into making the virtual environment accommodating and welcoming.[15]

The Physical Library Space

Print books and journals are now an uncommon site in the library. If public perception of this transition is not handled well, people start to question, "Why do we need a library?" Within the academic environment, non-library administrators could use this as an opportunity to reorganize the space into a classroom or create offices for other departments.[16] Forward-thinking library administrators work with planning committees and community members to retool the existing library space to include collaborative study areas, three dimensional printers, public access computers, and dedicated research space.[17, 18] They create meaningful spaces for their patrons. It is essential, whenever implementing changes, to get input from the community and to then market the new changes effectively so that patrons will talk about the changes favorably to each other and the community at large.[19, 20] Businesses like libraries grapple with the best way to capture the attention of outsiders. Soliciting and incorporating feedback while creating a comfortable multi-faceted space will lead to happy patrons, who feel ownership in the decision making process. Increased ownership frequently leads to increased use of the library.[21]

Collection Development and Collection Management

Today's patrons primarily use tablets, smartphones, and personal computers to access and navigate library resources. Liaison Librarians work diligently to suggest relevant journals, electronic books, or streaming videos that faculty, staff, and students will use for teaching classes or conducting research. Not all libraries, however, have the funding for librarians to put toward purchasing and renewals of such resources. Instead, a single person manages these tasks but takes into consideration outside recommendations.[22] Patron or demand driven acquisitions, for electronic books available from providers such as Ebrary or Rittenhouse, are popular among academic and public libraries. Connecting e-books to the discovery layer increases the use of such products and assists in justifying their costs. E-book platforms, which are very popular in health science libraries, are challenging collection development librarians to partner with departments and colleges due to constantly increasing prices.[23] Once the product is available, liaisons and scholarly communication librarians work closely to promote the resource, connect it to the library's catalog and databases, and to educate patrons on topics such as searching and copyright compliance.

Institutional Repositories

Digital publishing has opened the doors for faculty, staff, and students to permanently store their posters, papers, music, videos, and other file types within their campus-based institutional repository (IR).[24] An IR is an excellent opportunity for libraries to collaborate with their communities and to shape the evolution of scholarly communications.[25] Libraries are usually responsible for creating and maintaining such repositories and work with scholarly communications librarians and potentially the legal department to create guidelines and policies for the copyright of items contained within the IR. Liaisons are usually responsible for promoting the IR and educating interested faculty members on how to properly create records for IR items.[26]

Data Management

Data management is a new frontier for libraries. The mandate to create data repositories, if the researcher obtains federal funding, has created new opportunities for libraries. ORCID ID, Researcher ID, and other records are all part of the new initiative for keeping updated records for researchers and the publications they produce. Additionally, these systems are useful for encouraging collaboration among faculty members. The end goal of data management involves two parts. First, the researcher must decide how to collect and store their data. Second, they have to determine who needs access to the data and the best way to make it retrievable before, during, and after the project concludes.[27]

If time and staffing allow for it, data management support services could be developed to work with the research and grants offices on providing training for citation management tools, such as EndNote or RefWorks, and collaborative data collection and organization tools including RedCap or NVivo.[28] The library themselves may play a role in storing the data. Most librarians, unless they serve in an embedded role in research focused departments or as informationists in well-funded departments, lack the necessary training and skills to play active roles in this area. Librarians might choose to take additional coursework and change career directions to work more with data and less within traditional library areas (i.e., collection development and reference). Such an initiative requires commitment on the part of the library and institution as a whole to help their community meet federal requirements. This may mean letting go of underused services or practices to focus on this trending need.

RETOOLING AND RETHINKING THE LIBRARY SPACE AND LIBRARIAN'S ROLES

Library administrators are cognizant of the changes new trends and technologies present to space allocation, position titles, and systems within libraries. Many have responded by creating new roles, such as the embedded librarian, or reorganizing the organizational structure by areas, such as education, outreach, access services, and so forth. Some libraries are renovating existing spaces to include more areas for collaborative study. Others are embracing technology by creating library apps and purchasing 3D printers. Whenever possible, library administrators should provide professional development opportunities to assist employees in adjusting to these changes. By changing the existing organizational structure, libraries are positioned for new and exciting opportunities. Just as in commercial spaces, libraries must respond to demand with supply. Librarians and libraries need to prove their worth and justify established services. We have many established and well-honed services. A great deal of patrons are satisfied with existing services but at the same time question practices that are outdated. Many libraries now have a bigger role in their institution's strategic plan and are implementing the concept of value added to prove they are utilizing up-to-date data-driven decision making that shows a return on investment (ROI). Within the context of the library setting, value added refers to additional features that provide something extra to their institution, increasing their value to their community.[29] Additionally, being a part of the planning process gives library administrators opportunities to collaborate and network inside the university, community, or corporation, which lead to demonstrating ROI.

Library as Place and Library Spaces

Libraries are taking different approaches to solving space and renovation issues. This could mean creating collaborative study areas, moving computers to a different floor, or even redoing processes for collecting and maintaining statistics about how patrons are using journals and books. With primarily electronic collections, conducting usability studies in addition to analyzing usage statistics is worth considering. The usability study provides examples of patron behavior and the statistics show the numbers of people accessing and using a product or library space. Libraries will benefit from using more than one system for interpreting patron behavior and use of library resources.

Changes in the allocation of space and shifting collections from print to electronic resources are a communications test for library administrators and employees. If the communication between administration and department heads is clear, and adequate training provided, the transition is relatively easy to handle.[30] It is important for library directors or representatives to network and work directly with the space planners and departments to keep the library intact but redesigned, to best serve community members.[31] It is also crucial to inform the outside community about what is happening. Changes to library spaces are best communicated to communities by indicating the change and the opportunities created through implementation. A rapid removal of print collections could lead to inquiries about converting open spaces to offices rather than providing additional areas for collaborative study if poorly communicated. Library communications are best to remain ahead of such curves.

An important aspect of redesigning spaces is to incorporate input from the people who use the library most. Satisfied and excited patrons are the best and most cost-effective promoters for libraries.[32] If grants or funding are available to the institution for redesigning spaces, perhaps the library can capitalize on the opportunity to be involved with meetings from the beginning of the project. This makes marketing the future changes easier for colleagues, patrons, and community members.[33] At the University of California in San Francisco, nonlibrary community members agreed that a redesign of the library should only occur if it would maximize or improve the use of the space and library resources. The external planning committee included the library from the beginning in creating the strategic plan and making decisions about the planned redesign. Not every situation will go perfectly, but this is a great example of partnership and buy-in working out in the best possible way for an entire community.[34] Some libraries, forced by extenuating circumstances, make quick changes to library spaces without this luxury. In such instances all relevant library usage statistics available should be reviewed. This may provide minimal data to inform decision making but it may be all that is available on a tight timeline.[35]

Study results can serve as the impetus for restructuring and relabeling services to improve the patron experience and to increase the use of the library resources.[36] Time and money are required to restructure websites. Recognizing that changes take time, some libraries are creating timelines and meetings specific to completion of tasks. It also takes time to implement, accept, and adapt to the new design and decision-making process.[37] A usability study, as previously discussed in chapter 5, is a fantastic way to observe how patrons use the library. Websites and mobile devices occupy so much of people's time that it is worth considering redesigning a website or conducting a usability study to support the new way patrons use the library. In the following section, I discuss how specific librarian roles are developing to address some of these trends and technology in library spaces, and in some cases the rebounding impact on the library space.

Trending Librarian Roles

One response to trends and technology is to reorganize the library staff structure. For many years, the role of librarians coincided neatly with job titles and position descriptions. The circulation librarian was once responsible for the area or department overseeing the circulation of media (i.e., books, journals, audiobooks). A number of libraries have discontinued this position in response to the proliferation of electronic resources and have consolidated new and existing responsibilities into new roles such as the public services librarian. Depending on the staffing and funding of the library, this position may oversee paraprofessional staff responsible for troubleshooting issues with machines (i.e., printer, photocopier, scanner) available for public use for free or with minimal cost, reporting maintenance issues, or answering questions about accessing electronic resources. In the world of immediate access, these librarians handle impatient patrons and are responsible for answering quick questions from patrons via chat, email, and on the phone. They also coordinate with colleagues to handle questions that require a more in-depth response by scheduling a consult or directing patrons to contact the library liaison. Library front desks have seen many modifications overtime in staff, size, and service. Indeed, the new roles of librarianship involve librarians working outside the traditional physical space of a library.

Liaison Librarians, Embedded Librarians, and Informationists

A significant response to trends and technology in library spaces has been the evolution of the liaison librarian position. These librarians connect faculty, staff, and students to the library by teaching people how to search and navigate databases outside of the library space, usually in their own classroom or by scheduling one-on-one consultations. Faculty email questions to a liaison and expect tailored responses quickly. Some liaison librarians work directly within a department instead of having an office in the library, a dynamic impacting the library space. Additional roles, including the embedded librarian or informationist, have evolved from the liaison librarian position. The embedded librarian usually works in a department instead of the library. This position could include more research specific duties, such as creating and maintaining databases. It is not unusual for people in these positions to receive professional development funding and potentially a salary from the department instead of the library.[38] The informationist, by contrast, serves in a hospital or specialized department, depending on the size of the institution, and frequently possess degrees beyond that of the typical LIS. These positions may include some library duties that define them from embedded librarian positions. They take professional development classes for both librarianship and the group they support, go on rounds with clinicians, and attend research symposiums.[39] More recently, liaisons, called clinical medical librarians due to supporting primarily clinical departments, are challenging the informationist role. The duties of informationists, unlike liaisons and embedded librarians, vary greatly by the size and the needs of the library.[40, 41]

Liaisons, embedded librarians, and informationists frequently receive recommendations from faculty and students about books, journals, and databases.[42, 43, 44] Although tight budgets change the purchasing process for books and journals, encouraging the electronic resources librarian or discovery services librarian to discuss potential purchases with colleagues, who work daily with community members, is essential.[45] Whenever possible, it is best to communicate clearly the available budget for electronic purchases to faculty, staff, and students. It is always a good idea to make lists of recommended texts, which librarians can promise to consider as funds allow. If a department or college feels that getting the e-book platform or journal is essential, they are sometimes open to collaborating with the library to assist in paying for the product.[46]

Curricular changes are perfect opportunities for a library or librarian to reconsider the configuration of physical and virtual spaces and additional technology. To accomplish this, some libraries have the liaison librarians speak directly with programs to adjust what products a library makes available to assist the students in connecting more efficiently with library resources.[47] Liaisons may also use such opportunities to adjust the setup and the content of their lectures to make it more applicable for students.[48, 49] Some liaisons seize the opportunity to adapt the preclinical curriculum so that it includes content, which is emphasized during the second year and subsequent years of the medical school curriculum.[50] The changes in the standards for residents and fellow's professional activity, determined by the Accreditation Council for Graduate Medical Education, is leading to a more research-focused approach in medical school curricula.[51] Great opportunities exist for librarians to become more actively involved with implementation of new curricula.

In addition to new curricula, many academic institutions offer online-only, hybrid, and traditional classes. This provides both challenges and opportunities for liaison supporting these programs. To facilitate the creation of hybrid and online only classes, universities hire instructional designers (IDs) or curriculum instructional designers (CIDs). Individuals holding degrees in online environments such as an instructional design have experience creating and launching online courses in LMS. IDs work with faculty and staff on creating online courses for students. Enterprising liaison librarians, who lack experience or training with instructional design or course management systems, could seize the opportunity to meet with the IDs or CIDs to understand what role they play in the online education system. In most situations, IDs and CIDs are interested in collaborating with liaisons and could serve as a way for liaisons to integrate library resources more seamlessly into courses. CIDs and IDs, who are not usually as familiar with copyright, citations, or citation management systems, may direct faculty and students with questions on these topics to the liaisons. Sometimes CIDs and IDs may know about open access resources, which liaisons can promote to colleagues and consider making accessible to the greater community by connecting them to the listing of online journals, discovery system, and online library catalog. After establishing how the liaisons, IDs, and CIDs can support each other, arranging to meet on a semiregular basis to discuss issues and new developments could be beneficial for everyone.

Individual programs or schools may choose to incorporate the embedded or liaison librarian role for online programs. In this role, the librarians could monitor a chat box within an online course, located in an LMS, and use this as a way to provide reference support for online only or hybrid students. It is wise for a library to think carefully before implementing such services, particularly if staffing is an issue. Once a service exists and patrons are using it, the option to remove or adjust services is difficult without incurring the wrath of unhappy patrons.[52] Smaller libraries or solo librarians could consider creating videos and PDFs to demonstrate searching techniques and then upload these into the LMS or LibGuide they manage for a course or program. Another way to reach the online faculty, staff, and students is to offer virtual office hours using a web conferencing system such as Zoom, WebEx, or Free Conference Call.[53, 54] Additionally, it is great to ask patrons for suggestions on what the library can do to support them more effectively. It does not matter if your patron is in the physical or virtual library. Our jobs are first and foremost to ask what would be most useful for our patrons and then create programs, redesign services, and allocate funds to meet those needs.

Informationists, embedded librarians, hospital librarians, and clinical medical librarians are the bridge positions in health sciences librarianship. Each position contains some of the old (liaison duties, collection development) with a bit of the new (connecting with new departments, starting new programs, etc.). The threat of eliminating the library or moving the library's location, which happens more frequently than not in hospitals or association libraries, is a motivating factor for librarians to engage with new departments and to promote new programs or services.[55] Medical librarians play similar roles to hospital librarians but in an academic setting. Some, although not all clinical medical librarians, focus on supporting residents, fellows, clinicians, and students in the clinical portion of the health professional programs.[56] Other librarians, with the same title, focus on supporting both preclinical students and clinical students. Regardless of how much a position requires collaboration with other departments and entities, a good working relationship with area hospitals and hospital librarians is critical for librarian and student success.[57, 58, 59]

Liaisons, and their related counterparts, can also coordinate with the appropriate people on campus to establish patron friendly processes for entering data into existing databases. Some libraries are pursuing a partnership or training role to facilitate use of programs such as Red Cap or Qualtrics, which researchers can use to create surveys and store collected data. Determining what role the library should play is critical to discuss before launching events such as Data Days or scheduling regular training on these products.[60] A smaller and more manageable contribution to data management would be creating a list of faculty publications and making it searchable for the library and greater community. Departments, who manage funding for research and educational purposes, appreciate when libraries create and regularly update faculty publications lists. Collaborating with departments on such initiatives could lead to more participation opportunities for librarians on research and grant teams.

Committee participation by liaisons opens doors for libraries to connect to new community members and to promote services and resources the library provides. For instance, if serving on an institutional review board (IRB), librarians could be responsible for ensuring all members of the committee are familiar with citation management software. If serving on the facilities committee, librarians might have the chance to discuss ways to update existing spaces at no or minimal cost to the library. By participating on the curriculum committee, librarians could get recommendations for improving the library's collection and also form partnerships, which could lead to purchasing additional resources through a cost sharing agreement. Lastly, promotion and tenure is stressful for everyone, and librarians can assist faculty members in recognizing quality journals for potential publication, managing citations, and conducting literature searches to support the faculty research projects.

The presence of a librarian on a committee could lead to formation of new partnerships and eventually the development of new programs.[61]

Scholarly Communications Librarian

The emerging scholarly communications librarian role highlights the fact that librarians make pivotal grant and research team members because they excel at quickly locating the appropriate articles and related information for projects. By doing this, other team members focus on conducting research, drafting grant proposals, and revising protocols.[62, 63, 64] Copyright, with respect to managing and obtaining interlibrary loans, intellectual property, and obtaining permissions for use of images, citations, and figures are three areas that fall under the purview of the scholarly communications librarian.[65] Additionally, this position often works to develop policies for use, protection, and promotion of the IR. A librarian is a key player during library events such as Open Access Week and when instructing patrons on the importance of properly citing articles, books, videos, and so forth for writing papers, presenting at conferences, or publishing articles. Liaison librarians will be the first ones to answer uncomplicated questions, but the scholarly communications librarian will draft the policy and procedures for the library. They also will answer any questions or handle complex research patrons, whose issues require more expertise than a liaison can provide.[66] Scholarly communications librarians may also play a more personal role in connecting faculty members with common research interests. They, along with their liaison and related counterparts, are crucial for encouraging and explaining why faculty members and students should contribute to their institution's IR.

Libraries and universities with adequate facilities and staffing are able to host conferences on research reproducibility. Scholarly communications librarians could play a lead role in such events. Although important, study design and research do not always receive adequate attention in health professional programs. The focus instead might be communication with patients. The University of Utah is fortunate to have funding and space to host reproducibility conferences, which are available to the entire campus and the Salt Lake City community.[67] Such events, usually not funded entirely by the library, are excellent opportunities to form partnerships within the university and to improve the knowledge of faculty, staff, and students.

Assessment Librarian

Assessment of resources, library spaces, instruction, technology, and strengths and weaknesses are part of librarianship.[68,69] Some academic libraries now employ assessment librarians whose primary duty is to address assessment within the library. To support such efforts, the American College of Research Libraries (ACRL) has formed an assessment taskforce, which published the eleven areas most important to providing good assessment of programs, spaces, collections, and services.[70] When considering ways to conduct assessment, it is important for libraries to develop a scalable approach. By conducting usability studies, libraries can determine if the library website is adequately supporting patrons. Surveying students, faculty, and staff is also useful if a library is interested in getting the community perspective on the allocation of library space. It is also a way to get an outsiders opinion on how conducive the environment is for learning. Results of surveys and usability studies could be used by the library to make changes, improve the patron experience, and validate the value added of existing and prospective library services provided .[71, 72, 73]

The results of library assessments can also help influence library promotion initiatives. Librarians usually get opportunities to discuss library services and resources with new faculty, graduate students, residents, and fellows who arrive during the late summer or early fall each year. Identifying their needs related to the library space, course work, and so forth, through assessment surveys could help determine what services to promote to them and when. These initial opportunities often occur in small or large group orientations held in classrooms or the library. Throughout the academic year, however, the library should evaluate the best ways to promote library services. Liaison librarians provide consultations and small group meetings in addition to orientation sessions. Some argue that these are not effective because they occur sporadically rather than routinely. Others recognize that these meetings occur at a time when the faculty member or student recognizes a need to get assistance from a librarian. Such meetings have great potential for students and faculty returning to the library at a later point with additional questions and going on to promote the service they received to their peers and colleagues.

The perception and image of the library could change, depending on how librarians handle marketing of events and resources.[74] Libraries should consider collaborating with their institutions public relations or communications departments to seek promotion advice and streamline library promotion with institutional facets such as the institutions visual identity. Assessment librarians are a great resource for proving value added in the library, but it is a luxury not all institutions can afford. In such cases, designating a committee to handle assessment or having each department conduct routine assessment of services are feasible alternatives. An alternative would be to designate assessment to those leading the different areas of the library and collaboration amongst these leads as the data demands.

Health and Wellness Librarians

Health and wellness, which many interpret as going to rehabilitation centers, participating in weight management programs, or taking smoking cessation classes, are two topics many academic and health science libraries rarely discuss. Public libraries, by contrast, have many books on these topics, which health professional students will sometimes request from their health sciences library. Health sciences libraries may create a bulletin board talking about nutrition in the spring and health literacy in the fall, but rarely is time or money put toward these initiatives. In the United States' Affordable Care Act legislation, employers received money specifically to assist in health and wellness initiatives.[75] This, however, did not encourage libraries or many businesses to take action.

Community wellness provides libraries with an opportunity to collaborate with external and internal partners, create programs to lead new community members into the library, and change the perception about the services a library provides. In Texas, health science librarians formed a committee and created a fitness center in the workplace. This did not cost the library any money, and administrators thanked the library for offering this service.[76] Engineering librarians decided to offer LEGOS in a public space for students. By putting LEGOS in a common area, the noise did not disrupt the quiet study areas and it provided a way for students to take a break from preparing for exams.[77] Recognizing the popularity of board games, other libraries set up areas so that students could play games and take a break from studying and devices at the same time.[78] Lastly, recognizing how much time everyone, including librarians, spend on screens, another librarian introduced a program discussing the benefits of digital wellness.[79]

The burnout rate of students, physicians, and employees is peaking. Some businesses and institutions have decided to introduce fitness challenges and games as a way to improve the work environment and decrease stress. High-stress environments have high employee turnover rates.[80] Although wellness is a hot topic, and many employers offer programs, participation among employees, unless they enjoy exercise and fitness, is minimal.[81] While a health and wellness librarian may not be feasible in all health sciences libraries, these types of programs could be managed by the public services librarian who is designated to serve the institution's community at large.

Other Trending Titles

Emerging technology librarians, electronic resources librarians, online librarians, distance support librarians, or the first-year-experience librarians are the new frontier of librarian titles.[82] Changing user needs are paving the way for new titles, opportunities, and challenges for libraries. Emerging technology librarians, for instance, are responsible for trying out the latest technology and determining the appropriate online or physical tool to purchase for library personnel and the community. Frequently, the emerging technology and electronic resources librarian will work together from the outset on implementation of such resources. Internal and external collaboration are huge components of librarianship and limited budgets are emphasizing not minimizing these partnerships.[83] As mentioned in chapter 6, the Marston Science Library is rising to the challenge by including app development labs in the library to support institutional and student development of apps. Students, particularly in health professional programs, are using smartphones to answer questions from clinicians or to prepare for exams.[84, 85, 86, 87] Health Professionals are using apps and tablets to read the latest research articles on drug treatment protocols.[88, 89, 90] Some libraries develop apps so that patrons can easily access information at work.[91, 92] If a library does not have the money to develop and launch an app, redesigning the website to included responsive web design, which leads to improved accessibility of resources from tablets and smartphones, is an alternative way to tackle the same issue.

Online or distance support librarians work closely with students, faculty, and staff members, who may never venture into the physical library.[93] For this community, the physical design and layout of the library are not significant, but the importance of the website and the arrangement of content within the LMS are crucial.[94] Students, primarily, but also faculty and staff in online-only or hybrid learning environments often struggle to identify and to connect with the library. Springshare's LibGuides, which is a web-based software program that allows for quick editing and uploading of content with minimal training, is a great way to select and to promote materials specifically for online communities. It is important for librarians to reach and to support virtual communities and, whenever possible, to recreate the feeling of a physical library.[95, 96, 97]

PROFESSIONAL DEVELOPMENT OPPORTUNITIES, LIBRARY PROGRAMS, AND NEW HIRES

Professional Development

Education, librarianship, and research have different focuses but they share the common ingredient of lifelong learning. This is essential for librarians who find themselves taking on the aforementioned technologies, trends, and evolving roles. Depending on the fiscal situation, some professional development funds may be available on an annual basis. Many libraries only offer these funds for faculty or professionals. Staff are encouraged to also keep up with trends, however, they may need to be resourceful and seek out free educational sessions and opportunities to engage with colleagues, such as contributing to chats with others in the profession via Twitter and related social media.[98] Professional associations sometimes designate a hashtag (i.e., #medlibs) for Twitter discussions and host chats at specific times. The beauty of Twitter is that people can participate in discussions using most any device and continue the conversation outside of the designated time slots.

Presenting posters, giving presentations, or taking continuing education courses at conferences are three common ways to spend professional development funds. Continuing education courses allow participants to learn a new skill or refine an existing skill. Seeking out education in the above mentioned areas of technology, trends and emerging librarian roles is advised to keep pace with the current library climate. Table 9.1 includes opportunities for professional and paraprofessional development.

Library Programs and New Hires

Fiscal circumstances present challenges to employees and employers. Employers struggle to be optimistic but candid about the future, which makes

Table 9.1. Opportunities for professional and paraprofessional development

Organization	Opportunity	Website
Academy of Health Information Professionals (AHIP)	Work with a mentor and continue your professional development by taking classes, presenting at conferences, publishing, or serving on committees.	http://www.mlanet.org/p/cm/ld/fid=41
American Library Association (ALA)	Provides on-demand webinars on a variety of topics including building/facilities.	http://www.ala.org/educationcareers/elearning
Association of Independent Information Professionals	Participate in conferences, refine a new skill, or consider consulting as time allows.	https://www.aiip.org/
Association of Internet Research Specialists	Take online classes to be certified in searching legal databases, health sciences information, or become more comfortable with knowledge management.	https://www.airsassociation.org/
EBLIP: Evidence Based Library and Information Practice Conference	This conference takes place every other year and alternates locations between Europe, Canada, and the United States.	https://libguides.library.drexel.edu/EBLIP9/EBLIP10
Library Juice Academy	Take classes to learn how to become a better manager, manage organizational change, or on research data management.	http://libraryjuiceacademy.com/
Medical Library Association (MLA)	Recorded webinars on core competencies or trending topics.	http://www.medlib-ed.org/catalogs/mla-webinars
NASIG: Transforming the Information Community	This association specializes in technical services. It also offers online classes, webinars, and it hosts annual conferences.	http://www.nasig.org
NLM Biomedical Informatics Fellowship	Learn all about Informatics and how you can improve the practice of health care by taking this all-expenses-paid week long course!	https://www.nlm.nih.gov/news/biocourse.html
Special Libraries Association	This group hosts a yearly conference and specializes in providing legal and business information.	https://www.sla.org/

recruiting for new hires a challenge. Additionally, it makes moving between positions within librarianship not straightforward and could mean taking a pay cut. Employees may choose to stay in a comfortable position rather than trying for a more challenging role if they face unstable fiscal situations. As the number of experienced librarians retire, it is crucial for young professionals to learn from seasoned professionals but also adapt services and to develop skills necessary for thriving in our technology friendly world.[99, 100]

The master's in library science, master's of library and information science, or master's of science in information studies are just three of the degrees a professional librarian can obtain. These degrees could lead to working in an archive, academic, public, corporate, or health sciences library. "College of Information and Library Studies," or "iSchools," are the names of schools offering these programs. Whether enrolled in an LIS program or an iSchool, the provided degrees are the same. The "iSchool" identifier started to appear in 2005 within Academic Library Association–accredited programs in the United States. Some accredited programs, however, continue to use School of Information or School of Information and Library Studies as seen in table 9.2. Programs currently offer classes on instructional design, website management, research, data curation, and information services (i.e., reference). By including courses on topics relevant to all aspects of the information field, programs prepare students to transition smoothly and effectively from a master's program to the workplace.

Table 9.2.   Comparison of ten American Library Association library and information studies accredited programs

University	Online (O), face-to-face (F2F), hybrid (H), hybrid option not specified (HNS)*	Identifies as iSchool
Kent State University	O, F2F, HNS	No
McGill University	F2F, HNS	No
San Jose State University	O, F2F, HNS	Yes
University of British Columbia	F2F	No
University of Illinois at Champaign-Urbana	F2F, HNS	Yes
University of Maryland, College Park	O, F2F, H	Yes
University of Michigan	F2F, O, HNS	Varies
University of Pittsburgh	O, F2F, H	No
University of Toronto	F2F	Yes
Wayne State University	O, F2F, HNS	No

Are new graduates better prepared for the challenges of working in the field? Does the "I never learned that in library school" statement prevail during panel sessions with experienced professionals? To answer these questions, I have examined the websites, degrees offered, required courses, specializations, and pathways of ten different American Library Association accredited programs.[101] Seven programs are located in the United States and three programs are located in Canada. Table 9.3 summarizes the similarities and differences between programs.

Within the ten accredited programs discussed in table 9.2, professional specializations now include data curation, digital curation, information management, or knowledge management. Core courses for these programs, seen in table 9.3, reflect these specialties. The diversity in the information field is reflected in expertise of faculty members who teach classes and serve as advisers for students in these programs.[102]

Tables 9.2 and 9.3 touch on the similarities and differences between programs in the United States and Canada. iSchools exist in Europe and in the Asia-Pacific. The organization and requirements of these programs are similar to the masters and doctorate programs in Canada and the United States. The structure of courses for doctoral programs is quite different, and, for students enrolled in the Asia-Pacific, little flexibility exists. The European schools, by contrast, have a flexible curricula allowing students to study abroad at other schools within the European Union.[103] Additionally, some programs recognize the value of entrepreneurship and self-employment. These programs offer entire courses on the subjects. Faculty members recognize that entrepreneurial activities take time, involve heartache, and shape a person irrevocably.[104] These experiences often make a candidate well-rounded.

As mentioned in table 9.3, many programs are placing greater emphasis on preparing graduates for the work environment by providing courses in instructional design, important to liaison, distance support, or online librarians. A course such as "research for the information professional", for example, would be ideal for any graduate hoping to get a tenure-track position. Programs requiring students to create a portfolio or complete a master's thesis give new graduates an opportunity to showcase what they have learned for prospective employers. Some new hires have graduate teaching assistant experience prior to completing their master's, and this is a big advantage, especially if a candidate is pursuing a position in academia.[105] If a student goes

Table 9.3. Examples of professional specializations and core courses from ten American Library Association library and information studies accredited programs

University	Professional specializations	Core courses
Kent State University	<ul><li>Academic librarianship</li><li>Archival or special collections librarianship</li><li>Cataloging or metadata</li><li>Digital librarianship or digital initiatives</li><li>Digital preservation</li><li>Information technology and information science</li><li>K-12 School Librarianship</li><li>Library management</li><li>Museum studies</li><li>Public librarianship</li><li>Reference librarianship</li><li>Special librarianship</li><li>Youth services (Children's or Teen librarianship)</li></ul>	<ul><li>The information landscape</li><li>Information organization</li><li>People in the information ecology</li><li>Information institutions and professions</li><li>Research and assessment in library and information science</li><li>Master's portfolio in library and information science</li><li>Completion of an internship, project, paper, or thesis is required</li></ul>
McGill University	<ul><li>Archival studies</li><li>Knowledge management</li><li>Librarianship</li></ul>	<ul><li>Foundations of information studies</li><li>Information behavior and resources</li><li>Information systems design</li><li>Integrating research and practice</li><li>Organization of information practice</li></ul>

(continued)

Table 9.3. *(continued)*

University	Professional specializations	Core courses
San Jose State University	■ Academic librarianship ■ Data science ■ Digital curation ■ Digital services ■ Emerging technologies: Issues and trends ■ Information intermediation and instruction ■ Information organization, description, analysis, and retrieval ■ Leadership and management ■ management, digitization, and preservation of cultural heritage and records (archival studies and records management) ■ Public librarianship: A community hub for learning and literacy ■ Special librarianship ■ Teacher librarianship ■ Web programming and information architecture ■ Youth services	■ Advanced topics in library and information science (e-portfolio) or thesis ■ Applied research methods ■ Information communities ■ Information professions ■ Information retrieval system design ■ Online learning: Tools and strategies for success
University of British Columbia	■ Community and culture ■ Data services ■ Information interaction and design ■ Librarianship	■ Foundations of resource description and knowledge organization ■ Human information interaction ■ Information practices in contemporary society ■ Methods of research and evaluation in information organizations
University of Illinois at Champaign-Urbana	■ Archival and special collections ■ Data and asset management ■ Information organization and management ■ Knowledge management and competitive intelligence ■ Research and information services ■ Youth and K–12	■ Information organization and access ■ Libraries, information, and society

University		
University of Maryland, College Park	• Archives and digital curation (only face-to-face) • Diversity and inclusion (only face-to-face) • Individualized program plan (face-to-face, online) • School library (face-to-face, online) • Youth experience (face-to-face, online)	• Achieving organizational excellence • Creating information infrastructures • Designing principled inquiry • Serving information needs • Field study or thesis option
University of Michigan	• Data science, data analytics, computational social science • Digital archives and library science, preservation • User experience research and design, human computer interaction, social computing	• Cognate coursework (classes outside the iSchool) • UMSI internship program • Mastery course or master's thesis option program
University of Pittsburgh	• Archives and information science • Data stewardship • Library and information services	• Introduction to information technologies • Knowledge organization • Managing and leading information services • Understanding information
University of Toronto	• Archives and records management • Critical information policy studies • Culture and technology • Information systems and design • Information systems and design: Executive delivery option • Knowledge management and information management • User experience design	• Information workshop 1 and 2 • Representing, documenting, and accessing the cultural record • Communities and values • The information experience • Systems and infrastructures
Wayne State University	• Archives and digital content management • Information management • Library services	• Access to information • Information technology • Introduction to the information profession • Library administration and management • Organization of knowledge • Research for the information profession • School library media programs

straight from undergraduate school to graduate school, student worker positions, field experiences, and independent study opportunities are the resume building opportunities that will assist them in obtaining entry-level positions. As the job markets change, libraries are more open to hiring candidates with experience as a consultant or temporary employee. As with any program strengths and weaknesses exist among the ten schools listed in table 9.3, but it appears LIS and iSchools, along with libraries, are changing to embrace the new technology and trends impacting our discipline.

CONCLUSION

The perception and role of libraries and librarians continues to change. Being competent in traditional librarianship is no longer acceptable and instead librarians must provide ROI, design programs, implement new technology, provide excellent service, and contribute value added to the community. Teaching is both an art and a service. In academia, incorporating the library into the classroom is rare. Google and discovery layer systems, which allow people to search books, videos, journals, and databases at the same time, are the go-to resources for accessing information. These systems, promoted by libraries, are minimizing, at least in the eyes of faculty and students, the importance of the librarian's teaching role. By first talking to students and faculty about a product or resource that intrigues them, such as an app, librarians should adjust their conversations to include suggestions and techniques that are transferable to navigating and using databases and other library resources. Teaching and promotion opportunities can be found many places outside the traditional classroom environment.

Websites, electronic resources, and subscription databases are the modern tools of the trade in libraries. Deciding what to renew, drop, or consider for future years requires excellent communication and collaboration. Workflows may change to accommodate the shifts from print to electronic books and journals. By collaborating with each other and capitalizing on each librarians' strengths, the outcome leads to an improved experience for patrons.

Usability studies, data-driven decision making, and SWOT analyses are tools businesses use to assess what is working or to identify areas for improvement. As mentioned, directors and library administrators are beginning to use such tools when evaluating existing programs and creating strategic plans. The focus on data has grown tremendously and yet many people struggle to understand how librarians fit into the big data and data trends.[106] The data special interest group within the Medical Library Association is dedicated to discussing the latest trends and movements within this area of librarianship.[107] Colleges and universities are just beginning to develop data management and data lifecycle plans. Smaller libraries may struggle to find a place in the data world. Talking with patrons and conducting surveys on how patrons use and view the library are two options for all libraries to consider, before implementing changes. Libraries benefit from using this data to support decisions when choosing which journals, books, apps, and databases to purchase.

Space, place, and money are tight. Publishers are competing to introduce new platforms. Instead of creating additional content, however, many of these platforms simply combine e-books and other products into one platform. Such options limit what a library can do, particularly when the prices increase as the library budget decreases. Conversations with colleges always involve explaining that the library budget is not sufficient to supply all the resources, unless a department or school can assist in paying the subscription or the library receives additional funding. From a space perspective, a 3,000-square-foot library may shrink to 800 square feet and be merged with other departments. The loss of physical space should not prohibit creating an enhanced virtual space.

The future is murky, but the role of the information will always be important. The trick for librarians is to market our unique skills and services while continuing to prove our worth through value added opportunities, new roles, and enhanced skill sets regardless of our budget and physical space allocation. Libraries are the information hub and librarians are the key players for assisting patrons in locating, identifying, evaluating, and using information in all settings.

NOTES

1. Virginia M. Bowden, "Health Sciences Library Building Projects, 1998 Survey," *Bulletin of the Medical Library Association* 87, no. 4 (1999): 416–17.

2. Valerie A. Lynn, Marie FitzSimmons, and Cynthia K. Robinson, "Special Report: Symposium on Transformational Change in Health Sciences Libraries: Space. Collections, and Roles," *Journal of the Medical Library Association* 99, no. 1 (2011): 85–87, doi:10.3163/1536-5050.99.1.014.

3. Pauline S. Beam, Laura M. Schimming, Alan B. Krissoff, and Lynn K. Morgan, "The Changing Library: What Clinicians Need to Know," *Mt Sinai Journal of Medicine* 73, no. 6 (2006): 857–62.

4. Lucretia W. McClure, "When the Librarian was the Search Engine: Introduction to the Special Issue on New Roles for Health Sciences Librarians," *Journal of the Medical Library Association* 101, no. 4 (2013): 260, doi: 10.3163/1536-5050.101.4.006.

5. Heting Chu, "iSchools and non-iSchools in the USA: An Examination of Their Master's Programs," *Education for Information* 29, no. 1 (2012): 1–17, doi: 10.3233/EFI-2010-0908.

6. Michael Seadle, and Elke Greifeneder, "Envisioning an iSchool Curriculum," *Information Research* 12, no. 4 (2007), http://InformationR.net/ir/12-4/colis/colise02.

7. Laura Saunders, "Academic Libraries' Strategic Plans: Top Trends and Under-Recognized Areas," *The Journal of Academic Librarianship* 41, no. 3 (2015): 285–91, doi: 10.1016/j.acalib.2015.03.011.

8. Carol Perryman, "Assessment Related Skills and Knowledge Are Increasingly Mentioned in Library Job Postings," *Evidence Based Library & Information Practice* 10, no. 1 (2015): 98–100, doi: 10.18438/B8060T.

9. Ruth Browne, Kaye Lasserre, Jill McTaggart, Liz Bayley, Ann McKibbon, Megan Clark, Gerald J. Perry, and Jeannette Murphy, "International Trends in Health Science Librarianship: Part 1—The English Speaking World," *Health Information & Libraries Journal* 29, no. 1 (2012): 75-80, doi: 10.1111/j.1471-1842.2011.00973.x.

10. Bruce Massis, "Data-Driven Decision-Making in the Library," *New Library World* 117, no. 1/2 (2016): 131–34, doi:10.1108/NLW-10-2015-0081.

11. Saunders, "Academic Libraries' Strategic Plans," 285–91.

12. Eduardo P. Mayorga, "Webinar Software: A Tool for Developing More Effective Lectures (Online or In-Person)," *Middle East African Journal of Opthalmology* 21, no. 2 (2014): 123–27, doi: 10.4103/0974-9233.129756.

13. Rebecca Hedreen, "Time Zones, Screencasts, and Becoming Real: Lessons Learned as a Distance Librarian," *Urban Library Journal* 18, no. 1 (2012): 1–13, https://academicworks.cuny.edu/cgi/viewcontent.cgi?article=1114&context=ulj.

14. Lori S. Mestre, "Student Preference for Tutorial Design: A Usability Study," *Reference Services Review* 40, no. 2 (2012): 258–76, doi: 10.1108/00907321211228318.

15. John A. McArthur and Valerie Johnson Graham, "User-Experience Design and Library Spaces: A Pathway to Innovation?" *Journal of Library Innovation* 6, no. 2 (2015): 1–14.

16. Gary A. Freiburger, "'White Elephant' in the Library: A Case Study on Loss of Space from the Arizona Health Sciences Library at the University of Arizona," *Journal of the Medical Library Association* 98, no. 1 (2010): 29–31, doi: 10.3163/1536-5050.98.1.011.

17. Mary Joan Tooey, "Renovated, Repurposed, and Still 'One Sweet Library': A Case Study on Loss of Space from the Health Sciences and Human Services Library, University of Maryland, Baltimore," *Journal of the Medical Library Association* 98, no. 1 (2010): 40–43, doi: 10.3163/1536-5050.98.1.014.

18. Gail L. Persily and Karen A. Butter, "Reinvisioning and Redesigning 'A Library for the Fifteenth Through Twenty-First Centuries': A Case Study on Loss of Space from the Library and Center for Knowledge Management, University of California, San Francisco," *Journal of the Medical Library Association* 98, no. 1 (2010): 44–48, doi: 10.3163/1536-5050.98.1.015.

19. Camille Andrews, Sara E. Wright, and Howard Raskin, "Library Learning Spaces: Investigating Libraries and Investing in Student Feedback," *Journal of Library Administration* 56, no. 6 (2015): 647–72, doi: 10.1080/01930826.2015.1105556.

20. Cynthia K. Robinson, "Library Space in the Digital Age: The Pressure Is On," *Bottom Line* 22, no. 1 (2009): 5–8, doi: 10.1108/08880450910955369.

21. Saunders, "Academic Libraries' Strategic Plans," 285–91.

22. Karen Jensen, "No More Liaisons: Collection Management Strategies in Hard Times," *Collection Management* 42, no. 1 (2017): 1, 3–14, doi: 10.1080/01462679.2016.1263812.

23. Saunders, "Academic Libraries' Strategic Plans," 285–91.

24. Helen U. Emasealu and Susan N. Umeozor, "Training Librarians for 21st Century Repository Services: Emerging Trends," *Issues in Informing Science & Information Technology* 13 (2016): 187–94, http://iisit.org/Vol13/IISITv13p187-194Emasealu2639.pdf.

25. Canadian Association of Research Libraries (CARL), "Institutional Repositories," CARL, accessed April 15, 2018, http://www.carl-abrc.ca/advancing-research/institutional-repositories/.

26. Mary M. Case, "Partners in Knowledge Creation: An Expanded Role for Research Libraries in the Digital Future," *Journal of Library Administration* 48, no. 2 (2008): 141–56, doi: 10.1080/01930820802231336.

27. Manorama Tripathi, Archana Shukla, and Sharad Kumar Sonker, "Research Data Management Practices in University Libraries: A Study," *DESIDOC Journal of Library & Information Technology* 37, no. 6 (2017): 417–24, doi: 10.14429/djlit.37.11336.

28. Kevin Read and Fred Willie Zametkin LaPolla, "A New Hat for Librarians: Providing REDCap Support to Establish the Library as a Central Data Hub," *Journal of the Medical Library Association* 106, no. 1 (2018): 120–26, doi: 10.5195/jmla.2018.327.

29. Jennifer A. Barlett, "The Value-Added Organization: Beyond Business as Usual," *Library Leadership & Management* 30, no. 4 (2016): 1, https://uknowledge.uky.edu/cgi/viewcontent.cgi?article=1277&context=libraries_facpub.

30. Daniel M. Dollar, John Gallagher, Janis Glover, Regina K. Marone, and Cynthia Crooker, "Realizing What's Essential: A Case Study on Integrating Electronic Journal Management into a Print-Centric Technical Services Department," *Journal of the Medical Library Association* 95, no. 2 (2007): 147–55, doi: 10.3163/1536-5050.95.2.147.

31. Tooey, "Renovated, Repurposed, and Still," 40–43. 1536-5050.98.1.014.

32. Andrews, "Library Learning Spaces."

33. Robinson, "Library Space in the Digital Age."

34. Persily, "Reinvisioning and Redesigning."

35. Freiburger, "'White Elephant' in the Library."

36. Suzanna Conrad and Julie Shen, "Designing a User-Centric Web Site for Handheld Devices: Incorporating Data-Driven Decision-Making Techniques with Surveys and Usability Testing," *Journal of Web Librarianship* 8, no. 4 (2014): 349–83, doi: 10.1080/19322909.2014.969796.

37. Michael J. Dulock and Holley Long, "Digital Collections Are a Sprint, Not a Marathon," *Information Technology and Libraries Journal* 34, no. 4 (2015): 5–17, doi: 10.6017/ital.v34i4.5869.

38. Lindsay Blake, Frances M. Yang, Hutton Brandon, Benjamin Wilson, and Renee Page, "A Clinical Librarian Embedded in Medical Education: Patient-Centered Encounters for Preclinical Medical Students," *Medical Reference Services Quarterly* 37, no. 1 (2018): 19–30, doi: 10.1080/02763869.2018.1404384.

39. Susan C. Whitmore, Suzanne F. Grefsheim, and Jocelyn A. Rankin, "Informationist Programme in Support of Biomedical Research: A Programme Description and Preliminary Findings of an Evaluation," *Health Information and Libraries Journal* 25, no. 2 (2008): 135–41, doi: 10.1111/j.1471-1842.2007.00756.x.

40. Mark Aaron Polger, "The Informationist: Ten Years Later," *Journal of Hospital Librarianship* 10, no. 4 (2010): 363–79, doi: 10.1080/15323269.2010.514556.

41. Lisa Federer, "The Librarian as Research Informationist: A Case Study," *Journal of the Medical Library Association* 101, no. 4 (2013): 298–302, https://www.ncbi.nlm.nih.gov/pmc/articles/PMC3794685/.

42. Selinda A. Berg and Michelle Banks, "Beyond Competencies: Naming Librarians' Capacity for Research," *Journal of Academic Librarianship* 42, no. 4 (2016): 469–71, https://www.sciencedirect.com/science/article/pii/S009913331630074X.

43. Bedi, "Transforming Roles," 314–27.

44. Michael R. Kronenfeld, R. Curtis Bay, and William Coomb, "Survey of User Preferences from a Comparative Trial of UpToDate and ClinicalKey," *Journal of the Medical Library Association* 101, no. 22 (2013): 151–54, doi: 10.3163/1536-5050.101.2.011.

45. Jensen, "No More Liaisons," 3–14.

46. Dulock, "Digital Collections are a Sprint," 5–17.

47. Steven S. Harris, Benjamin Barden, H. Kenneth Walker, and Martin A. Reznek, "Assessment of Student Learning Behaviors to Guide the Integration of Technology in Curriculum Reform," *Information Services & Use* 29, no. 1 (2009): 45–52, doi: 10.3233/ISU-2009-0591.

48. Jonathan D. Eldredge, David G. Bear, Sharon J. Wayne, and Paula. P. Perea, "Student Peer Assessment in Evidence-Based Medicine (EBM) Searching Skills Training: An Experiment," *Journal of the Medical Library Association* 101, no. 4 (2013): 244–51, doi: 10.3163/1536-5050.101.4.003.

49. Melissa J. Kash, "Teaching Evidence-Based Medicine in the Era of Point-of-Care Databases: The Case of the Giant Bladder Stone," *Medical Reference Services Quarterly* 35, no. 2 (2016): 230–36, doi: 10.1080/02763869.2016.1152148.

50. Blake, "A Clinical Librarian Embedded," 19-30.

51. Larry Gruppen, et al., "Toward a Research Agenda for Competency-Based Medical Education," *Medical Teacher* 39, no. 6 (2017): 623–30, doi: 10.1080/0142159x.2017.1315065.

52. Erika Bennett and Jennie Simning, "Embedded Librarians and Reference Traffic: A Quantitative Analysis," *Journal of Library Administration* 50, no. 5/6 (2010): 443–57, doi: 10.1080/01930826.2010.491437.

53. Mestre, "Student Preference for Tutorial," 258–76.

54. Hedreen, "Time Zones, Screencasts," 1–14.

55. Layla S. Heimlich, "New and Emerging Roles for Medical Librarians," *Journal of Hospital Librarianship* 14, no. 1 (2014): 24–32, doi: 10.1080/15323269.2014.859995.

56. Kay Cimpl Wagner and Gary D. Byrd, "Evaluating the Effectiveness of Clinical Medical Librarian Programs: A Systematic Review of the Literature," *Journal of the Medical Library Association* 100, suppl. 4 (2012): 14–33, https://www.ncbi.nlm.nih.gov/pmc/articles/PMC3571670/.

57. Yini Zhu, Mina Ghajar, and Ermira Mitre, "SHARE: Spreading Health Awareness with Resources and Education—Librarians' Role in Patient Education, A Case Study," *Journal of Hospital Librarianship* 16, no. 4 (2016): 319–27, doi: 10.1080/15323269.2016.1221280.

58. Lauren A. Maggio, Olle ten Cate, David M. Irby, and Bridget C. O'Brien, "Designing Evidence-Based Medicine Training to Optimize the Transfer of Skills from the Classroom to Clinical Practice: Applying the Four Component Instructional Design Model," *Academic Medicine* 90, no. 11 (2015): 1457–61, doi: 10.1097/acm.0000000000000769.

59. Lindsay Blake and Darra Balance, "Teaching Evidence-Based Practice in the Hospital and the Library: Two Different Groups, One Course," *Medical Reference Services Quarterly* 32, no. 1 (2013): 100–10, doi: 10.1080/02763869.2013.749143.

60. Read, "A New Hat for Librarians."

61. Kathy A. Zeblisky, et al., "Rethinking Your Involvement: A Survey on Hospital Library Committee Participation," *Journal of Hospital Librarianship* 13, no. 1 (2013): 47–58, doi: 10.1080/15323269.2013.743361.

62. Marshall Breeding, "Data-Driven Libraries," *Computers in Libraries* 34, no. 7 (2014): 23–26, https://librarytechnology.org/repository/item.pl?id=19695.

63. Koltay Tibor, "Are You Ready? Tasks and Roles for Academic Libraries in Supporting Research 2.0," *New Library World* 117, no. 1/2 (2016): 94–104, doi: 0.1108/NLW-09-2015-0062.

64. Shailoo Bedi, and Christine Walde, "Transforming Roles: Canadian Academic Librarians Embedded in Faculty Research Projects," *College & Research Libraries* 78, no. 3 (2017): 314–27. doi: 10.5860/crl.78.3.16590.

65. Emasealu, "Training Librarians for 21st Century," 187–94.

66. Jingfeng Xia and Yue Li, "Changed Responsibilities in Scholarly Communication Services: An Analysis of Job Descriptions," *Serials Review* 41, no. 1 (2015): 15–22, doi: 10.1080/00987913.2014.998980.

67. Melissa L. Rethlefsen, Mellanye J. Lackey, and Shirley Zhao, "Building Capacity to Encourage Research Reproducibility and #MakeResearchTrue," *Journal of the Medical Library Association* 106, no. 1 (2018): 113–19, doi: 10.5195/jmla.2018.273.

68. Perryman, "Assessment Related Skills," 98–100.

69. Browne, "International Trends in Health," 75–80.

70. American Library Association (ALA), "ACRL Proficiencies for Assessment Librarians and Coordinators," ALA, accessed April 22, 2018, http://www.ala.org/educationcareers/accreditedprograms/directory.

71. Harris, "Assessment of Student Learning," 45–52.

72. Paolo Gardois, Nicoletta Colombi, Gaetano Grillo, and Maria C. Villanacci, "Implementation of Web 2.0 Services in Academic, Medical and Research Libraries: A Scoping Review," *Health Information & Libraries Journal* 29, no. 2 (2012): 90–109, doi: 10.1111/j.1471-1842.2012.00984.x.

73. Anne M. Houston, "Revisiting Library as Place," *Reference & User Services Quarterly* 55 no. 2 (2015): 84–86, https://journals.ala.org/index.php/rusq/article/viewFile/5852/7366.

74. Ryan Harris, Alexa Mayo, James D. Prince, and Mary J. Tooey, "Creating Shared Campus Experiences: The Library as Culture Club," *Journal of the Medical Library Association* 101, no. 4 (2013): 254–56, doi: 10.3163/1536-5050.101.4.005.

75. Laura Anderko, et al., "Promoting Prevention Through the Affordable Care Act: Workplace Wellness," *Preventing Chronic Disease* 9 (2012): E175.   doi: 10.5888/pcd9.120092.

76. Beatriz G. Varman and Adela V. Justice, "The Unfunded Worksite Wellness Program," *Journal of Hospital Librarianship* 15, no. 3 (2015): 284–95, doi: 10.1080/15323269.2015.1049065.

77. Megan Lotts, "Playing with LEGO®, Learning About the Library, and 'Making' Campus Connections: The Rutgers University Art Library Lego Playing Station, Part One," *Journal of Library Administration* 56, no. 4 (2016): 359–80, doi: 10.1080/01930826.2016.1168252.

78. Daniel Newton, "Releasing Steam: Stressbusters to Market the Library as Place," *Public Services Quarterly* 7, no. 3/4 (2011): 169–72, doi: 10.1080/15228959.2011.622648.

79. Amber T. Loos, "The Role of Librarians in Promoting Digital Wellness: A Case Study," *Public Services Quarterly* 13, no. 1 (2017): 32–40, doi: 10.1080/15228959.2016.1268943.

80. Jie Tang, Min-Shi Liu, and Wen-Bin Liu, "How Workplace Fun Influences Employees' Performance: The Role of Person-Organization Value Congruence," *Social Behavior & Personality: An International Journal* 45, no. 11 (2017): 1787–1801, https://www.sbp-journal.com/index.php/sbp/article/view/6240.

81. Hangsheng Liu, et al., "Do Workplace Wellness Programs Reduce Medical Costs? Evidence from a Fortune 500 Company," *Inquiry: The Journal of Health Care Organization, Provision, and Financing* 50, no. 2 (2013): 150–58, doi: 10.1177/0046958013513677.

82. Emasealu, "Training Librarians for 21st Century," 187–94.

83. Susan Nash Simpson, Jeffrey G. Coghill, and Patricia C. Greenstein, "Electronic Resources Librarian in the Health Sciences Library: An Emerging Role," *Journal of Electronic Resources in Medical Libraries* 2, no. 1 (2005): 27–39, https://www.tandfonline.com/doi/abs/10.1300/J383v02n01_03.

84. Cecilia Lau and Venkata Kolli, "App Use in Psychiatric Education: A Medical Student Survey," *Academic Psychiatry* 41, no. 1 (2017): 68–70, doi: 10.1007/s40596-016-0630-z.

85. Anna. M. Seifert, Nicole Stotz, and Alexia E. Metz, "Apps in Therapy: Occupational Therapists' Use and Opinions," *Disability Rehabilitation Assistive Technology* 12, no. 8 (2017): 772–79, doi: 10.1080/17483107.2016.1262912.

86. Maged N. Boulous, Steve Wheeler, Carlos Tavares, and Ray Jones, "How Smartphones are Changing the Face of Mobile and Participatory Healthcare: An Overview, with Example from eCAALYX," *BioMedical Engineering OnLine* 10 (2011): 24, doi: 10.1186/1475-925x-10-24.

87. Julie Youm and Warren Wiechmann, "Medical Student Use of the iPad in the Clerkship Curriculum," *The Clincal Teacher* 12, no. 6 (2015): 378–83, doi: 10.1111/tct.12381.

88. Boulos, "How Smartphones are Changing," 24.

89. Jill T. Boruff and Dale Storie, "Mobile Devices in Medicine: A Survey of How Medical Students, Residents, and Faculty Use Smartphones and Other Mobile Devices to Find Information," *Journal of the Medical Library Association* 102, no. 1 (2014): 22–30, doi: 10.3163/1536-5050.102.1.006.

90. Douglas Archibald, Colla J. Macdonald, Judith Plante, Rebecca J. Hogue, and Javier Fiallos, "Residents' and Preceptors' Perceptions of the Use of the iPad for Clinical Teaching in a Family Medicine Residency Program," *BMC Medical Education* 14 (2014): 174, doi: 10.1186/1472-6920-14-174.

91. Michael R. Kronenfeld and Harold S. Bright, "Library Resource Discovery," *Journal of the Medical Library Association* 103 no. 4 (2015): 210–13, doi: 10.3163/1536-5050.103.4.011.

92. Nicole Hennig, "Mobile Apps in Library Programs," *Library Technology Reports* 50, no. 8 (2014): 18–22, https://journals.ala.org/index.php/ltr/article/view/4652.

93. Yingqi Tang, "Distance Education Librarians in the United States: A Study of Job Announcements," *Journal of Academic Librarianship* 39, no. 6 (2013): 500–505, doi: 10.1016/j.acalib.2013.08.012.

94. Elizabeth L. Black and Betsy Blankenship, "Linking Students to Library Resources through the Learning Management System," *Journal of Library Administration* 50, no. 5/6 (2010): 458–67, doi: 10.1080/01930826.2010.488587.

95. Rosie Croft and Naomi Eichenlaub, "E-mail Reference in a Distributed Learning Environment: Best Practices, User Satisfaction, and the Reference Services Continuum," *Journal of Library Administration* 45, no. 1–2 (2006): 117–47, doi: 10.1300/J111v45n01_07.

96. Christopher Diaz, "Academic Library Services to Distance Learners: In Consideration of Costs, Technology, and Stability," *Urban Library Journal* 18, no. 1 (2012), https://academicworks.cuny.edu/ulj/vol18/iss1/2/.

97. Rachel E. Cannady, "Fostering Library as Place for Distance Students: Best Practices from Two Universities," *Journal of Electronic Resources Librarianship* 23, no. 3 (2011): 286–89. doi: 10.1080/1941126x.2011.601242.

98. Judi Moreillon, "#schoollibrarians Tweet for Professional Development: A Netnographic Case Study of #txlchat," *School Libraries Worldwide* 21, no. 2 (2015): 127–37.

99. Scott T. Plutchak, "Breaking the Barriers of Time and Space: The Dawning of the Great Age of Librarians," *Journal of the Medical Library Association* 100, no. 1 (2012): 10–19, doi: 10.3163/1536-5050.100.1.004.

100. Linda Ashcroft, "Developing Competencies, Critical Analysis and Personal Transferable Skills in Future Information Professionals," *Library Review* 53, no. 2 (2004): 82–88, doi: 10.1108/00242530410522569.

101. American Library Association (ALA), "American Library Association Directory of Accredited and Candidate Programs," ALA, accessed March 15, 2018, http://www.ala.org/educationcareers/accreditedprograms/directory.

102. Zhiya Zuo, Kang Zhao, and David Eichmann, "The State and Evolution of U.S. iSchools: From Talent Acquisitions to Research Outcome," *Journal of the Association for Information Science & Technology* 68, no. 5 (2017): 1266–77, doi: 10.1002/asi.23751.

103. Michael Seadle, "The European iSchools," *Bulletin of the Association for Information Science & Technology* 42, no. 4 (2016): 26–30, https://onlinelibrary. wiley.com/doi/full/10.1002/bul2.2016.1720420408.

104. Michael R. Kristiansson and Henrik Jochumsen, "How to Implement Entrepreneurship in LIS Education: A Danish Example," *BiD*, no. 35 (2015): 16–21, doi: 10.1344/BiD2015.35.21.

105. Cynthia Kane, Kellie Meehlhause, and Marianne Ryan, "GTA = Great Teaching Adventure!" *Reference & User Services Quarterly* 54, no. 1 (2014): 12–16, doi: 10.5860/rusq.54n1.12.

106. Rebecca L. Harris-Pierce and Yan Quan Liu, "Is Data Curation Education at Library and Information Ccience Schools in North America Adequate?" *New Library World* 113, no. 11/12 (2012): 598–613, doi: 10.1108/03074801211282957.

107. Medical Library Association (MLA), "Data Special Interest Group," MLA, accessed March 2018, http://www.mlanet.org/p/cm/ld/fid=213.

Nickel and Diming Library Space Improvements with the Annual Library Budget

ALANNA CAMPBELL AND PATTY FINK

Since the 2008 recession hit, many libraries can identify with struggling to maintain a strong collection and still make improvements to their library spaces. But what do you do when you don't have a budget or grant to improve your library space? Well, you do what we have been doing at the Health Sciences Library at the Northern Ontario School of Medicine (NOSM) for years. You nickel and dime it with the annual budget! In the absence of a dedicated budget line, we have found strategic ways to enhance our space including managing noise, adopting new technologies, improving signage, upgrading furnishings, and more. Some of these improvements have come with minimal costs while more expensive items have required waiting for the right year. Patty Fink has been the director of the Health Sciences Library since 2007 after joining the school in 2004. Alanna Campbell joined NOSM as a librarian in 2009, and has been responsible for public services since 2013. We have worked on a number of space improvement projects together and we're excited to share them with you here.

The Northern Ontario School of Medicine is co-located at Lakehead University in Thunder Bay and Laurentian University in Sudbury. The Health Sciences Library primarily serves undergraduate medical students, dietetic interns, residents, faculty, and staff. We also support the members of our host institutions Lakehead University and Laurentian University. We maintain a small physical collection of 8,472 hardcopy titles while we have 13,266 electronic resources. Our collection priority is digital resources as the majority of our users are distributed throughout the 843,853 square kilometers of Northern Ontario. Each Health Sciences Library location staffs two librarians and one library technician. At our Lakehead location, we also have our library coordinator, and at our Laurentian location we have our administrative assistant and director.

Our two campus libraries are physically different, and the spaces present different challenges and opportunities. This includes layout, lighting, aesthetic, and location within the medical school buildings. Our Lakehead library space is 2,223 square feet and located on the second floor of the building. It also includes staff offices, a small storage room, a work room with kitchenette, and one small library study room making up an additional 853 square feet. There are also two videoconference meeting rooms managed by NOSM Facilities within the library. Head 965 kilometers southeast and you'll arrive at our Laurentian location. The main library space is 2,925 square feet and located on the main floor of the school. In addition to this the library contains staff offices and a work room with kitchenette making up an ad-

FIGURE 10.1.
The NOSM Health Sciences Library at Laurentian.

FIGURE 10.2.
The NOSM Health Sciences Library at Lakehead.

ditional 574 square feet. Our square footage has been maintained since our inception in 2005.

We are a publicly funded organization, with the majority of that funding allocated from two provincial ministries. Our budget year is May 1 to April 30, and the budget planning cycle for the coming year commences the preceding fall. Proposals are submitted for allocations that are made across the medical school, with final approvals from our board of governors. We are not permitted to roll funds forward from year to year; dollars must be expensed within a fiscal cycle.

The Health Sciences Library receives two pockets of funds, one for operating expenses and one for maintaining the collection. It is within the operating funds that we need to find dollars for space improvement. After salary and collection dollars, the available funds total 3.05 percent of the overall budget (2017–2018 budget). Those operating funds can cover promotional activities and space improvements only after the core maintenance and support licenses are paid (e.g., ILS fees). It is a small pocket of funds to work with on an annual basis, and usually the exact figure is not known until the last quarter (January–April) once all those other expenses are accounted for.

We also seek internal partnerships for space improvement. For example, we approached our Indigenous department to purchase a display cabinet that would house select artifacts from a related archival fonds. They agreed, and contributed several thousand dollars to the project. We also look to our facilities department to combine dollars for certain space improvements, such as accessibility retrofits, and have recently begun to work with our advancement department to propose donor funded opportunities for space improvements.

Based on our experience we have broken this chapter down into three main sections.

1. *Responding to Users* will address how our users use our space, the ways in which we have received and processed their feedback, and how we have responded through space improvements including furnishings, sound barriers, technology enhancements, and accessibility.
2. *Public Relations Opportunities* will look at how we have enriched promotional opportunities in the library space including related purchases for the space and branding.
3. *Recent Service and Workflow Changes* discussess initiatives such as getting rid of our gates and opening up our reserves collection.

As you can likely understand trying to enhance two library spaces by nickel and diming the annual library budget has meant that transforming our library spaces has been slow. Prioritizing improvements between two sites, on one budget, has been a balancing act based on user and staff feedback, library initiatives, other contributing factors and if funds are even available. This can be a frustrating process which we actively work not to piecemeal together but rather to fit into a larger vision. At the end of the day, each improvement to the library space has come with positive feedback, insights for future improvements and resulted in an overall enhanced space of benefit to our users. You may be frustrated yourself by trying to enhance your library space on a budget, but as Diana Rendina (2015) notes in her article, "How to Transform Your Library Space on a Budget," "still dream big."[1] Whether only working with an annual budget or actively attempting to find funding to finance big purchases, do not let the dollars and cents inhibit your creativity and motivation to improve your library space.[2] *Where there is a will there is a way,* and we'll show you what we've willed here.

RESPONDING TO USERS AND STAFF

User Feedback

Our users visit the library space for a variety of standard tasks. This includes group study, individual study, lounging, printing, photocopying and scanning, accessing course reserves, perusing and borrowing from our hardcopy collection, borrowing our equipment booking technology, using our public PCs, and stopping in to ask directional, quick reference, and specialist reference questions. Both our locations are defined as quiet study spaces as we currently are unable to offer silent study space.

Over the years, we have collected and responded to user feedback regarding our spaces through a few methods. First, we receive self-initiated user comments about our spaces via email, instant message, and at our information desk. Second, we have sought feedback through the Health Sciences Library Advisory Group. The committee comprises elected representatives from our three faculty divisions, an undergraduate learner, a postgraduate resident, and a health sciences learner. Lastly, in January 2017, we ran a five-week library feedback survey open to all NOSM members which included questions specific to the library space. These included the following: "What activities do you engage in most frequently when visiting one of the Library's spaces?" and "what improvements would you suggest to the library's physical spaces?"

Based on our most recent survey and our ongoing forms of acquiring feedback, the issues to be addressed can be divided into three main categories.

1. Noise
2. Power outlets
3. Furniture

Many of the desired improvements that fall under these three categories have yet to be resolved in their entirety due to lack of funding, however we have been able to mediate many of them with our current strategy of nickel and diming it along with a little help from our friends in facilities!

Noise

Sound carries very well in our space and implementing aftermarket sound barriers is an annual discussion in the library. A frequent complaint that we had at our Laurentian campus location was noise from the staff cubicles and work room located behind our information desk. While staff did their very best to go about their everyday work quietly, including frequent teleconferences due to the nature of our distributed learning environment, the situation had become frustrating even for them. Additionally, since the entryway and information desk are not isolated from the rest of the library space, visitors entering with friendly greetings do not often realize that they've been disruptive to those studying. With the staff cubicles behind our information desk these greetings were often projected even further. In an attempt to mediate this, we began selling earplugs for twenty-five cents in 2011. The earplugs were purchased in bulk and sales paid for them over time.

While this attempt was helpful, and we do continue to sell earplugs to compensate for our lack of silent study space, it was apparent that we needed a more permanent fix. Three quarters through the 2014 fiscal year, the director and our facilities department allocated available funds to construct a sound barrier between the information desk and staff cubicles. We then began to act quickly to ensure the barrier was installed prior to the end of the 2015 fiscal year. The project involved working with multiple outside vendors, NOSM's facilities, and Laurentian University's facilities department. A glass Teknion wall (6 feet 2 inches × 9 feet) was purchased and scheduled for installation in March 2015. In preparation for the disruption installation would cause to staff, meeting rooms were booked as temporary offices. A temporary information desk was set up opposite our front entry. For a practical and fun spin on the disruption the temporary information desk was outfitted with free earplugs and cookies for the day. A week in advance of the installation we announced to users the pending disruption including a Facebook post outlining what services would be available during renovations. The installation was a success and we no longer receive complaints from users or staff about the noise from behind our information desk.

Power Outlets

Although the medical school buildings were built in 2004, an era of emerging digital resources and an increase in student laptop usage, the library

FIGURE 10.3.
The glass Teknion wall behind our information desk.

spaces were not equipped with an adequate amount of accessible power outlets. Adding numerous outlets to our spaces in one fell swoop is cost prohibitive, however we have been able to address the issue in a few different ways. In 2015, we purchased an M8 wall-mounted charging station for each library location through the company KwikBoost. Users are able to charge three Apple lightning, one Apple 30-pin, and four micro USB devices at once using the station. Beyond the practicalities of the station its other main selling features were that it did not take up any additional floor space, only required a single outlet for installation, and was aesthetically customizable (which will be discussed further in the next section, Public Relations Opportunities).

In 2017, we purchased one portable charging device for each campus. It allows users to charge any device with an AC adapter anywhere in the library. The portable charging devices are kept behind our information desk and are available for four-hour in-house use loans. They can be booked in advance through our online equipment booking system or requested at the information desk. When not in use the devices are plugged in to recharge in preparation for the next borrower. In 2017, we were also able to add two wall outlets at our Thunder Bay location as part of a small furniture refresh. The two outlets were installed to complement the height of the new furniture, allowing library users direct table level access to the combined AC/USB wall outlets.

Furniture

Updated and functional furniture is a big ticket wish list item for the library and our users. Over the years we have been able to make small space enhancements with furniture acquired from other areas of the school by modifying our existing furnishings and newly purchased items. In 2014 (Laurentian location) and 2015 (Lakehead location), we replaced the bulky and uncomfortable castor desk chairs that were located at all our group tables and carrel booths. With the support of facilities, we were able to split the cost of the chairs at our Laurentian location and at the Lakehead location they were fully covered by facilities. Working with another department that is also responsible for school spaces is incredibly helpful when you just don't have the funds to do it on your own.

In 2017, we were able to purchase new furnishings for a small area at our Lakehead location. In preparation for the enhancement we reorganized the public terminals and photocopier area. The existing decade old bulky scanner was replaced with a small footprint Fujitsu ScanSnap ix50 as recommended by our IT department. The new scanner was installed near our public terminals area, resulting in the removal of a PC in our photocopier area and one of the public terminals. The microfiche reader kept in our photocopier area was allocated to a cart, which can be brought out as needed for researchers.

All of this allowed for the clearing of a space under a windowed wall where two sets of booths including tables were installed. The booth seating attracted users upon installation with people taking a seat nearly immediately. The colors selected for the booths were a neutral modern gray, and tables were selected in mahogany and black to match the existing bookshelves and furniture. The hope is that in 2018 we will be able to update the lounge area next to the new booths with coordinating lounge chairs and remove the older couches we repurposed from another area of the school.

In 2017, we were also able to purchase an electronic stand up desk for our Lakehead location. Over the last couple of years, we have received quite a few requests for stand up desks in the library as a result of the school installing these in lecture rooms and some small group based learning rooms. The purchase of the stand-up desk also aligns with our mission to enhance the accessibility of the library space (see A Note on Accessibility box).

FIGURE 10.4.
Booth seats added to our Lakehead location in 2017.
Marian Diamond, Library Coordinator at NOSM's Health Sciences Library

A NOTE ON ACCESSIBILITY

The accessibility of the Health Sciences Library spaces and our resources is a top priority. To ensure compliance with provincial accessibility standards in our physical and virtual library spaces we follow standards including the following:

- Ensuring a standard egress between furniture, bookcases, and walls

- Providing library users with accessible study tables and public PC terminals

- Photocopying and scanning services via information desk staff

- Automated door entry
- Loaner laptops with Kurzweil 3000
- Formatting our website, LibGuides, and LibAnswers so that they are readable by text to speech and related software

RECOMMENDED RESOURCES

Visit your provincial, state or national library associations to see training and resources specific to your local legislation.

Access Forward. "Getting Started." Access Forward/Vers Accessibilité: Training for an Accessible Ontario. Accessed May 23, 2017. http://accessforward.ca/.

Association of College & Research Libraries. "Getting Started with this Toolkit." Web Accessibility Tool Kit: Making Digital Resources Useable and Accessible in Research Libraries. Accessed May 3, 2017. http://accessibility.arl.org/standards-best-practices/.

Council of Ontario Universities. "Customer Service Standard." Accessible Campus. Accessed May 25, 2017. http://www.accessiblecampus.ca/tools-resources/administrators-tool-kit/iasr/customer-service-standard/.

Reilly, Bernard F., Jr. "The Future of Cooperative Collections and Repositories." *Library Management* 34, no. 4/5 (2013): 342–51. doi: 10.1108/01435121311328681.

Wentz, Brian, Paul T. Jaeger, and John C. Bertot, eds. *Advances in Librarianship: Accessibility for Persons with Disabilities and the Inclusive Future of Libraries.* Bingley, UK: Emerald Group Publishing Ltd, 2015.

Staff Specific Feedback

While the majority of the feedback we get is about our public spaces, library staff have a particularly keen eye for what goes on behind the scenes and its impact on the look and feel of the library. A problem at both our locations was that there was nowhere for our part-time student assistants to store their personal gear when they arrived for their shift. Often it would be placed on our back counter (Laurentian location), visible from the information desk, or somewhere in our storage room/kitchenette where it posed a workflow problem or tripping hazard. To resolve this, we purchased lockers in 2013 (Lakehead location) and 2014 (Laurentian location). The banks each included three lockers. One was reserved for student assistants during their shift (items are not to be left when not working), and two were reserved for our two staff members who work from office cubicles to provide more storage space and security for items.

PUBLIC RELATIONS OPPORTUNITIES

Our visual identity is as important to space improvements as furniture and paint. In order to create a distinct presence, we embarked on a branding

FIGURE 10.5.
Bank of three lockers for staff and student assistants.

exercise in 2011. Working with our communications department, in particular our graphic artist, we developed a distinct visual identity. A logo was first created, followed by custom designs for signage, publicity materials, and the website. Of course, this meant an update to existing signage, ensuring all visible materials had the new logo. We wanted to create a recognizable brand, so that in both the physical and virtual library spaces, our users would always identify those as part of our library. We created banners and images for our website, LibGuides, YouTube channel, and so forth, all based on this new visual identity. Although this exercise took several months, the budgetary impact was minimal. We purchased inexpensive Plexiglas signage, and the virtual updates were cost neutral. That being said, the time investment by staff was significant.

Following the branding exercise, we installed digital displays at both campuses. This gave us another opportunity to impact the space by pushing branded promotional materials to our users. We wall mounted two flat screen TVs with external hard drives attached via a USB connection. A scrolling PowerPoint presentation displays events, policies, and general library info. In

FIGURE 10.6.
Branded Plexiglas signage is shown to the right of our Laurentian location entry.

particular, this information helps us to remind users of space etiquette (e.g., food and drink are permitted, but be clean, keep noise to a whisper, or buy earplugs). We developed a white background template with consistent font and image requirements. The PowerPoint slide deck is updated monthly to keep the content fresh, although the space related policy slides are on permanent rotation.

Prior to the digital displays, we purchased inexpensive digital photo frames. The concept was the same, a set of scrolling images was displayed, and the frames were positioned on the counters at our information desks. This was a low cost option at less than $200 CAD, in contrast to the TV displays. However, the visibility was less than optimal. The size of the frame (approximately 12 inches) offered a limited view, and only those interacting at the information desks could see the material.

Whenever we adopt a new technology or create new displays we ensure a central focus on our branding. When we installed the mobile device charging stations, the ability to incorporate our aesthetic was an important criterion when selecting the product. Each mobile charging station is recognizable by our logo while fulfilling a basic need—providing more power options. Our loaner technology (laptops, projectors, iPads, etc.) and our portable charging devices also sport decals with our logo. The image is recognizable, thereby easily identifiable as a library resource.

Annually we purchase promotional materials, and the visual identity is central. Some items might promote our social media spaces, our website or simply our contact info. Each item is selected to enhance a space, whether branded pencils available at our information desks for student use, or bookmarks with our website URL. We thoughtfully consider how these promo items represent us. For example, we purchased pockets that adhere to the back of cell phones that strikingly focus on our social media address. The pockets serve a useful purpose, letting you carry credit card size cards with your phone, and act as a great continual reminder that you can access us via the social media apps on that very phone.

We also have physical cork bulletin boards. They are a dated approach to promotions, but not easily removed or replaced. We've tried to upscale the visible content even if this is a less interactive type of promotion. The bulletin boards are updated monthly, and we consistently use color posters promoting select resources and subject guides to quickly attract the eye. The letter

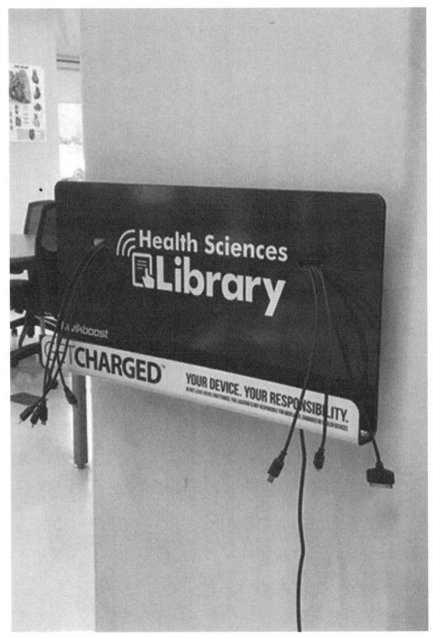

FIGURE 10.7.
Our customized mobile device charging station.

FIGURE 10.8.
Cell phone pockets with our Facebook and Twitter handles.

size printouts include QR codes, so that the resources promoted can be easily accessed.

To draw people to the space, we try to link with school wide events or activities. These are a great opportunity to showcase our space, and increase the foot traffic. We set up a display table, with information targeted to the event's audience, and have purchased a promotional banner to dress up the display area. For example, for our annual open house we printed a glossy postcard sized handout that outlines two consumer help apps. As this event is open to the general public, we chose freely available consumer health apps that can be useful tools for this audience. The librarians demonstrate how to use the apps on an iPad, and the visitors take away the cards for future reference. The cards include our branding and website URL, and we also provide details about donation opportunities. The cards were inexpensive to print (less than $100 CAD), and the banner was an investment that we have been able to reuse for events both internal and external to the library (approximately $150 CAD).

Annually, we spend about $1,500 CAD on promotional and signage materials. In small increments, we have improved the promotional items available in the library and the visibility of our branding. Each item enhances the aesthetic, promotes interactivity, and even increases traffic to both our physical and virtual spaces.

SERVICE AND WORKFLOW CHANGES

Information Desk Enhancements

Some of the changes we have made in the library space have directly impacted our services and workflows. In 2015, we made one of our largest furniture enhancements, a new information desk for our Lakehead location. The previous desk had been a large square desk that tended to act as a catchall for clutter instead of being streamlined and service oriented. It was the library's first impression and was not very welcoming. The new desk is circular and proportionate to the space. The desk was designed with the functions of a library in mind. It collects less clutter and is far more welcoming. Additionally, it includes a stand up desk component that meets accessibility standards.

At our Laurentian location, our information desk has had a number of enhancements over time. This has included replacing a large ancient book

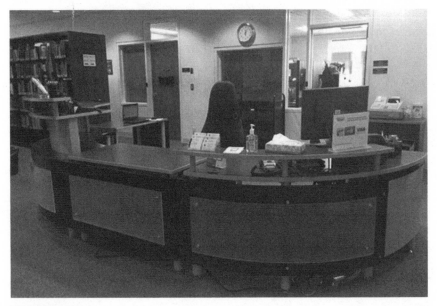

FIGURE 10.9.
Our upgraded information desk with built-in standing desk.

FIGURE 10.10.
Two aftermarket under counter shelves hold our outgoing equipment.

desensitizer and a wired barcode scanner with a wireless model. One small addition we made in 2015 was the installation of custom shelves under our information desk. This aided in the workflow of our equipment booking process. Each evening our student assistants are expected to prepare and check any equipment reserved for the following day. If there is an item reserved, the student verifies the equipment is charged and includes all components (AC adapter, mouse, etc.). In the past, the equipment was then placed on our back counter. The counter was becoming cluttered, and, since it is now behind the Teknion wall, accessibility was inhibited. The simple fix of adding the two shelves under our information desk to set aside the readied equipment has kept the visible areas clear and workflow streamlined. The shelves were purchased custom through our host university's facilities department and match the existing wood grain of the information desk.

Open Reserves

In hopes of breaking down barriers to service for our users in 2014, we began planning an open-reserves system in our main library spaces. Previously reserves were kept behind our information desk and learners and faculty would have to request the four-hour loan material from a staff member. In addition to employee time, the cost for this project was a few Plexiglas signage stands. Existing shelves at our Laurentian campus were converted from display shelves to standard bookshelves. At our Lakehead campus, it was just a matter of shifting our newspapers. The open reserves system allows users to read and photocopy reserve materials in the library at their leisure. We have designated a spot for users to place material to be reshelved and we track the in-house usage through our ILS. If a user wants to borrow the item, they bring it to the information desk as they would any other hardcopy material and we check it out for them.

Security Gates and Visitor Statistics

In a bold move, we've begun removing our security gates. In our experience the need for security gates in our library has been minimal. It is normally only by accident that users walk out with an item, and even that is rare. In recent years, the only thing stopping us from removing the gates has been that they count our visitors. Previously, information desk staff and students were responsible for collecting the visitor count from the security gate at the end of each desk shift. The number was entered in our desk statistics form and compiled by our library coordinator, annually. In 2016, however, we purchased two sets of very petite wall-mounted people counters for each of our locations. These devices track library foot traffic hourly and data can be extracted via a USB cable monthly by designated staff at each of our locations. The people counters were trialed for six months in 2016 to determine their accuracy compared to the existing gates.

As there was minimal disparity between the two systems, in late winter 2017, we switched our statistics collection to the people counters. Information desk staff no longer need to collect the numbers after each shift, which has reduced human error. Around the same time, we switched to the people counters the opportunity to have the gate removed from the entryway at our Lakehead location presented itself. The gate and a boxed-in wall that had been installed to direct the flow of traffic through the gate were removed. This opened up the entryway immensely and has already had a positive impact on library visibility from the hallway, particularly during in-house events. The entry seems far less enclosed and is incredibly more welcoming for all. We plan to do the same in the coming year or so at the Laurentian location.

Preparing for Change

Currently our access services librarian is working on weeding the Lakehead collection, which is composed of thirty-two bays of books. This weeding project will allow for the additional lounge space we have planned for our Lakehead location. Next year the Laurentian campus collection will be weeded and hopefully we will be able to remove a minimum of twenty-four of our fifty-five bays. This would clear up room for a variety of space enhancements including additional seating, building out a silent study room, or even adding a new service. Along with this reduction in hardcopy books, we've begun to examine the need for our ILS and investigate alternative options for a very small hard copy collection.

Also on our list of priorities this fiscal year is to look at alternatives to removing our cash register. Our primary cash sales include copy cards, photocopies, ear plugs, and fines. Revenue from fines is minimal and we are considering doing away with them. Ideally we'd like to piggyback on our host universities' one-card systems, which allows university members to load their ID with funds electronically and use it to purchase food, print and copy, pay for parking, and more. We are looking forward to seeing what options there are for reducing the workflow and security measures required to maintain the cash registers.

CONCLUSION

We held a blue sky planning session at our annual library in person planning meeting held in February 2017. Our in-person meeting brings together all the library staff from both locations for training and strategic planning for the upcoming academic year. This blue sky session was an opportunity for staff to reimagine the space. The team was split into two groups and asked to imagine rebuilding the library from scratch. What would the building look like? What services would we offer? What would the library space offer our users? What would be the tone or ambience of the space? The session was a great opportunity to gather our diverse team members' thoughts. Results of the session included ideas such as enhanced convenience services, natural enhancements to the library space expressed through furniture and installation pieces, collaboration opportunities within the space with external departments, noise management, diversified study spaces, and wellness services. We are looking forward to taking the feedback from this session and integrating it into our long term and short term nickel and dime planning.

During 2015, I, Alanna took a six-month research sabbatical. As lead of public services, and with an interest in library spaces, a resulting sabbatical goal was to develop a library spaces report. To create this report, three academic libraries with recent or in progress renovations were visited, a literature search on health science library spaces was conducted, and members of the Association of Academic Health Sciences Libraries (AAHSL), who had removed at least one bookshelf in the last five years, were surveyed. The results of this survey were presented in Toronto at Mosaic 2016 in a poster presentation entitled, "Less Shelves More What? How Are Academic Health Sciences Libraries Replacing Their Shelves?"[2]

The final report was composed of a summary of visits and survey results, as well as a list of recommendations for the library moving forward. This included the following:

- *Collect user feedback*—It was recommended that we survey our users for feedback on the library space. Suggested methodologies included an online survey, focus groups, and consulting with the library advisory group. (We have since completed an online survey and consulted with the advisory committee.)
- *Electrical outlets*—It was suggested that the library consider enhancing electrical outlet access at both locations. An affordable option would be to assess ceiling dropped electrical outlets, which would not require drilling through the floor. (We have since made some progress on this recommendation via our portable chargers and installation of two new electrical outlets at our Lakehead location.)
- *Establishing a funding source*—It was recommended that the library source additional funds beyond the annual budget to support significant space enhancements. This would include fund-raising, grant sourcing, and so forth.

- *3D printing*—It was recommended that the library consider acting as a hub for 3D printing and possibly collaborating with the research department who may have a more immediate need for the service. Many academic libraries are able to offer the service for free upon start up with a grant. Some eventually transition to a materials based fee. This service would require the development of a policy and procedures as well as additional training for staff.
- *Lighting*—It was suggested that the library remove bookshelves to enhance natural light at both locations. This would provide more natural light to the lounge and study areas. Light, both artificial and natural, is a functional and architectural element that should be used constructively in the library space. Should the arrangement of tables, carrels, or walls change it is best to assess if lighting needs have changed as well.
- *Study carrels*—It was recommended that we build out a silent study as our carrels are currently immediately next to our group study tables. There are also a variety of carrel options on the market that are sound proof.
- *Group study rooms*—It was suggested that we build out a group study room equipped with smart screen technology at our Laurentian location, while our Lakehead location does have a small group study room. It would benefit from furnishings best suited to a narrow space and similar technology enhancements.

A major recommendation made in the library spaces report, and for readers, is to develop a multitiered space improvement plan: Plan A, B, and C. These would each have a different required budget with A being the ideal full renovation plan, B a modified version, and C a plan of small improvements that can be made each year. We're already actively working under a plan C each year, but what if your library did receive a one-time grant? What if your push for a major overhaul to the space was finally recognized and money directed your way? Having thought through what you want will be imperative to securing those funding sources and easing the planning process. Dream big and know what you want!

TIPS ON LIBRARY SPACE A, B, C PLANNING

PLAN A

This is your ideal library space improvement plan. The idea with Plan A is to be prepared for opportunities that may allow for a complete renovation.

Points to consider include the following:

- Have on hand existing usage statistics and user and staff feedback in case you need to act quickly.

- Consider the tone you want for the library space. Are you reinventing the overall feel of the library or simply upgrading?

- Look at how you could use lighting, furnishings, flow of traffic, and study space to impact the tone and function of the space.

- Write down your major wish list items (more group study rooms, more outlets, more lighting, less humidity, less noise, etc.).

- Examine what changes to services and policies a significant library transformation could allow for. Think about taking advantage of the upheaval of a large renovation to purge what isn't necessary or working and bring in new services and policies.

- Earmark what key library staff members should sit on a renovation committee to ensure library input is included in planning.

- Have an idea of what you don't want by looking at other library spaces. Consider the lessons learned presented in this book.

- Assess what time of year would be best for the most disruptive components of a major renovation and how to support users during less disruptive periods (e.g., a separate entrance to study spaces, free earplugs, access to necessary materials, etc.).

PLAN B

This is for cases where you've got enough funds available to complete a partial rendition of Plan A. As a result, you'll want to take into consideration the points in Plan A as well as the following:

- What are the key wish list items from Plan A that you want to accomplish sooner than later? What are you willing to let go of or wait on?
- If you can't renovate your entire library space, what areas are most important to focus on? This could mean only renovating one floor of your space or a portion if you only have one floor.
- Taking Plan A and breaking it down into three or more years of renovations may help with prioritizing in Plan B.

PLAN C

This is your nickel and dime plan. It's your Plan B broken down into what you can afford each year. Consider the following when it comes to your Plan C.

- What from your Plan B do you want to complete this year? What would give you the biggest return on investment when it comes to improving services and user satisfaction?
- Can you extend a project from Plan B over a few years allowing you to build on it each year?
- What projects from Plan B cost more? Can those be done this fiscal year? Consider saving the less expensive projects for when there are other financial pressures such as the collection, staffing, and so forth.

NOTES

1. Diana Rendina, "How to Transform Your Library Space on a Budget. Knowledge Quest," accessed May 4, 2017, http://knowledgequest.aasl.org/transform-library-space-budget/.

2. Alanna Campbell, "Less Shelves, More What? How Are Academic Health Sciences Libraries Choosing to Replace Their Shelves?" (poster presented, MLA/CHLA joint conference Mosaic '16, Toronto, ON, May 13–18, 2016).

Epilogue: To Be a Building or Not to Be

Looking Toward the Future

Jean Shipman and Alanna Campbell

As illustrated by many of the authors of this book, one of today's pivotal questions is this: Does a library need to be in a building to be a library, or, phrased differently, can librarians be more effective by being placed in context or distributed with those they work with rather than being centrally located. If there is no library building, are there still librarians? These questions have yet to be fully answered, as there are very few institutions that have tried such on a permanent scale.

Beyond the pages of this book we must continue to ask, what would be the challenges of moving in this direction? What are the benefits? Why would a library not want to own a building or a designated space? In the last few pages of this book, these questions are discussed to encourage librarians to think differently about their futures and their practice environments.

For the positives, not having to maintain and fund a facility would save expenditures of library budgets. It also enables staff to be repurposed from taking care of building details to being more focused on professional activities. Not having a building eliminates the recent trend of sharing library space with different institutional units, which brings along with it challenges of offering public space to individuals while providing collaborative workspaces for employees that can be noisy. Not having a building might also help with changing the stereotype of librarians from being *ssshhhers* and meek, quiet individuals. The main advantage of being co-located, or meeting users where *they* are, is that users do not have to disrupt their workflows nor are impeded by accessibility issues to seek help with their information or organizational needs. Often, users do not know what they do not know or how to ask in an effective manner for the assistance they need. Librarians in context can directly observe the need and address it immediately where the need originates. This places the emphasis of librarianship on the value of our skills and knowledge (expertise) that we contribute rather than the traditional library space.

On the flipside, having a building or a dedicated space gives definition to what services are going to be available to users. Users, in most cases, have a fond affiliation when they think of libraries. They see them as places to retreat to in order to get work done, to have a chance to leave behind their daily obligations to reflect on new directions, to seek answers to their questions, or to meet with fellow colleagues. Libraries have become common gathering places or community centers in many cases, offering space for collaboration, for making, and for groups to gather. They house events such as exhibits, journal clubs, innovation spaces, wellness activities, and so forth. If libraries no longer existed, where would these university activities occur?

The other main benefit of having a central space for a library is the ability to collide with professional colleagues to bounce ideas off, plan activities, discuss the latest findings in information science, and so forth. Technology can be applied to replicate this closeness, but librarians still find solace and efficiency in collaborating face-to-face. If a building is not part of the picture, means for conducting such informal communications need to be implemented to not harm the collegiality that exists amongst librarians. Indeed, the greatest benefit of practicing within context with one's users is potentially negated by not being in close context with one's peers. Where can librarians gather to meet, where should core library staff be situated—can technological and financial support be offered from a distance? How would allowing staff to work from home benefit family life, save on transportation costs, commuting stress, and the environment? What policies and home facilities need to be offered to employees who work from their homes?

To be a building or not to be—the answer is not universal, as it depends on the university or institution within which one works. Distances between campuses and the expanse of central campus have required librarians to offer distance user services. The globalization of campuses has also mandated that libraries reach out beyond a building to meet their users' needs. As more universities partner or form coalitions, librarians will need to determine the most effective and efficient means of capturing and addressing increased numbers of users' information and organizational needs. As universities offer more self-guided instruction and the ability to learn from homes, offices, and beaches, the library building becomes more obsolete as these learners may never step foot within such a space.

This book addresses many issues and trends in current library buildings and spaces. We challenge you to identify what such spaces offer and how to emulate these key functions when library buildings are either nonexistent or are only occupied by library staff. How should such a transformation of our practice context change our professional name—is it time to reidentify ourselves by our expertise and not our buildings? We encourage you to reread this book with this idea in mind, to start to measure the impact sans building might have on your futures.

Appendix

CHAPTER 3: 2016-SPRING-24/5 ASSESSMENT MSL—OVERNIGHT

Q1. The purpose of this study is to evaluate library usage and space. Your participation in this study is completely voluntary and you can withdraw from the study at any time. By completing this survey you imply your consent to participate in the study.

Q2. Today's Date
- ☐ 01/25/16–Monday
- ☐ 01/26/16–Tuesday
- ☐ 01/27/16–Wednesday
- ☐ 01/28/16–Thursday
- ☐ 01/29/16–Friday
- ☐ 02/22/16–Monday
- ☐ 02/23/16–Tuesday
- ☐ 02/24/16–Wednesday
- ☐ 02/25/16–Thursday
- ☐ 02/26/16–Friday
- ☐ 04/04/16–Monday
- ☐ 04/05/16–Tuesday
- ☐ 04/06/16–Wednesday
- ☐ 04/07/16–Thursday
- ☐ 04/08/16–Friday

Q3. Current Time
☐ 1:00 a.m.– 2:00 a.m.
☐ 2:00 a.m.–3:00 a.m.
☐ 3:00 a.m.–4:00 a.m.
☐ 4:00 a.m.–5:00 a.m.
☐ 5:00 a.m.–6:00 a.m.
☐ 6:00 a.m.–7:00 a.m.
☐ 7:00 a.m.–8:00 a.m.

Q4. Does Marston Science Library meet your needs in the following areas?

1. Open hours
   Never   Rarely   Sometimes   Often   All of the time
2. Power outlets
   Never   Rarely   Sometimes   Often   All of the time
3. Computers
   Never   Rarely   Sometimes   Often   All of the time
4. Printing
   Never   Rarely   Sometimes   Often   All of the time
5. Scanning
   Never   Rarely   Sometimes   Often   All of the time
6. Course reserves (textbooks for checkout)
   Never   Rarely   Sometimes   Often   All of the time
7. Temperature
   Never   Rarely   Sometimes   Often   All of the time
8. Individual study space
   Never   Rarely   Sometimes   Often   All of the time
9. Group study space
   Never   Rarely   Sometimes   Often   All of the time
10. Desk surface space
    Never   Rarely   Sometimes   Often   All of the time
11. Seating comfort
    Never   Rarely   Sometimes   Often   All of the time
12. Seating amount
    Never   Rarely   Sometimes   Often   All of the time
13. Noise level
    Never   Rarely   Sometimes   Often   All of the time

14. Lighting
   Never   Rarely   Sometimes   Often   All of the time
15. Cleanliness: bathrooms
   Never   Rarely   Sometimes   Often   All of the time
16. Cleanliness: building
   Never   Rarely   Sometimes   Often   All of the time
17. Personal safety
   Never   Rarely   Sometimes   Often   All of the time

Q5. Which of the following do you use when visiting the library overnight (Marston Science Library or previously Library West, 1:00 a.m.–8:00 a.m.) (Choose all that apply)?
☐ Books/print materials
☐ Course reserves (textbooks)
☐ Computers/technology
☐ Printing/scanning
☐ Study rooms
☐ Group study areas (not study rooms)
☐ Individual study areas (tables/carrels)
☐ Starbucks
☐ Other _____

Q6. Which library do you most often use?
☐ Marston Science Library
☐ Library West
☐ Smathers Library (formerly Library East)
☐ Education Library
☐ Architecture and Fine Arts Library
☐ Health Science Center Library
☐ Law Library

Q7. Where do you usually study in Marston Science Library? (Choose all that apply)

1st Floor (Collaboration Commons)
☐ Study Rooms
☐ Open Study Tables
☐ Computers
☐ Individual Study Desks (Carrels)

2nd Floor (The floor you walk in on)
☐ Study Rooms
☐ Open Study Tables
☐ Computers
☐ Individual Study Desks (Carrels)

3rd Floor (Group study)
☐ Study Rooms
☐ Open Study Tables
☐ Computers
☐ Individual Study Desks (Carrels)

4th Floor (Quiet study)
☐ Study Rooms
☐ Open Study Tables
☐ Computers
☐ Individual Study Desks (Carrels)

5th Floor (Silent study/grad student carrels)
☐ Study Rooms
☐ Open Study Tables
☐ Computers
☐ Individual Study Desks (Carrels)

Q8. How often do you use Marston Science Library?
Never
☐ Once a year
☐ Once a semester
☐ 2–3 times a semester
☐ Once a month
☐ 2–3 times a month
☐ Once a week

☐ 2–3 times a week
☐ 4–6 times a week
☐ Daily

Q9. What hours do you usually use Marston Science Library? (Choose all that apply)
☐ 12:00 p.m.–1:00 a.m.
☐ 1:00 a.m.–2:00 a.m.
☐ 2:00 a.m.–3:00 a.m.
☐ 3:00 a.m.–4:00 a.m.
☐ 4:00 a.m.–5:00 a.m.
☐ 5:00 a.m.–6:00 a.m.
☐ 6:00 a.m.–7:00 a.m.
☐ 7:00 a.m.–8:00 a.m.
☐ 8:00 a.m.– 9:00 a.m.
☐ 9:00 a.m.–10:00 a.m.
☐ 10:00 a.m.–11:00 a.m.
☐ 11:00 a.m.–12:00 p.m.
☐ 12:00 p.m.–1:00 p.m.
☐ 1:00 p.m.–2:00 p.m.
☐ 2:00 p.m.–3:00 p.m.
☐ 3:00 p.m.–4:00 p.m.
☐ 4:00 p.m.–5:00 p.m.
☐ 5:00 p.m.–6:00 p.m.
☐ 6:00 p.m.–7:00 p.m.
☐ 7:00 p.m.–8:00 p.m.
☐ 8:00 p.m.–9:00 p.m.
☐ 9:00 p.m.–10:00 p.m.
☐ 10:00 p.m.–11:00 p.m.
☐ 11:00 p.m.–12:00 a.m.

Q10. Before tonight, have you used Marston Science Library overnight (1:00 a.m.–8:00 a.m.)?
☐ Yes
☐ No

Q11. In past semesters, did you use Library West overnight (1:00 a.m.–8:00 a.m.)?

☐ Yes
☐ No

Q12. What is your status?

☐ Undergraduate student
☐ Graduate student
☐ Staff
☐ Faculty
☐ Santa Fe student
☐ Other _____

Q13. What is your major/department/college?

_____

Q14. What do you like about Marston Science Library?

_____

_____

Q15. What would you like to see changed or improved at Marston Science Library?

_____

_____

Q16. Describe your ideal library space.

_____

_____

Bibliography

Aben, Kathrina, Kevin Adams, Ennis Barbery, Allison Bayley, Anne Bowser, Alexander Carson, Kendall Concini, et al. "Ethnographic Research on College Schoolwork and Libraries: A Study Completed by Graduate Students in the Methods of Cultural Analysis (ANTH606) Department of Anthropology, University of Maryland." Study Report, College Park, MD, 2011.

Access Forward. "Getting Started." Access Forward/Vers Accessibilité: Training for an Accessible Ontario. Accessed May 23, 2017. http://accessforward.ca/.

Allan, Barbara. *Emerging Strategies for Supporting Student Learning: A Practical Guide for Librarians and Educators.* London, United Kingdom: Facet Publishing, 2016.

American Library Association (ALA). "About." Libraries Transform: An Initiative of the American Library Association. Accessed April 15, 2018. http://www.ilovelibraries.org/librariestransform/about.

———. "ACRL Proficiencies for Assessment Librarians and Coordinators." ALA. Accessed April 22, 2018. http://www.ala.org/educationcareers/accreditedprograms/directory.

———. "American Library Association Directory of Accredited and Candidate Programs." ALA. Accessed March 15, 2018. http://www.ala.org/educationcareers/accreditedprograms/directory.

———. "Libraries Transform: About." American Library Association. Last updated 2015. http://www.ilovelibraries.org/librariestransform/about.

Anderko, Laura, Jason S. Roffenbender, Ron Z. Goetzel, John Howard, Francois Millard, Kevin Wildenhaus, Charles DeSantis, and William Novelli. "Promoting Prevention Through the Affordable Care Act: Workplace Wellness." *Preventing Chronic Disease* 9 (2012): E175. doi: 10.5888/pcd9.120092.

Andrews, Camille, Sara E. Wright, and Howard Raskin. "Library Learning Spaces: Investigating Libraries and Investing in Student Feedback." *Journal of Library Administration* 56, no. 6 (2015): 647–72. doi: 10.1080/01930826.2015.1105556.

Archibald, Douglas, Colla J. Macdonald, Judith Plante, Rebecca J. Hogue, and Javier Fiallos. "Residents' and Preceptors' Perceptions of the Use of the iPad for Clinical Teaching in a Family Medicine Residency Program." *BMC Medical Education* 14 (2014): 174. doi: 10.1186/1472-6920-14-174.

Ashcroft, Linda. "Developing Competencies, Critical Analysis and Personal Transferable Skills in Future Information Professionals." *Library Review* 53, no. 2 (2004): 82–88. doi: 10.1108/00242530410522569.

Association of College & Research Libraries. "Getting Started with this Toolkit." Web Accessibility Tool Kit: Making Digital Resources Useable and Accessible in Research Libraries. Accessed May 3, 2017. http://accessibility.arl.org/standards-best-practices/.

Association of Research Libraries. "LibQUAL+®" Association of Research Libraries. Accessed February 8, 2018. http://www.arl.org/focus-areas/statistics-assessment/libqual#.WnyzYU3rvIU.

Avolio, Bruce J., John J. Soski, Surinder S. Kahai, and Bradford Baker. "E-Leadership: Re-Examining Transformations in Leadership Source and Transmission." *Leadership Quarterly* 14 (2014): 111. doi: 10.1016/j.leaqua.2013.11.003.

Bardyn, Tanya P., Elizabeth Atcheson, Colleen Cuddy, and Gerald J. Perry. "Managing and Revitalizing Your Career as a Medical Librarian: A Symposium Report." *Journal of Hospital Librarianship* 13, no. 3 (2013): 220–30. doi:10.1080/15323269.2013.798770.

Barlett, Jennifer A., "The Value-Added Organization: Beyond Business as Usual," *Library Leadership & Management* 30, no. 4 (2016): 1–4. https://uknowledge.uky.edu/cgi/viewcontent.cgi?article=1277&context=libraries_facpub.

Bartlett, Doreen, Lisa A. Chiarello, Tina Hjorngaard, and Barbara Sieck Taylor. "Moving From Parent 'Consultant' to Parent 'Collaborator': One Pediatric Research Team's Experience." *Disability and Rehabilitation* 39, no. 21 (2017): 2228–35. doi: 10.1080/09638288.2016.1219402.

Beam, Pauline S., Laura M. Schimming, Alan B. Krissoff, and Lynn K. Morgan. "The Changing Library: What Clinicians Need to Know." *Mt Sinai Journal of Medicine* 73, no. 6 (2006): 857–63.

Bedi, Shailoo, and Christine Walde. "Transforming Roles: Canadian Academic Librarians Embedded in Faculty Research Projects." *College & Research Libraries* 78, no. 3 (2017): 314–27. doi: 10.5860/crl.78.3.16590.

Bennett, Erika, and Jennie Simning. "Embedded Librarians and Reference Traffic: A Quantitative Analysis." *Journal of Library Administration* 50, no. 5/6 (2010): 443–57. doi: 10.1080/01930826.2010.491437.

Bennis, Warren. "Authentic Leaders Engage More in Creative Collaboration." *Leadership Excellence Essentials* 23, no. 8 (2006): 3–4.

———. "Leadership Competencies." *Leadership Excellence Essentials* 27, no. 2 (2010): 20.

Berg, Selinda A., and Michelle Banks. "Beyond Competencies: Naming Librarians' Capacity for Research." *Journal of Academic Librarianship* 42, no. 4 (2016): 469–71. https://www.sciencedirect.com/science/article/pii/S009913331630074X.

Black, Elizabeth L., and Betsy Blankenship. "Linking Students to Library Resources through the Learning Management System." *Journal of Library Administration* 50, no. 5/6 (2010): 458–67. doi: 10.1080/01930826.2010.488587.

Blake, Lindsay, and Darra Balance. "Teaching Evidence-Based Practice in the Hospital and the Library: Two Different Groups, One Course." *Medical Reference Services Quarterly* 32, no. 1 (2013): 100–110. doi: 10.1080/02763869.2013.749143.

Blake, Lindsay, Frances M. Yang, Hutton Brandon, Benjamin Wilson, and Renee Page. "A Clinical Librarian Embedded in Medical Education: Patient-Centered Encounters for Preclinical Medical Students." *Medical Reference Services Quarterly* 37, no. 1 (2018): 19–30. doi: 10.1080/02763869.2018.1404384.

Blanchard, Ken, and Susan Fowler. *Self Leadership and the One-Minute Manager Revised Edition: Gain the Mindset and Skillset for Getting What You Need to Succeed.* New York, NY: William Morrow, 2017.

Blum, Susan D. *My Word! Plagiarism and College Culture.* Ithaca, NY: Cornell University Press, 2010.

Bolles, Mark E., and Richard N. Bolles. "Skills." In *What Color is Your Parachute: Guide to Job Hunting Online*, 39–56. Berkeley: Ten Speed Press, 2011.

Boosinger, Marcia, Bonnie MacEwan, Denise Baker, Ashley Goerke, Adelia Grabowsky, Cory Latham, Kasia Leousis, et al. "Reconfiguring Auburn University's Main Library for Engaged Active Student Learning." Ithaka S+R Libraries & Scholarly Communications Research Report, New York, NY, 2016. doi: 10.18665/sr.284239.

Boruff, Jill T., and Dale Storie. "Mobile Devices in Medicine: A Survey of How Medical Students, Residents, and Faculty Use Smartphones and Other Mobile Devices to Find Information." *Journal of the Medical Library Association* 102, no. 1 (2014): 22–30. doi: 10.3163/1536-5050.102.1.006.

Boulos, Maged N. Kamel, Steve Wheeler, Carlos Tavares, and Ray Jones. "How Smartphones Are Changing the Face of Mobile and Participatory Healthcare: An Overview, with Example from eCAALYX." *BioMedical Engineering OnLine* 10 (2011): 24. doi: 10.1186/1475-925x-10-24.

Bowden, Virginia M. "Health Sciences Library Building Projects, 1998 Survey." *Bulletin of the Medical Library Association* 87, no. 4 (1999): 415–36.

Braude, Robert M. "Virtual of Actual: The Term Library is Enough." *Bulletin of the Medical Library Association* 87, no. 1 (1999): 85–87. https://www.ncbi.nlm.nih.gov/pmc/articles/PMC226533/.

Breeding, Marshall. "Data-Driven Libraries." *Computers in Libraries* 34, no. 7 (2014): 23–26. https://librarytechnology.org/repository/item.pl?id=19695.

——. "Relationship with Discovery." *Library Technology Reports* 51, no. 4 (2015): 22–25. https://journals.ala.org/index.php/ltr/article/view/5688.

Browne, Ruth, Kaye Lasserre, Jill McTaggart, Liz Bayley, Ann McKibbon, Megan Clark, Gerald J. Perry, and Jeannette Murphy. "International Trends in Health Science Librarianship: Part 1—The English Speaking World." *Health Information & Libraries Journal* 29, no. 1 (2012): 75–80. doi: 10.1111/j.1471-1842.2011.00973.x.

Campbell, Alanna. "Less Shelves, More What? How Are Academic Health Sciences Libraries Choosing to Replace Their Shelves?" Poster presentation at the MLA/CHLA joint conference Mosaic '16, Toronto, ON, May 13–18, 2016.

Campbell, Graeme. "Tying it all together with an MLIS." *Access* 15, no. 4 (2009): 40–41.

Canadian Association of Research Libraries (CARL). "Institutional Repositories." CARL. Accessed April 15, 2018. http://www.carl-abrc.ca/advancing-research/institutional-repositories/.

Cannady, Rachel E. "Fostering Library as Place for Distance Students: Best Practices from Two Universities." *Journal of Electronic Resources Librarianship* 23, no. 3 (2011): 286–89. doi: 10.1080/1941126x.2011.601242.

Case, Mary M. "Partners in Knowledge Creation: An Expanded Role for Research Libraries in the Digital Future." *Journal of Library Administration* 48, no. 2 (2008): 141–56. doi: 10.1080/01930820802231336.

Chamberlain University. "Our History and Heritage." Chamberlain University. Accessed February 6, 2018. http://www.chamberlain.edu/about/history.

Choy, Fatt Cheong, and Su Nee Goh. "A Framework for Planning Academic Library Spaces." *Library Management* 37, no. 1/2 (2016): 13–28. doi:10.1108/LM-01-2016-0001.

Chu, Heting. "iSchools and non-iSchools in the USA: An Examination of Their Master's Programs." *Education for Information* 29, no. 1 (2012): 1–17. doi: 10.3233/EFI-2010-0908.

Chusmir, Leonard H., Christine S. Koberg, and Joan Mills. "Male-Female Differences in the Association of Managerial Style and Personal Values." *Journal of Social Psychology* 129, no. 1 (1989): 65–78. doi: 10.1080/00224545.1989.9711700.

Connolly-Brown, Maryska, Kim Mears, and Melissa E. Johnson. "Reference for the Remote User through Embedded Librarianship." *Reference Librarian* 57, no. 3 (2016): 165–81. doi: 10.1080/02763877.2015.1131658.

Conrad, Suzanna, and Julie Shen. "Designing a User-Centric Web Site for Handheld Devices: Incorporating Data-Driven Decision-Making Techniques with Surveys and Usability Testing." *Journal of Web Librarianship* 8, no. 4 (2014): 349–83. doi: 10.1080/19322909.2014.969796.

Cosgrove, Tracey. L. "Planetree Health Information Services: Public Access to the Health Information People Want." *Bulletin of the Medical Library Association* 82, no. 1 (1994): 57–63. http://www.ncbi.nlm.nih.gov/pubmed/8136762.

Council of Chief Librarians Electronic Access and Resources Committee. "Discovery Comparison." Review Document, s.n., 2016. https://cclibrarians.org/sites/default/files/reviews/Documents/DiscoveryComparisonCCLEAR16.pdf.

Council of Ontario Universities. "Customer Service Standard." Accessible Campus. Accessed May 25, 2017. http://www.accessiblecampus.ca/tools-resources/administrators-tool-kit/iasr/customer-service-standard/.

Croft, Rosie, and Naomi Eichenlaub. "E-mail Reference in a Distributed Learning Environment: Best Practices, User Satisfaction, and the Reference Services Continuum." *Journal of Library Administration* 45, no. 1–2 (2006): 117–47. doi: 10.1300/J111v45n01_07.

Cunningham, Heather V., and Susanne Tabur. "Learning Space Attributes: Reflections on Academic Library Design and Its Use." *Journal of Learning Spaces* 1, no. 2 (2012). http://libjournal.uncg.edu/jls/article/view/392.

Delcore, Henry D., James Mullooly, and Michael Scroggins. "The Library Study at Fresno State." Institute of Public Anthropology Publication, Fresno, CA, 2009. http://fresnostate .edu/socialsciences/anthropology/ipa/thelibrarystudy.html.

Detlefsen, Ellen G. "Teaching About Teaching and Instruction on Instruction: A Challenge for Health Sciences Library Education." *Journal of the Medical Library Association* 100, no. 4 (2012): 244–50. doi: 10.3163/1536-5050.100.4.005.

Dettmar, Nicole. "Where to Start? Needs Assessment." *The Medical Library Association Guide to Providing Consumer and Patient Health Information*, ed. Michelle Spatz, Lanham, MD: Rowman & Littlefield, 2014: 11–26.

Diaz, Christopher. "Academic Library Services to Distance Learners: In Consideration of Costs, Technology, and Stability." *Urban Library Journal* 18, no. 1 (2012). https://academicworks.cuny.edu/ulj/vol18/iss1/2/.

Dollar, Daniel M., John Gallagher, Janis Glover, Regina K. Marone, and Cynthia Crooker. "Realizing What's Essential: A Case Study on Integrating Electronic Journal Management into a Print-Centric Technical Services Department." *Journal of the Medical Library Association* 95, no. 2 (2007): 147–55. doi: 10.3163/1536-5050.95.2.147.

Drucker, Peter F. "What Makes an Effective Executive." *Harvard Business Review* 82, no. 6 (2004): 58–63, 136. https://hbr.org/2004/06/what-makes-an-effective-executive.

Duke, Lynda M., and Andrew D. Asher. *College Libraries and Student Culture: What We Now Know*. Chicago, IL: American Library Association, 2012. e-book.

Dulock, Michael J., and Holley Long. "Digital Collections Are a Sprint, Not a Marathon." *Information Technology and Libraries Journal* 34, no. 4 (2015): 5–17. doi: 10.6017/ital.v34i4.5869.

Eldredge, Jonathan. D., David G. Bear, Sharon J. Wayne, and Paula. P. Perea. "Student Peer Assessment in Evidence-Based Medicine (EBM) Searching Skills Training: An Experiment." *Journal of the Medical Library Association* 101, no. 4 (2013): 244–51. doi: 10.3163/1536-5050.101.4.003.

Emasealu, Helen U., and Susan N. Umeozor. "Training Librarians for 21st Century Repository Services: Emerging Trends." *Issues in Informing Science & Information Technology* 13 (2016): 187–94. http://iisit.org/Vol13/IISITv13p187-194Emasealu2639.pdf.

Federer, Lisa. "The Librarian as Research Informationist: A Case Study." *Journal of the Medical Library Association* 101, no. 4 (2013): 298–302. https://www.ncbi.nlm.nih.gov/pmc/articles/PMC3794685/.

Fields, Erin. "Making Visible New Learning: Professional Development with Open Digital Badge Pathways." *Partnership: The Canadian Journal of Library & Information Practice & Research* 10, no. 1 (2015): 1–10. http://www.irss.uoguelph.ca/index.php/perj/article/viewFile/3282/3514.

Flippin, Candace Steele. "The Glass Ceiling Is Breaking, Now What?" *Generations* 41, no. 3 (2017): 34–42. http://www.ingentaconnect.com/content/asag/gen/2017/00000041/00000003/art00006.

Foster, Nancy Fried, ed. *Studying Students: A Second Look*. Chicago, IL: Association of College & Research Libraries, 2013.

Foster, Nancy Fried, Teresa Balser, Rae Lynn Boes, Dianna Deputy, William Ferrall, Michael Fosmire, and Jeremy R. Garritano et al. "Participatory Design of Purdue University's Active Learning Center Final Report." Libraries Reports, West Lafayette, IN, 2013. http://docs.lib.purdue.edu/libreports/1.

Foster, Nancy Fried, and Susan Gibbons. "Understanding Faculty to Improve Content Recruitment for Institutional Repositories." *D-Lib Magazine* 11, no. 1 (2005). doi:10.1045/january2005-foster.

———, eds. *Studying Students: The Undergraduate Research Project at the University of Rochester*. Chicago, IL: Association of College & Research Libraries, 2007. e-book.

Freiburger, Gary A. "'A White Elephant' in the Library: A Case Study on Loss of Space from the Arizona Health Sciences Library at the University of Arizona." *Journal of the Medical Library Association* 98, no. 1 (2010): 29–31. doi: 10.3163/1536-5050.98.1.011.

Gardois, Paolo, Nicoletta Colombi, Gaetano Grillo, and Maria C. Villanacci. "Implementation of Web 2.0 Services in Academic, Medical and Research Libraries: A Scoping Review." *Health Information & Libraries Journal* 29, no. 2 (2012): 90–109. doi: 10.1111/j.1471-1842.2012.00984.x.

General Electric Company. "GE Annual Report." Annual Report, Fairfield, CT, 2000. http://www.ge.com/annual00/download/images/GEannual00.pdf.

Gleason, Ann Whitney. *New Methods of Teaching and Learning in Libraries.* New York, NY: Rowman & Littlefield, 2017.

Gombeski, William R., Jr., Joe O. Claypool, Michael Karpf, Jason Britt, Mark Birdwhistell, Karen Riggs, Tanya Wray, and Jan Taylor. "Hospital Affiliations, Co-branding, and Consumer Impact." *Health Marketing Quarterly* 31, no. 1 (2014): 65–77. doi: 10.1080/07359683.2014.874873.

Gonzalez, Sara Russell, and Denise Beaubien Bennett. "Planning and Implementing a 3D Printing Service in an Academic Library." *Issues in Science and Technology Librarianship* 78 (2014): 1–14. doi:10.5062/F4M043CC.

Gorman, Michael. *Our Enduring Values: Librarianship in the 21st Century.* Chicago: American Library Association, 2000.

Groenwald, Susan L. *Designing and Creating a Culture of Care for Students and Faculty: The Chamberlain University College of Nursing Model.* Philadelphia: Wolters Kluwer, 2018.

Gruppen, Larry, Jason R. Frank, Jocelyn Lockyer, Shelley Ross, M. Dylan Bould, Peter Harris, Farhan Bhanji, et al. "Toward a Research Agenda for Competency-Based Medical Education." *Medical Teacher* 39, no. 6 (2017): 623–30. doi: 10.1080/0142159x.2017.1315065.

Guédon, Jean-Claude. "The Digital Library: An Oxymoron?" *Bulletin of the Medical Library Association* 87, no. 1 (1999): 9–19. https://www.ncbi.nlm.nih.gov/pmc/articles/PMC226505/.

Harris, Ryan, Alexa Mayo, James D. Prince, and Mary J. Tooey. "Creating Shared Campus Experiences: The Library as Culture Club." *Journal of the Medical Library Association* 101, no. 4 (2013): 254–56. doi: 10.3163/1536-5050.101.4.005.

Harris, Steven S., Benjamin Barden, H. Kenneth Walker, and Martin A. Reznek. "Assessment of Student Learning Behaviors to Guide the Integration of Technology in Curriculum Reform." *Information Services & Use* 29, no. 1 (2009): 45–52. doi: 10.3233/ISU-2009-0591.

Harris-Pierce, Rebecca L., and Yan Quan Liu. "Is Data Curation Education at Library and Information Science Schools in North America Adequate?" *New Library World* 113, no. 11/12 (2012): 598–613. doi: 10.1108/03074801211282957.

Hazen, Dan. "Rethinking Research Library Collections: A Policy Framework for Straitened Times, and Beyond." *Library Resources & Technical Services* 54, no. 2 (2010). https://dash.harvard.edu/handle/1/4111039.

Hedreen, Rebecca. "Time Zones, Screencasts, and Becoming Real: Lessons Learned as a Distance Librarian." *Urban Library Journal* 18, no. 1 (2012): 1–13. https://academicworks.cuny.edu/cgi/viewcontent.cgi?article=1114&context=ulj.

Heimlich, S. Layla. "New and Emerging Roles for Medical Librarians." *Journal of Hospital Librarianship* 14, no. 1 (2014): 24–32. doi: 10.1080/15323269.2014.859995.

Hennig, Nicole. "Mobile Apps in Library Programs." *Library Technology Reports* 50, no. 8 (2014): 18–22. https://journals.ala.org/index.php/ltr/article/view/4652

Hennig, Nicole, Tracy Gabridge, Millicent Gaskell, Maggie Bartley, Darcy Duke, Christine Quirion, Stephen Skuce, Amy Stout, and Ellen Finnie Duranceau. "User Needs Assessment of Information Seeking Activities of MIT Students—Spring 2006." D-Space @ MIT Archived Report, Cambridge, MA, 2006. http://dspace.mit.edu/handle/1721.1/33456.

Hogan, "Leader Focus." Hogan, accessed April 16, 2018, www.hoganleaderfocus.com.

Holland, Dorothy C., and Margaret A. Eisenhart. *Educated in Romance: Women, Achievement, and College Culture.* Chicago, IL: University of Chicago Press, 1990. e-book.

Homan, J. Michael. "Eyes on the Prize: Reflections on the Impact of the Evolving Digital Ecology on the Librarian as Expert Intermediary and Knowledge Coach, 1969–2009." *Journal of the Medical Library Association* 98, no. 1 (2010): 49–56. doi: 10.3163/1536-5050.98.1.016.

Houston, Anne M. "Revisiting Library as Place." *Reference & User Services Quarterly* 55 no. 2 (2015): 84–86. https://journals.ala.org/index.php/rusq/article/viewFile/5852/7366.

Jarvis, Christy, Joan M. Gregory, and Jean P. Shipman. "Books to Bytes at the Speed of Light: A Rapid Health Sciences Collection Transformation." *Collection Management* 39, no. 2–3 (2014): 6–76. doi: 10.1080/01462679.2014.910150.

Jensen, Karen. "No More Liaisons: Collection Management Strategies in Hard Times." *Collection Management* 42, no. 1 (2017): 1, 3–14. doi: 10.1080/01462679.2016.1263812.

Joseph, Claire, and Helen-Ann Brown Epstein. "Proving Your Worth/Adding to Your Value." *Journal of Hospital Librarianship* 14, no. 1 (2014): 69–79. doi: 10.1080/15323269.2014.860842.

Kane, Cynthia, Kellie Meehlhause, and Marianne Ryan. "GTA = Great Teaching Adventure!" *Reference & User Services Quarterly* 54, no. 1 (2014): 12–16. doi: 10.5860/rusq.54n1.12.

Kash, Melissa J. "Teaching Evidence-Based Medicine in the Era of Point-of-Care Databases: The Case of the Giant Bladder Stone." *Medical Reference Services Quarterly* 35, no. 2 (2016): 230–36. doi: 10.1080/02763869.2016.1152148.

King, Samuel, Erica Cataldi-Roberts, and Erin Wentz. "Meeting at the Crossroads: Collaboration between Information Technology Departments and Health Sciences Libraries." *Journal of the Medical Library Association* 105, no. 1 (2017): 27–33. doi: 10.5195/jmla.2017.104.

Koop, Maggie Gallup. "Academic Libraries, Institutional Missions, and New Student Recruitment: A Case Study." *Reference Services Review* 41, no. 2 (2013): 192–200. doi: 10.1108/00907321311326192.

Kristiansson, Michael R., and Henrik Jochumsen. "How to Implement Entrepreneurship in LIS Education: A Danish Example." *BiD*, no. 35 (2015): 16–21. doi: 10.1344/BiD2015.35.21.

Kronenfeld, Michael R., R. Curtis Bay, and William Coombs. "Survey of User Preferences from a Comparative Trial of UpToDate and ClinicalKey." *Journal of the Medical Library Association* 101, no. 22 (2013): 151–54. doi: 10.3163/1536-5050.101.2.011.

Kronenfeld, Michael R., and Harold S. Bright. "Library Resource Discovery." *Journal of the Medical Library Association* 103 no. 4 (2015): 210–13. doi: 10.3163/1536-5050.103.4.011.

Lau, Cecilia, and Venkata Kolli. "App Use in Psychiatric Education: A Medical Student Survey." *Academic Psychiatry* 41, no. 1 (2017): 68–70. doi: 10.1007/s40596-016-0630-z.

Link, Jeanne, and Jonna Peterson. "Replicating Rochester: Developing a Feasible Multi-Institution Study of User Information Needs in the Health Sciences." Council on Library and Information Resources Reports, Washington, DC, 2014. https://www.clir.org/wp-content/uploads/sites/6/pub161.pdf.

Liu, Hangsheng, Soeren Mattke, Katherine M. Harris, Sarah Weinberger, Seth Serxner, John P. Caloyeras, and Ellen Exum. "Do Workplace Wellness Programs Reduce Medical Costs? Evidence from a Fortune 500 Company." *Inquiry: The Journal of Health Care Organization, Provision, and Financing* 50, no. 2 (2013): 150–58. doi: 10.1177/0046958013513677.

Loos, Amber T. "The Role of Librarians in Promoting Digital Wellness: A Case Study." *Public Services Quarterly* 13, no. 1 (2017): 32–40. doi: 10.1080/15228959.2016.1268943.

Lotts, Megan. "Playing with LEGO®, Learning about the Library, and 'Making' Campus Connections: The Rutgers University Art Library Lego Playing Station, Part One." *Journal of Library Administration* 56, no. 4 (2016): 359–80. doi: 10.1080/01930826.2016.1168252.

Lynn, Valerie A., Marie FitzSimmons, and Cynthia K. Robinson. "Special Report: Symposium on Transformational Change in Health Sciences Libraries: Space. Collections, and Roles." *Journal of the Medical Library Association* 99, no. 1 (2011): 82–87. doi:10.3163/1536-5050.99.1.014.

Maggio, Lauren A., Olle ten Cate, David M. Irby, and Bridget C. O'Brien. "Designing Evidence-Based Medicine Training to Optimize the Transfer of Skills from the Classroom to Clinical Practice: Applying the Four Component Instructional Design Model." *Academic Medicine* 90, no. 11 (2015): 1457–61. doi: 10.1097/acm.0000000000000769.

Massis, Bruce. "Data-driven decision-making in the library." *New Library World* 117, no. 11/2 (2016): 131–34. doi:10.1108/NLW-10-2015-0081.

Mautz, Scott. "8 Powerful Ways to Lead from the Heart: Here's How to Roll Up Your Sleeves and Wear Your Heart on Them." *Leadership Excellence Essentials* 34, no. 11 (2017): 5. https://www.hr.com/en/magazines/leadership_excellence_essentials/november_2017_leadership.

Mayorga, Eduardo P. "Webinar Software: A Tool for Developing More Effective Lectures (Online or In-Person)." *Middle East African Journal of Opthalmology* 21, no. 2 (2014): 123–27. doi: 10.4103/0974-9233.129756.

McArthur, John A., and Valerie Johnson Graham. "User-Experience Design and Library Spaces: A Pathway to Innovation?" *Journal of Library Innovation* 6, no. 2 (2015): 1–14.

McClure, Lucretia W. "When the Librarian was the Search Engine: Introduction to the Special Issue on New Roles for Health Sciences Librarians." *Journal of the Medical Library Association* 101, no. 4 (2013): 257–60. doi: 10.3163/1536-5050.101.4.006.

Medaille, Ann, Molly Beisler, Tara Radniecki, Maggie Ressel, Heidi Slater, Danielle Copper, and Nancy Fried Foster. "Exploring Group Study at the University of Nevada, Reno." Ithaka S+R Libraries & Scholarly Communications Research Report, New York, NY, 2015. http://www.sr.ithaka.org/publications/exploring-group-study-at-the-university-of-nevada-reno/.

Medical Library Association (MLA). "Data Special Interest Group." MLA. Accessed March 2018. http://www.mlanet.org/p/cm/ld/fid=213.

Mestre, Lori S. "Student Preference for Tutorial Design: A Usability Study." *Reference Services Review* 40, no. 2 (2012): 258–76. doi: 10.1108/00907321211228318.

Mi, Misa. "Factors that Influence Effective Evidence-based Medicine Instruction." *Medical Reference Services Quarterly* 32, no. 4 (2013): 424–33. doi: 10.1080/02763869.2013.837733.

Mitchell, Emily, and Brandon West. "Collecting and Applying Usability Data from Distance Learners." *Journal of Library & Information Services in Distance Learning*, 11 no. 1 (2017): 1–12. doi:10.1080/1533290X.2016.1223963.

Moffatt, Michael. *Coming of Age in New Jersey: College and American Culture.* New Brunswick, NJ: Rutgers University Press, 2000.

Montgomery College Libraries. "Montgomery College Libraries Ethnography Study: Home." Montgomery College Libraries. Last updated June 13, 2017. http://libguides.montgomerycollege.edu/ethnographic.

Moreillon, Judi. "#schoollibrarians Tweet for Professional Development: A Netnographic Case Study of #txlchat." *School Libraries Worldwide* 21, no. 2 (2015): 127–37.

Nash, Meredith, Amanda Davies, and Robyn Moore. "What Style of Leadership Do Women in STEMM Fields Perform: Findings from an International Survey." *PLoS One* 12, no. 10 (2017): e1085727. https://www.ncbi.nlm.nih.gov/pubmed/?te rm=nash%5Bau%5D+PLoS+STEMM.

Nathan, Rebekah. *My Freshman Year: What a Professor Learned by Becoming a Student.* New York, NY: Penguin Books, 2014. e-book.

National Archives and Record Administration. "TIP 13: Using Technology to Safeguard Archival Holdings." Specifications and Research Document, College Park, MD, 1997. https://www.archives.gov/files/preservation/technical/tip13.pdf.

National Center for Education Statistics. "3.2.2 Net Assignable Area (Net Assignable Square Feet-NASF)," National Center for Education Statistics. Accessed March 23, 2018, https://nces.ed.gov/pubs2006/ficm/content.asp?ContentType=Section&c hapter=3&section=2&subsection=2.

Newton, David. "Releasing Steam: Stressbusters to Market the Library as Place." *Public Services Quarterly* 7, no. 3/4 (2011): 169–72. doi: 10.1080/15228959.2011.622648.

O'Connor, Richard. "Seeing duPont within Sewanee and Student Life." Task Force Final Report for the Jessie Ball duPont Library, Sewanee, TN, 2005. https://www. pdffiller.com/13341550--Seeing-duPont-within-Sewanee-and-Student-Life-Ringling-College.

Office of Disease Prevention and Health Promotion. "HealthyPeople.gov." Office of Disease Prevention and Health Promotion. Accessed February 6, 2018, https:// www.healthypeople.gov/.

Ontario Library Association. "Accessible Library Services for Persons with Disabilities." Ontario Library Association. Accessed May 3, 2017. http://www. accessola.org/web/OLA/IssuesAdvocacy/Accessible_Services.aspx.

Pacifico, Michele F., ed. *Archival and Special Collections Facilities: Guidelines for Archivists, Librarians, Architects and Engineers.* Chicago, IL: American Library Association, 2009.

Perryman, Carol. "Assessment Related Skills and Knowledge Are Increasingly Mentioned in Library Job Postings." *Evidence Based Library & Information Practice* 10, no. 1 (2015): 98–100. doi: 10.18438/B8060T.

Persily, Gail L., and Karen A. Butter. "Reinvisioning and Redesigning 'A Library for the Fifteenth Through Twenty-First Centuries': A Case Study on Loss of

Space from the Library and Center for Knowledge Management, University of California, San Francisco." *Journal of the Medical Library Association* 98, no. 1 (2010): 44–48. doi: 10.3163/1536-5050.98.1.015.

Pink, Daniel H. *To Sell is Human: The Surprising Truth About Moving Others.* New York, NY: Riverhead Books, 2013.

Plutchak, T. Scott. "Breaking the Barriers of Time and Space: The Dawning of the Great Age of Librarians." *Journal of the Medical Library Association* 100, no. 1 (2012): 10–19. doi: 10.3163/1536-5050.100.1.004.

Polger, Mark Aaron. "The Informationist: Ten Years Later." *Journal of Hospital Librarianship* 10, no. 4 (2010): 363–79. doi: 10.1080/15323269.2010.514556.

Putnam, Samuel R., and Sara Russell Gonzalez. "Getting Real in the Library: A Case Study at the University of Florida." *The Code4Lib Journal* 39 (2018). http://journal.code4lib.org/articles/13201.

Read, Kevin, and Fred Willie Zametkin LaPolla. "A New Hat for Librarians: Providing REDCap Support to Establish the Library as a Central Data Hub." *Journal of the Medical Library Association* 106, no. 1 (2018): 120–26. doi: 10.5195/jmla.2018.327.

Reilly, Bernard F., Jr. "The Future of Cooperative Collections and Repositories." *Library Management* 34, no. 4/5 (2013): 342–51. doi: 10.1108/0143512131132 8681.

Rendina, Diana. "How to Transform Your Library Space on a Budget. Knowledge Quest." Accessed May 4, 2017. http://knowledgequest.aasl.org/transform-library-space-budget/.

Rethlefsen, Melissa L., Mellanye J. Lackey, and Shirley Zhao. "Building Capacity to Encourage Research Reproducibility and #MakeResearchTrue." *Journal of the Medical Library Association* 106, no. 1 (2018): 113–19. doi: 10.5195/jmla.2018.273.

Robinson, Cynthia K. "Library Space in the Digital Age: The Pressure Is On." *Bottom Line* 22, no. 1 (2009): 5–8. doi: 10.1108/08880450910955369.

Roksandic, Stevo. "Enhancing Health Information Services in Franklin County, Ohio Public Libraries: Consumer Health Information Project (CHIP)." (unpublished manuscript, 2008).

———. "Mount Carmel Health System Library Services: Health Sciences Librarianship Gains its Momentum!" *Ohio Libraries Quarterly* (2014a):

14–15. https://library.mchs.com/images/pdf/MCHSLPubs/201407-OhioLibrariesQuarterly-MCHSLArticle.pdf

———. "Revitalized Library Services: Redefining and Maximizing Operational Efficiency and Excellence." *Doody's Core Title* (2014b). https://library.mchs.com/images/pdf/MCHSLPubs/Revitalized_Library_Services-Roksandic.pdf.

Rosenberg, Merrick. "Which Bird Are You? Taking Flight with the DISC Styles." Training: The Source for Professional Development. Last modified September 10, 2014. https://trainingmag.com/which-bird-are-you-taking-flight-disc-styles.

Rosener, Judy B. "Ways Women Lead." *Harvard Business Review* 68, no. 6 (1990): 119–25. https://hbr.org/1990/11/ways-women-lead.

Sandy, John H., Mangala Krishnamurthy, and Vincent F. Scalfani. "Repurposing Space in a Science and Engineering Library: Considerations for a Successful Outcome." *Journal of Academic Librarianship* 40, no. 3/4 (2014): 388–93. doi: 10.1016/j.acalib.2014.03.015.

Saunders, Laura. "Academic Libraries' Strategic Plans: Top Trends and Under-Recognized Areas." *The Journal of Academic Librarianship* 41, no. 3 (2015): 285–91. doi: 10.1016/j.acalib.2015.03.011.

Seadle, Michael. "The European iSchools." *Bulletin of the Association for Information Science & Technology* 42, no. 4 (2016): 26–30. https://onlinelibrary.wiley.com/doi/full/10.1002/bul2.2016.1720420408.

Seadle, Michael, and Elke Greifeneder. "Envisioning an iSchool Curriculum." *Information Research* 12, no. 4 (2007). http://InformationR.net/ir/12-4/colis/colise02.

Seifert, Anna. M., Nicole Stotz, and Alexia E. Metz. "Apps in Therapy: Occupational Therapists' Use and Opinions." *Disability Rehabilitation Assistive Technology* 12, no. 8 (2017): 772–79. doi: 10.1080/17483107.2016.1262912.

Sens, Thomas. "12 Major Trends in Library Design." Building Design and Construction. Accessed February 15, 2018. https://www.bdcnetwork.com/12-major-trends-library-design.

Seo, Hilary T., and Tanya Zanish-Belcher. "Pitfalls, Progress and Partnership." *Collection Management* 30, no. 3 (2006): 3–19. doi: 10.1300/J105v30n03_02.

Shipman, Jean P., and Barbara A. Ulmer, eds. *Information and Innovation: A Natural Combination for Health Sciences Libraries.* Lanham, MD: Rowman & Littlefield, 2017.

Sidlofsky, Michael, Tim Tripp, and Jennifer M. Bayne. "Usage and Impact of a Teaching Hospital Virtual Library." *Journal of Hospital Librarianship* 3, no. 3 (2003): 1–11. doi:10.1300/J186v03n03_01.

Silver, Howard. "Library as Place: Rethinking Roles, Rethinking Space, Council on Library and Information Resources, Washington, DC (2005) ISBN 1932326138 81 Pp. $20." *Library & Information Science Research* 28, no. 2 (2006): 336–37. doi: 10.1016/j.lisr.2006.03.012.

Simpson, Susan Nash, Jeffrey G. Coghill, and Patricia C. Greenstein. "Electronic Resources Librarian in the Health Sciences Library: An Emerging Role." *Journal of Electronic Resources in Medical Libraries* 2, no. 1 (2005): 27–39. https://www.tandfonline.com/doi/abs/10.1300/J383v02n01_03.

Smith, Sarah, and Mark Duman. "The State of Consumer Health Information: An Overview." *Health Information & Libraries Journal* 26, no. 4 (2009): 260–78. doi: 10.1111/j.1471-1842.2009.00870.x.

Spatz, Michele. *The Medical Library Association Guide to Providing Consumer and Patient Health Information.* Lanham, MD: Rowman & Littlefield Publishers, 2014.

Steele, Patricia A., David Cronrath, Sandra Parsons Vicchio, and Nancy Fried Foster. *The Living Library: An Intellectual Ecosystem.* Chicago, IL: Association of College & Research Libraries, 2015.

Stoker, John R. "Leadership Lessons from the River of No Return—8 Questions to Assess the Qualifications of Your Leadership." *Leadership Excellence Essentials* 34, no. 11 (2017): 6–7. https://www.hr.com/en/magazines/leadership_excellence_essentials/november_2017_leadership

Suarez, Doug. "What Students Do When They Study in the Library: Using Ethnographic Methods to Observe Student Behavior." *Electronic Journal of Academic and Special Librarianship* 8, no. 3 (2007). http://southernlibrarianship.icaap.org/content/v08n03/suarez_d01.html.

Sullivan, Louis H. "The Tall Office Building Artistically Considered." *Lippincott's Monthly Magazine*, 339 (1896): 403–9. https://archive.org/details/tallofficebuildi00sull.

Tang, Jie, Min-Shi Liu, and Wen-Bin Liu. "How Workplace Fun Influences Employees' Performance: The Role of Person-Organization Value Congruence." *Social Behavior & Personality: An International Journal* 45, no. 11 (2017): 1787–1802. https://www.sbp-journal.com/index.php/sbp/article/view/6240.

Tang, Yingqi. "Distance Education Librarians in the United States: A Study of Job Announcements." *Journal of Academic Librarianship* 39, no. 6 (2013): 500–5. doi: 10.1016/j.acalib.2013.08.012.

Texas A&M University Libraries. "How We Build Our World Class Collections." Texas A&M University Libraries. Accessed January 19, 2018, https://library.tamu. edu/research/how_build.html.

Texas Historical Commission. "Basic Guidelines for the Preservation of Historical Artifacts." Guideline, Austin, TX, 2013. http://www.thc.texas.gov/public/upload/ publications/Basic%20Guidelines%20for%20the%20Preservation%20of%20 historic%20artifacts%202013.pdf.

The Association of Specialized and Cooperative Library Agencies. "Library Accessibility Toolkits: What you need to know." ASCLA. Accessed May 4, 2017. http://www.ala.org/ascla/resources/tipsheets.

Thibodeau, Patricia L. "When the Library Is Located in Prime Real Estate: A Case Study on the Loss of Space from the Duke University Medical Center Library and Archives." *Journal of the Medical Library Association* 98, no. 1 (2010): 25–28. doi: 10.3163/1536-5050.98.1.010.

Tibor, Koltay. "Are You Ready? Tasks and Roles for Academic Libraries in Supporting Research 2.0." *New Library World* 117, no. 1/2 (2016): 94–104. doi: 0.1108/NLW-09-2015-0062.

Tod, Angela M., Beverly Bond, Niamh Leonard, Irene J. Gilsenan, and Simon Palfreyman. "Exploring the Contribution of the Clinical Librarian to Facilitating Evidence-Based Nursing." *Journal of Clinical Nursing* 16, no. 4 (2007): 621–29. doi: 10.1111/j.1365-2702.2006.01726.x.

Tooey, Mary Joan. "Renovated, Repurposed, and Still 'One Sweet Library': A Case Study on Loss of Space from the Health Sciences and Human Services Library, University of Maryland, Baltimore." *Journal of the Medical Library Association* 98, no. 1 (2010): 40–43. doi: 10.3163/1536-5050.98.1.014.

Tooey, Mary Joan, and Gretchen N. Arnold. "The Impact of Institutional Ethics on Academic Health Sciences Library Leadership: A Survey of Academic Health Sciences Library Directors." *Journal of the Medical Library Association* 102, no. 4 (2014): 241–46. doi: 10.3163/1536-5050.102.4.005.

Tripathi, Manorama, Archana Shukla, and Sharad Kumar Sonker. "Research Data Management Practices in University Libraries: A Study." *DESIDOC Journal of Library & Information Technology* 37, no. 6 (2017): 417–24. doi: 10.14429/ djlit.37.11336.

Trivette, Karen Jamison. "Historical Holdings and New Dimensions: The Fashion Institute of Technology—SUNY Library Unit of Special Collections and College Archives." *Art Libraries Journal* 42, no. 3 (2017): 140–47. doi: 10.1017/alj.2017.20.

Twiss-Brooks, Andrea B., Ricardo Andrade, Jr., Michelle B. Bass, Barbara Kern, Jonna Peterson, and Debra A. Werner. "A Day in the Life of Third-Year Medical Students: Using an Ethnographic Method to Understand Information Seeking and Use." *Journal of the Medical Library Association* 105, no. 1 (2017): 12–19. doi:10.5195/jmla.2017.95.

U.S. News & World Report. "The 10 Best Public Universities in America." *U.S. News & World Report.* Accessed February 19, 2018. https://www.usnews.com/best-colleges/rankings/national-universities/top-public.

Varman, Beatriz G., and Adela V. Justice. "The Unfunded Worksite Wellness Program." *Journal of Hospital Librarianship* 15, no. 3 (2015): 284–95. doi: 10.1080/15323269.2015.1049065.

Waddell, Stacie. "The Road to Virtual: The Sauls Memorial Virtual Library's Journey." *Medical Reference Services Quarterly,* 33, no. 1 (2014): 92–101. doi: 10.1080/02763869.2014.866493.

Wagner, Kay Cimpl, and Gary D. Byrd. "Evaluating the Effectiveness of Clinical Medical Librarian Programs: A Systematic Review of the Literature." *Journal of the Medical Library Association* 100, suppl. 4 (2012): 14–33. https://www.ncbi. nlm.nih.gov/pmc/articles/PMC3571670/

Wagner, Sarah S. "Published Environmental Standards." Standards Document, Washington, DC, 2011. http://siarchives.si.edu/sites/default/files/pdfs/ SummaryStorageStandards_0.pdf.

Welch, Jennifer M., Susan D. Hoffius, and E. Brooke Fox. "Archives, Accessibility and Advocacy: A Case Study of Strategies for Creating and Maintaining Relevance." *Journal of the Medical Library Association* 99, no. 1 (2011): 57–60. doi: 10.3163/1536-5050.99.1.010.

Wentz, Brian., Paul T. Jaeger, and John C. Bertot, eds. *Advances in Librarianship: Accessibility for Persons with Disabilities and the Inclusive Future of Libraries.* Bingley, UK: Emerald Group Publishing Ltd., 2015.

Whitmore, Susan C., Suzanne F. Grefsheim, and Jocelyn A. Rankin. "Informationist Programme in Support of Biomedical Research: A Programme Description and Preliminary Findings of an Evaluation." *Health Information and Libraries Journal* 25, no. 2 (2008): 135–41. doi: 10.1111/j.1471-1842.2007.00756.x.

Wilsted, Thomas P. "Renovating Special Collections Facilities." *Journal of Library Administration* 52, no. 3–4 (2012): 321–31. doi. 10.1080/01930826.2012.684530.

Woodward, Orrin. "Warren Bennis Six Personal Qualities of Leadership." *Orrin Woodward on LIFE & Leadership*. April 18, 2008. http://orrinwoodwardblog. com/2008/04/18/warren-bennis-six-personal-qualities-of-leadership/.

Xia, Jingfeng, and Yue Li. "Changed Responsibilities in Scholarly Communication Services: An Analysis of Job Descriptions." *Serials Review* 41, no. 1 (2015): 15–22. doi: 10.1080/00987913.2014.998980.

Youm, Julie, and Warren Wiechmann. "Medical Student Use of the iPad in the Clerkship Curriculum." *The Clincal Teacher* 12, no. 6 (2015): 378–83. doi: 10.1111/tct.12381.

Zeblisky, Kathy A., Rebecca A. Birr, April L. Aguiñaga, David Drachman, and Kathleen Mathieson. "Rethinking Your Involvement: A Survey on Hospital Library Committee Participation." *Journal of Hospital Librarianship* 13, no. 1 (2013): 47–58. doi: 10.1080/15323269.2013.743361.

Zhu, Yini, Mina Ghajar, and Ermira Mitre. "SHARE: Spreading Health Awareness with Resources and Education—Librarians' Role in Patient Education, A Case Study." *Journal of Hospital Librarianship* 16, no. 4 (2016): 319–27. doi: 10.1080/15323269.2016.1221280.

Zuo, Zhiya, Kang Zhao, and David Eichmann. "The State and Evolution of U.S. iSchools: From Talent Acquisitions to Research Outcome." *Journal of the Association for Information Science & Technology* 68, no. 5 (2017): 1266–77. doi: 10.1002/asi.23751.

Index

Note: All page numbers in *italics* refer to figures or tables.

About the Editor
and Contributors

EDITOR

Alanna Campbell, MISt, is the public services librarian *with* the Health Sciences Library at the Northern Ontario School of Medicine (NOSM). She has a BA in history with minor in biology from Brock University and received her MISt from the University of Toronto. Her research interests include library spaces, user engagement, and evidence-based medicine. In 2015, Alanna took a six-month research sabbatical focused on library spaces. She visited North American library spaces with varying budgets, specialties, and space provisions that had been recently renovated. Additionally, Alanna conducted a survey of AAHSL members who had removed one or more library shelves in the last five years to determine the impact on their library spaces, services, usage, and more. The results of this study were shared in a poster presentation titled "Less Shelves, More What? How Are Academic Health Sciences Libraries Choosing to Replace Their Shelves?" at the MLA/CHLA joint conference in Toronto, Ontario, in May 2016. Alanna has also presented multiple posters, sessions, a lightning talk and coauthored a journal article on topics related to library spaces, embedded librarianship, and mobile technologies.

CONTRIBUTORS

Dr. Neelam Bharti is the chemical sciences and engineering librarian with the Marston Science Library at the University of Florida. She has a PhD in chemistry and worked as a research scientist for ten years. Prior to her current position, she was involved in a NIH drug development project, which led to several peer-reviewed publications and patents, and directed three drugs to clinical trials. In her current position, she has been actively involved in teaching chemical literacy, research strategy, responsible conduct in research, and 3D-printing technology in the library and the community. Neelam has presented at numerous national and international conferences and earned recognition for her articles, which have been published in top science and information journals, including *Chemical Reviews* and the *Journal of Chemical Education*. She is also a member of the editorial boards of many leading international chemistry journals. Her research interests include critical information literacy in sciences and emerging technology.

Lisa S. Blackwell, MLS is the national director of library services for Chamberlain University, based in Downers Grove, Illinois. She manages library operations and services for all Chamberlain campus and online programs, which include twenty-one physical campuses in fifteen states, online RN to BSN, MSN, FNP, DNP, and MPH programs. Lisa has overseen and implemented the transition of library operations, staffing, resources, and services from physical campus-based libraries to a cohesive, primarily virtual, enterprise-wide library operational infrastructure.

Adam Brown is a ten-year veteran of the University of Florida's (UF) information technology services. He is the current operations manager with the academic technology unit. Adam attended UF for his undergraduate studies and he will be graduating this year with a master's of business administration from his alma mater. He looks forward to his first published work.

Nancy G. Burford is the veterinary collections curator and was the Medical Sciences Library (MSL) project manager for the special collections renovation project at Texas A&M. She has also been on the MSL renovation team for the two general collection spaces projects. She is currently the project manager for a staff spaces renovation project to be completed in 2018.

Shannon Butcheck, MLIS, is the head of electronic resources and bibliographic control at the Cleveland Health Sciences Library at Case Western Reserve University. In addition to managing the library's e-resources, Shannon heads the cataloging department and serves as the library's fiscal officer. After completing her bachelor's degree in art history from the University of Maryland, Baltimore County, she returned to Ohio to pursue her MLIS at Kent State University. Throughout her career in library-land, she has worked in a variety of departments, including special collections, archives, and interlibrary loan. Shannon served as the team leader during the 2015 Cleveland Health Sciences Library space reallocation project.

Esther E. Carrigan has been director of the Medical Sciences Library (MSL) for over ten years. During that time, five distinct library renovation projects have been undertaken. Two of the projects were to update staff spaces from their original 1980s workspace configurations. Three of the projects have focused on user spaces, one for the general MSL user and collection spaces, one to create a graduate and professional study zone (with ID access required), and one to reimagine the special collections area.

Jessica DeCaro is the senior user services librarian with the Cleveland Health Sciences Library at Case Western Reserve University where she engages with medical, nursing, and dental medicine students, faculty, researchers, and staff in a range of services from teaching the ins and outs of navigating library-land to systematic reviews. In her downtime at work, Jessica enjoys learning about genetics, data management, bioinformatics, and leadership. She is also involved with a variety of committees and responsibilities in MLA, the Midwest Chapter of MLA, and the Academic Library Association of Ohio. Jessica received her MLIS from Kent State University and attended Hiram College for her undergraduate degree. In her previous career, Jessica was a certified athletic trainer, which makes health sciences librarianship a perfect fit.

Helen-Ann Brown Epstein, in her over forty years as a librarian, has been a health sciences librarian, working as a hospital librarian, trainer for the National Library of Medicine, and a private vendor, library school professor, and clinical librarian for a major academic medical center. NLM has recognized her as a rock star librarian. She is a fellow of the Medical Library Association. Currently, Helen-Ann is the informationist at virtual health in south New Jersey. She successfully manages a virtual library serving a three-hospital system with 9,000 employees.

Allison Erlinger, RN/BSN, MA, MLIS, AHIP, is a medical reference librarian and registered nurse. Allison worked at the Mount Carmel Health Sciences Library (MCHSL) for several years as a volunteer, library assistant, and finally reference librarian and was actively involved in many of the transformative projects at MCHSL. She now works as a reference librarian at the Nationwide Children's Hospital Grant Morrow III Medical Library.

Patty Fink holds an MA (history) from Laurentian University, an MLIS from Western University, and is a senior member of the Academy of Health Information Professionals. In 2004, Patty joined the Northern Ontario School of Medicine (NOSM) as the e-resources librarian. She helped establish the medical school libraries at Laurentian University and Lakehead University, and has developed a distributed model of library service that spans the vast geography of Northern Ontario. Patty is currently the director of research and the Health Sciences Library at NOSM.

Sara Russell Gonzalez is the physical sciences, mathematics, and visualization librarian at the Marston Science Library at the University of Florida. She oversees the UF libraries' 3D-printing service and is the former director of the MADE@UF software development lab. A former geophysicist, her research interests include emerging technologies in libraries, modeling and visualization of data, and scientific literacy instruction. She holds a PhD from the University of California, Santa Cruz, in seismology, and a MLIS from Florida State University.

Margaret A. Hoogland, MLS, AHIP, serves as the clinical medical librarian in the Mulford Health Sciences Library at the University of Toledo. In this position, she conducts research, applies all the skills and techniques she gathered over the years, and works to ensure health professional students graduate with the skills necessary to excel and provide the best possible patient care. From 2012 to 2016, she served as a distance support librarian and was responsible for creating and maintaining a program to support a completely online school providing degrees in public health, health education, health adminis-tration, health sciences, and kinesiology.

In 2014–2016, she codeveloped and coinstructed, "Expand Your Library Instruction Toolkit: An Introduction to Online Learning and Distance Sup-port" at the MLA Annual Meetings and Conferences in Austin, Texas, and Toronto, Canada, with Virginia Pannabecker. In July 2017, Margaret became the chair-elect of MLA's educational media and technologies section.

Mellanye Lackey, MSI, is the associate director for education and research at the Spencer S. Eccles Health Sciences Library at the University of Utah. She is professionally interested in library administration, embedding librarian ex-pertise into systematic reviews, and partnering with health sciences educators and researchers. When not at work, Mellanye enjoys hiking with her wife and her greyhound, the Velcro-dog.

Valrie Minson, chair of the Marston Science Library, provides leadership for the only nonmedical science library at the University of Florida (UF), with 1.5 million visitors per year and supporting forty-two departments across three colleges. She oversees the work of twenty-two employees and builds strategic partnerships through the development of new projects and services. Prior to her current position, she was an Agricultural Outreach Librarian at UF and also a Collection and Research Services Librarian at Dickinson College (2003–2005). She has an MLS from Florida State University.

Stevo Roksandic joined the Mount Carmel Health System (MCHS) in 2003, and since 2006 has served as regional director of library services at MHCS, Columbus, Ohio. Stevo received *Library Journal's* "Movers & Shakers" award, Class 2015–Advocates. He led and created the design of the Consumer Health Library and Consumer Health Information Center(s) within MCHS as "Libraries without Shelves." He has assisted and worked with professional designers on all other renovation projects of Mount Carmel Library Services (MCLS) under financial and other constraints associated with large corpo-rate settings. He is inspired by such challenges and recommends focusing on rethinking, redoing, and repurposing existing environments. He is continu-ously redesigning diverse MCLS spaces to reinforce and to tie together the library identity and the MCHS institutional mission and vision. His research interests include the evaluation of diverse user communities that foster the integration of elements of emerging library design trends and future organizational development. His working and living philosophy is this: "It's not about me, it's about we." MCLS has joined the ALA "Libraries Transforms" campaign. Current projects are preparing the library for their great transformational milestone which they plan to reach by their hundred-year birthday celebration in 2021.

Camille Salmond has worked at the Eccles Health Sciences Library for over twenty-seven years. She has worked as the interlibrary loan supervisor and is now the electronic resources coordinator. Her duties have included Docline training classes for NN/LM Region 4, metadata entry for the University of Utah's institutional repository and cataloging. Additionally, Camille has served on Eccles Library Space planning task forces and participated in the patron survey process.

Darell Schmick, MLS, AHIP, is the founding director of library services at the University of the Incarnate Word (UIW) School of Osteopathic Medicine. In this role he is responsible for establishing the physical and digital library spaces for the School of Osteopathic Medicine, as well as providing instruction and curriculum support for the programs offered on UIW's medical campus. Previously, Darell worked at the University of Utah Eccles Health Sciences Library in Salt Lake City, Utah, as research librarian, where he worked with researchers, clinicians, and innovators along all aspects of the research life cycle. Darell has also worked at the University of Missouri Health Sciences Library in Columbia, Missouri. He holds a MLS degree from Emporia State University and a graduate certificate in organizational change from the University of Missouri.

Jean P. Shipman, MSLS, AHIP, FMLA, is the vice president, global library relations for Elsevier. Prior to that she was the executive director, knowledge management and Spencer S. Eccles Health Sciences Library; director of the MidContinental Region and National Training Office of the National Network of Libraries of Medicine; director for information transfer, Center of Medical Innovation; and adjunct faculty of the Department of Biomedical Informatics, School of Medicine; all at the University of Utah. She has also been employed by the John Hopkins University, Greater Baltimore Medical Center, University of Maryland, University of Washington, and Virginia Commonwealth University. She served as president of the Medical Library Association for 2006–2007 and on the board of directors for the Society for Scholarly Publishing from 2013 to 2016. She was a member and co-chair of the Chicago Collaborative, a group of publishers, librarians, and editors who met to discuss issues regarding scholarly communications. She is the co-editor of two books: *Information and Innovation: A Natural Combination for Health Sciences Libraries* and *Strategic Collaborations in Health Sciences Libraries* (in press).

Christine Driver Yip is the access services and collections manager at Marston Science Library at the University of Florida. She leads a unit of nine staff members and over fifteen student employees in providing patron services and collection access to the 1.5 million visitors the library receives each year. She has fourteen years of academic library experience and specializes in workflow development, team building, library space assessment, and project management. She holds an MA in criminology, law, and society from the University of Florida.